The Christian School and Philanthropy

From Secular Transaction to Biblical Relationship

SIMON JEYNES, MED, MA

CHRISTIAN SCHOOL MANAGEMENT

CSM
partnership · leadership · transformation

WESTBOW
PRESS®
A DIVISION OF THOMAS NELSON
& ZONDERVAN

WestBow Press books may be ordered through booksellers or by contacting:

WestBow Press
A Division of Thomas Nelson & Zondervan
1663 Liberty Drive
Bloomington, IN 47403
www.westbowpress.com
844-714-3454

New International Version (NIV)
Holy Bible, New International Version®, NIV® Copyright ©1973, 1978, 1984, 2011 by Biblica, Inc.® Used by permission. All rights reserved worldwide.

ISBN: 979-8-3850-3758-2 (sc)
ISBN: 979-8-3850-3759-9 (e)

Library of Congress Control Number: 2024923530

Print information available on the last page.

WestBow Press rev. date: 12/04/2024

Mission
For Jesus, through mission, with students

Vision
A Christian education for children everywhere

Motto
"On earth as it is in heaven" (Matthew 6)

Key Words
Partnership, Leadership, Transformation

Driving Force
To reverse the tragic decline in Christian Education

partnership · leadership · transformation

THE PHILANTHROPIST'S PRAYER

Praise be to you, Lord,
the God of our father Israel,
from everlasting to everlasting.
Yours, Lord, is the greatness and the power
and the glory and the majesty and the splendor,
for everything in heaven and earth is yours.
Yours, Lord, is the kingdom;
you are exalted as head over all.
Wealth and honor come from you;
you are the ruler of all things.
In your hands are strength and power
to exalt and give strength to all.
Now, our God, we give you thanks,
and praise your glorious name.

But who am I, and who are my people, that we should be able to give as generously as this? Everything comes from you, and we have given you only what comes from your hand. We are foreigners and strangers in your sight, as were all our ancestors. Our days on earth are like a shadow, without hope. Lord our God, all this abundance that we have provided for building you a temple for your Holy Name comes from your hand, and all of it belongs to you. I know, my God, that you test the heart and are pleased with integrity. All these things I have given willingly and with honest intent. And now I have seen with joy how willingly your people who are here have given to you. Lord, the God of our fathers Abraham, Isaac and Israel, keep these desires and thoughts in the hearts of your people forever, and keep their hearts loyal to you. And give my son Solomon the wholehearted devotion to keep your commands, statutes and decrees and to do everything to build the palatial structure for which I have provided (1 Chronicles 29:10-19).

Amen. May our hearts be drawn to serve the Lord as in the time of Solomon. Amen.

PERSPECTIVES FROM OUR READERS

"*The Christian School and Philanthropy* should be in the hands of every Christian school leader and its Board. Reading and applying the principles and practices of this book will not be for the faint of heart – Simon Jeynes calls for a radical rethinking of the why and how of all aspects of fundraising in our schools.

"With principles emerging from theological and biblical truth, we are challenged to approach all donors relationally, not transactionally, and to let that drive the "what" that governs everything we do to get and use other people's resources. Thankfully, Simon clearly delineates the 'how tos required to be successful.

"May leaders have the courage to reexamine current practices in light of this visionary and enlightening approach to funding our schools."

Dr. Deborah Miller
Former Head of School and ACSI Regional Director

"Simon Jeynes and his team at CSM have provided a wonderful service to the growing Christian School world. This book is steeped in biblical insight on the task of true relationship fundraising. If you are a skeptic on the motive and means of 'biblical fundraising,' this volume will provide insight and encouragement in this critical task for every Christian School. The breadth of coverage and insight is quite remarkable. Annual Funds, endowments, planned giving, events, staffing, and much more are covered in practical detail.

"This is not a cover-to-cover read, but, I would say, an invaluable handbook on every aspect of raising money for your school in a God-honoring way. The detailed table of contents can be your guide to just the questions you may be asking.

"This is an important resource for every Head of School (after all, you are, regardless of the size of your Development Team, the chief fundraising officer of your school!). The new Development Officer, or seasoned one, will turn to this guide time and time again through the years as the inevitable challenges of your important work present themselves. Don't just read *The Christian School and Philanthropy*, wear it out!"

R. Mark Dillon
Senior VP/Founder
Generis Advancement
Author: *Giving and Getting in the Kingdom: a Field Guide*

I really enjoyed the book. It takes the CSM philanthropy Principle and makes it simple, easy to understand, and well reasoned. I especially liked how every part of the process begins with the Bible and flows from there. This book gives great guidance both to the philanthropy newcomer and the experienced professional. As a school board member heading up the philanthropy committee I particularly value that every part of the process begins with the Bible and constantly goes back to Scripture. The book's invitation to be part of the work God is doing in Christian schools inspired me. Simon lays out guiding principles and detailed steps with a simplicity and clarity that makes accessible a process that can seem daunting and scary. I feel better equipped to do well the task I am privileged to do.

Darrin Crow, Board member, Cedar Valley Christian School, IA

CSM offers a refreshing perspective on philanthropy, advocating for a shift from transactional fundraising to transformative giving and fostering a culture of philanthropy. This book is not just another collection of fundraising ideas and strategies. It represents a complete redefinition of stewardship and philanthropy within the Christian school context. My copy is filled with notes and tabs for future reference, reflecting its valuable insights.

The book provides a strategic roadmap for building a professional team to coordinate database and advancement activities, support enrollment and recruitment efforts, and develop a culture of philanthropy. It outlines the different roles necessary for this development, offers a calendar of communications for donor outreach, and emphasizes that philanthropy is fundamentally about relationships.

One key affirmation from this book is the importance of covering the budget with tuition through disciplined tithing, maintaining operational reserves, and managing expenses effectively. The funds raised should directly benefit the students. Implementing the ideas presented in this book will undoubtedly be challenging and require a significant leap of faith. Shifting from traditional fundraising methods to a more relational and transformative approach involves changing long-standing mindsets and practices. However, the potential rewards for our school community are immense. As we plan for the future of our school, our focus has shifted towards the Annual Fund, Comprehensive Campaign, and Endowment, guided by the principles outlined in this book.

Dr. Deborah Samuelson, Head of School, Faith Heritage School, NY.

"*The Christian School and Philanthropy: From Secular Transaction to Biblical Relationship* is practical, empathetic, and inspiring. Different constituencies will find it enlightening, as it commissions a holistic and sequenced response to nurture a thriving Christian school."

Greg Deja former Head of School Grand Rapids Catholic High School and now Executive Director of the Catholic Foundation of West Michigan

Stewardship of a Christian school's mission entails engaging philanthropy. It's not an add on or an afterthought. It's as integral a part of stewarding the school's mission as is aligning budget dollars or selecting curriculum. Accordingly, it should be done with excellence. Moreover, when approached from a biblical perspective, it's also discipleship. Jeynes reminds readers that the mission we pursue in our schools is God's mission. The resources are his. Through the work of cultivating philanthropy, we get to be part of the ongoing story of his provision, and we get to be part of the ongoing story of drawing the hearts of his followers closer to him.

Dr. Daniel Wesche, Head of School, Landmark Christian School, GA

Overall, this provides an excellent format for the creation and ongoing support of Christian school philanthropy. I found it extremely valuable.

Gwenn Sorber, Board Chair, Faith Heritage School, NY

CONTENTS

FOREWORD

First, I must thank Jenny Knight and Martin Riggs, fellow collaborators and consultants at Christian School Management, who worked with me on the True Stories in this book and encouraged me in this work. Unless given specific attribution, we have told these stories from our own experiences. They have edited, made suggestions, critiqued, and done all the things that friends do. My gratitude is endless. We spent a fruitful couple of days together thinking and talking and writing. They have spent time reading and re-reading sections and chapters. What an inestimable treasure it is to have co-workers in the Kingdom who will take the time to "think" with you! Jenny and Martin are true friends. They deserve great credit for this book. Thank you.

Second, I must thank Terri Gillespie, CSM's editor since the earliest days. She has forced me to use a style guide that she constantly updates and improves. She finds all my inconsistencies and advocates for "em" and "en" dashes. What writer does not have an unimaginable debt of gratitude to their editor? While all the errors are my own responsibility, there would have been hundreds more without Terri's eagle eye. She has not only been my editor but nurtured my children, celebrated with our family, pushed me to be better as a person and as a professional. Thank you.

Thirdly, CSM is deeply grateful to Martin Riggs, Chief Generosity Officer at Landmark Christian School, GA, for permission to use and adapt the Golden Rule Cycle. When I was looking for insight to understand the relationship between the donor and the steward, Marty provided the solution. His deep spirituality led me to understand the primacy of prayer in the relationship. His insight, borne of decades of experience and study in the field, provided the steps that became the Golden Rule Cycle. Thank you.

INTRODUCTION

We want you to care about money, raising money, using money, on behalf of children to forward your school's mission. We want you to care about it in a way that begins with Jesus' own appreciation for his philanthropy committee. We want you to be successful at it in the way God the Father Almighty himself was successful in the evoking of His people's generosity in the building of the Tabernacle. We want you to have the resources you need to deliver the mission with excellence. That's a lot of wants.

We provide you with a framework for thinking about philanthropy and a lot of details about how to do it, some in excruciatingly minute detail. Use the book as a handbook; check out the index – it's pretty thorough. Read the parts that are of particular use to you. Have someone at the school or on the Philanthropy Committee read the whole thing because it hangs together. We don't 'insist' you do it exactly the way we say. We're trying to give you practical ways that have worked at other schools. But here's the center that you cannot stray from. Raising money is not about money. Raising money is about the relationships that you have and foster. It's about loving people and asking them to love your children. It's about connecting Jesus' love for the child to Jesus' love for each one of us to our gratitude and loving God and our neighbor back. We want to bless you with this book so that you raise so much money that you have to say: "Stop! We have enough!" Philanthropy is a serious enterprise. That doesn't mean we shouldn't have a lot of fun doing it. If it stops being fun, you're doing something wrong. Go back to the relationship. It's all about the relationship. Blessings!

Secular Philanthropy

We can do philanthropy, and do it well, without being a Christian. It's like talking with people. Have you ever been to one of those communication seminars? They teach us how to be with people in a way that makes the other person feel valued and welcomed to the conversation. And they are full of techniques that "work."

- Make eye contact, smile, and be enthusiastic.
- Have an open body posture.
- Lean forward slightly.
- Make affirming sounds.

Those techniques are good ones and they do work! We know that the opposite closes people down and makes them regard us with suspicion. The impact of nonverbals on trust is significant, and the way in which people see us matters.

Secular philanthropy also has many helpful insights. For example, talking with a donor or potential donor can begin well or poorly depending on how that person 'sees' us. Mirroring language – responding to a smile with a smile, for example – has been shown to have an immediate, positive impact in our brains.

You don't have to be a Christian to utilize this kind of information and knowledge. You don't even have to be a Christian to understand the ethical issues in the manipulative use of these techniques that are inauthentic and can lead to fraud and abuse.

This can also be illustrated in the kinds of asks (invitations to invest) that charities routinely make. Such requests may be face-to-face, but typically they are in our mailboxes. We are continuously inundated by requests for money. The typical mailed request includes the following secular techniques:

- Personalized letter in a window envelope
- Gift inside, from a dime coin to return address envelopes to Christmas cards
- A long letter explaining why you should give
- A mechanism for giving – a form to fill out and send back and instructions for online giving

These requests are definitely not based on any kind of connection between the charity and us. The vast majority clearly come from a 'bought' mailing list where, when you gave to one charity, other charities learned about it and thought you would therefore be generous to them as well.

A 2006 study by Carmody and Lewis showed that the use of our own names activated very specific regions of the brain including the "middle frontal cortex, middle and superior temporal cortex, and cuneus." Personalization is an excellent technique to get and keep someone's attention.

Giving a gift provokes a reciprocal action. That's an extension of Cialdini's work on persuasion and the idea that if someone does something for you, you are more likely to do something for them. For example, the mint on the bill at a restaurant is a classic reciprocal action and apparently increases the tip offered manyfold.

The long letter will talk about the objective of the charity and the work your gift will make possible. It will also talk about how you are joining a group of people, by implication like you, who are engaged in this very important work. This plays on a number of concepts including the idea of social proof, the idea that you want to do what other people do. Social media today is only the most obvious example.

The mechanism for giving is all about convenience – an envelope is provided and you often don't have to put a stamp on it. Fill in the form, put it in the envelope, and it's done. Or go online. As *Forbes* put it in a 2020 article: "*To create convenience, business owners must find ways to eliminate that 'friction' that could pop up anywhere in the process when a potential customer is interacting with or buying from your brand.*" Friction is bad!

There are many ways to do philanthropy that don't require you to be a Christian! You need to be well-read, understand the basic marketing principles (cf. Dr. Robert Cialdini's Seven Principles of Influence and Persuasion), test them in your marketplace and, voila, you have a basic philanthropy program.

It obviously works. The Lilly Family School of Philanthropy puts out its *Giving USA* report annually, identifying what is happening in the world of giving. The 2024 report (for the year 2023) said: "In 2023, giving from individuals, bequests, foundations, and corporations reached an estimated $557.16 billion, growing 1.9 percent over 2022. The stock market and GDP buoyed total giving – both performed better than many economists initially expected in 2023. The new total represented a high in current dollars, but did not outpace the higher-than-average inflation rate of 4.1 percent." (Giving USA: The Annual Report on Philanthropy for the Year 2023 (2024). Chicago: Giving USA Foundation.)

There are two pieces of good news here. One is that giving continues to increase. The second is that Americans and Canadians like to give. And giving is done predominantly by individuals. When we put individuals, bequests, and foundations together (that are largely individual driven), individuals comprise 96 percent of all givers (p. 22 of the report).

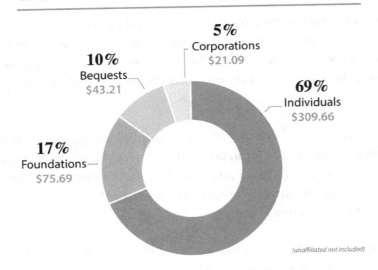

2019 Contributions: $449.64 billion by source of contributions (in billions of dollars - all figures are rounded)

5%
Corporations
$21.09

10%
Bequests
$43.21

69%
Individuals
$309.66

17%
Foundations
$75.69

(unaffiliated not included)

And that giving has increased in inflation-adjusted numbers (p. 33 of the report).

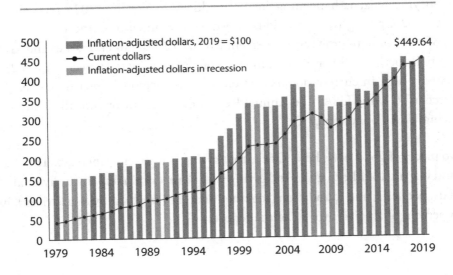

Total giving, 1979-2019 (in billions of dollars)

Inflation-adjusted dollars, 2019 = $100
Current dollars
Inflation-adjusted dollars in recession

$449.64

Imagine Canada reports similar findings. The 2018 report *30 Years of Giving in Canada*, with ups and downs, also shows an upward trend based on tax returns (p. 5):

- **Phase 1 (1985 to 1990):** Rapid growth (equivalent to approximately 4.4% annually). Total donations claimed went from $4.0 billion to $4.9 billion, an increase of 24%.

- **Phase 2 (1990 to 1995):** Stagnation. Claimed donations increased just 2% (to $5.0 billion) over the entire period.

- **Phase 3 (1995 to 2007):** Even more rapid growth (equivalent to approximately 5.6% annually). Total claimed donations reached $9.6 billion just prior to the economic downturn of 2008.

- **Phase 4 (2007 to 2014):** Instability. Total annual donation amounts fluctuated year to year. Only in 2014 did claimed donations return to 2007 levels.

Figure 4: Donations claimed 1985 - 2014, constant 2014 dollars.

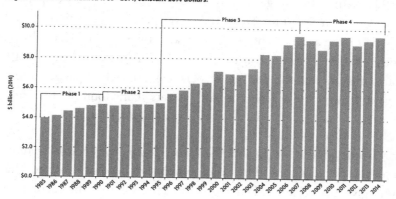

And both Canada and the USA are in the top three most generous countries in the world, according to this same report (p. 4):

Figure 3: Levels of Individual giving to charities as percentage of GDP, various years.

The upshot is that philanthropy is alive and well. You don't have to be a Christian to understand the field and how to be successful in it, and there are numerous sources of excellent information that you can access in order to be well-read.

There is also some bad news. Generosity has been declining steadily. Robert Putnam writes in *Bowling Alone* (2020): "In 1960 we gave away about $1 for every $2 we spent on recreation; in 1997 we gave away less than $0.50 for every $2.00 we spent on recreation" (p. 123). In addition, the table above shows giving as a percentage of GDP at 1.44% for the USA, which is very generous compared with other nations. However, it used to be 2.26% in 1964, 1.61% in 1998. It continues to decline. Putnam suggests that the decline in social capital, lack of participation, and the reality that the current generation is not a generation of "joiners" contribute significantly to this drop in philanthropy.

We can finish with some good news, in that the "joiner" is more generous than the one who does not join. From a secular point of view, if I can get someone to become involved, that person is more likely to give and to give more. Hence, Penelope Burk's finding that the current donor wants more direct interaction – the hands-off approach is not attractive. Secular organizations understand this reality and involve their donors in the charity's doing.

But Christian philanthropy is not secular philanthropy. None of the above is "wrong." Done ethically and with the purest motives, all of the above and more is useful. Indeed, we would be wise to include some of the best practices followed by our secular colleagues, while weaving in the spiritual lessons and interactions that drive our Christ-centered work.

And, as Christian philanthropists, we need to go deeper.

Summary

- You can be a secular organization and fundraise well.
- The principles of secular fundraising are well known and based on human behavior research.
- People like to give.
- The USA and Canada are two of the top three most generous nations in the world.

CHRISTIAN PHILANTHROPY

Putting the word Christian in front of anything has a transformative effect. As Christians we are God's people, listen to his voice, and respond to his promptings. Philanthropy is one of the ways in which that "listening" deepens our own personal relationship with God. How do we uncover that effect in our schools? The answer is explored more deeply below in the Mary Principle, founded on Luke 8:3. In this introduction, suffice it to say that the Lukan narrative identifies five operating principles for Christian philanthropy:

1. Giving is in gratitude for what God has done for each one of us.
2. Giving is done by people who are intimately involved with the action.
3. Giving includes involvement, not just the act of giving itself.
4. Giving galvanizes possibilities that otherwise could not be imagined.
5. Giving is recognized and honored.

Giving is in gratitude: we love because he first loved us (1 John 4:19). This is not a reciprocal act – God does something for us and so we do something for him, as if he needed it. Being able to love is **made possible** by God's love for us. "Dear friends, let us love one another because love comes from God. Everyone who loves has been born of God and knows God" (v. 7). Because God is love and has demonstrated that in giving his own Son (v. 10), we are enabled / empowered by the Spirit (v. 13) to demonstrate that same love now made alive in us to our neighbor, in this case, through philanthropy. In this way, we become like Jesus (v. 17).

Giving is done by people who are intimately involved with the action: Mary Magdalene, the name given to the Mary Principle, was not someone who showed up once a year to a thank-you reception. She actually followed Jesus where he went on his ministry. She was with him to the end, standing at the foot of the cross. She was blessed by being at the tomb and being one of the first to understand

and believe that Jesus was resurrected. Inspired donors are insiders, not peripheral to the action. Intimacy does not mean power or running the show; intimacy means connected to the action.

Giving includes involvement, not just the act of giving itself. The Christian life is not a spectator sport. The involvement of donors is both in deed as well as in word. They are advisers and asked for their input. They are part of committees. They may sit on the Board. They are volunteers. The one who gives money is also the one who gives time. Giving is not an outward action but one that comes from who the person is. Jesus is the paradigm of this, a "prophet powerful in word and deed" (Luke 24:19).

Giving galvanizes possibilities that otherwise could not be imagined. Gifts are possible because of the donor's own stewardship and value system. The widow's gift (Mark 12:41-44) is not picked out by Jesus because she gave all that she had; it was a symbol of the value system that the Scribes in the previous verses clearly did not live up to. This aspect of "yes" and "no" is important. Donors should not have to make up for the school's poor stewardship – for example, in failing to care for infrastructure or in not charging enough tuition, leaving operating deficits. Donors want their gifts to matter, whether they are given from poverty or from wealth. The objective of the gift is to make something possible, to change reality.

Giving is recognized and honored. Most importantly, giving is recognized and honored by God. Where giving is "generous" and "cheerful" (2 Corinthians 9:7), God will bless the donor and the gift. The donor brings the loaves and fish and God feeds the 5,000. This must be echoed by the school in its relationship with the donor. Of course, the school cannot judge the donor's heart. And it is not required to.

The school must bless the donor, giving thanks and honor. What of the passage where Jesus noted that giving should be such that no one knows it is happening (Matthew 6:1-4), with the promise that God sees all and will reward? One interpretation of this passage suggests that its intent is to protect the recipient of the gift, i.e., to not shame the poor person who came by in secret. Our donors give to the school and, unless it is specifically for financial aid, there is no fear of embarrassing the recipient, the school. As they honor God by using his wealth to bless the school, so we are God's hands in recognizing and honoring our donors.

The Mary Principle

The prince of this world lives and occupies an alternate and transient reality. The Christian reality is eternal. So philanthropy is not a secular concept. It is a profoundly Christian concept. Philanthropy represents the Creator of the heavens and the earth. It prefigures a new heaven and a new earth (Isaiah 65:17).

The notion that we might and should help those who are not related to us, not connected to us geographically or socially, indeed may be different ethnicities and live in places far from us, is profoundly Christian. This is particularly so when connected to the notion that the act of philanthropy is selfless, with no benefit intended or attached to the giver. Jesus says: "Do not let your left hand know what your right hand is doing" (Matthew 6:3). And Jesus blessed those who were ignored by others – the foreigner, the possessed, the low in prestige. The Christian reality is that all are loved by God just as God knows even the sparrow that is sold for less than a penny (Luke 12:6).

Christian schools need supporters who will give of their abundance (at whatever level that indicates) in order to further the work of the school. Tuition and fees must pay for all operational expenses of the school. We will come back to that. Operational expenses typically do not include the purchase of property, the building of new facilities or renovating old, or providing items that are over and above normal everyday expenses. Strategically, every Christian school needs a culture of philanthropy in order to raise money over and above operating income. The Mary Principle calls the Christian school to enjoy raising money, to treat donors honorably and respectfully, and to follow the highest ethical standards.

From our perspective at CSM, it is no casual statement to call this the Mary Principle. (See the Appendix for the full Principle.) It is based on the third verse of chapter 8 where Luke identifies Jesus' very own Philanthropy Committee: "Mary (called Magdalene) from whom seven demons had come out; Joanna the wife of Chuza, the manager of Herod's household; Susanna; and many others. These women were helping to support them out of their own means."

The women mentioned in Luke's Gospel had been "cured of evil spirits and diseases" (v. 2). They had experienced an astonishing change in their circumstances and were giving out of gratitude for deliverance. These women were the same ones who, in Luke 23 and 24, gave Jesus' body its final ministrations and were the first at the tomb the next day. Certainly, having someone as wealthy as Joanna in the ranks would have been enormously important in order to cover the expenses of this work. It is one of the great ironies of history to note that Jesus' ministry was funded in part by Herod!

Why pick the name Mary? Mary Magdalene, a member of this influential group, is so important that she is mentioned at least 12 times in the Gospels, more than many of the apostles, and mentioned in connection with the key events of Jesus' life. She and the other women were not just appurtenances, but key and vital members of Jesus' work. They offered characteristics that one might find in other Bible passages, such as Proverbs 31 ("A wife of noble character who can find?" v. 10). Connecting philanthropy to these women is to establish important principles buttressing the work of raising money for Christian schools.

We don't know if these women were asked to give or if they initiated the conversation. We can imagine, however, that once someone like Mary had been healed, she asked in what way she could be part of what was going on with Jesus. There was obviously some kind of organizational structure to Jesus' ministry such that, when he arrived at a place, there had been preparations made: food bought for the road, fresh clothing to replace what was wearing out, new sandals on occasion, even transportation, such as the special time that Jesus told his disciples to seek out the ass for his entrance into Jerusalem.

It can't have been a simple thing for 13 men and other followers to travel around the countryside living a peripatetic lifestyle. Each of these women would have been gratefully welcomed into the company of donors who kept things on an even keel. Maybe she asked; maybe she was asked. What we do know is that she and others (many others) were thought important enough to be specifically honored through Luke's narrative.

Giving for Christian education needs to follow the five operating principles outlined above. In the past, caring for the money of others has not been a strong practice on the part of Christian schools. Actual and potential Christian donors often (very often) became disillusioned because their money, given thoughtfully and hopefully, vanished into a black hole that has these characteristics:

- It is not accountable – how it was spent is not identified.
- It does not solve problems; in fact, it merely papers over the problems the school continually fails to address.
- It does not move the school forward. It does not create space for creative solutions or visionary possibilities. Far from opening up opportunity, it reaffirms the school in thinking that its "faithful prayer" has been answered. The future is not a new day but only the present day repeated.
- It does not support building capacity in the teachers, staff, and administration of the school. The gift is used to cover deficits in the current budget. It does not fund "moving forward" items such as providing significant professional development, impacting the child's experience, building endowment, supporting the impactful use of consulting services, professionalizing operations, or implementing technology systems to collect and manage data.
- Even when it is applied to new buildings and renovations, it often papers over the reality that it is actually funding deferred maintenance, i.e., poor stewardship.

4

Following the five operating principles is an opportunity for Christian schools to manage and think about gifts in a different way. Christian schools must know how to look after the gift legally and ethically. Christian schools are wise to use the gift in a way that moves the school from the present into the future. Even the manna in the desert enabled the Jewish people to move toward the Promised Land! Gifts that only serve the present, by definition, mask underlying management and leadership problems that the Board of Trustees and Principal / School Head are not addressing effectively. Gifts are not about the present. They are about future and about vision and about direction.

Interestingly, Christian schools have trouble asking people for money. But it would seem that Jesus and his disciples were not shy about it. Mary, Joanna, and **many others** supported their work. The Mary Principle explicitly states that many want to support the work of Jesus in the Christian school and need to be asked. Penelope Burk in her research into giving says that, for example, "9 to 10 percent of people say they have put bequests in their wills, but more than 30 percent say they would definitely do it or take it under serious consideration if asked." James says in chapter 4: "You do not have because you do not ask God." If we do not ask, with right action and the right motives, we will not receive. Scripture says so.

Scriptural reality is borne out in secular research. The donor has no problem with giving but wants to be asked. Donors want their philanthropy to be an excellent investment in the future. They want to be asked within the context of a plan, to be included appropriately in the conversation, to be thanked, to be told that their gift was used as asked, and to be given evidence that children benefited as a result of the gift.

When donors are treated in this way, they will want to be equally or more generous the following year. A "tired" donor is typically someone for whom these things have not happened. Burnout among donors is a result of bad practice, not a waning of generosity.

It is clear that our schools do not have the confidence, or they do not think it is right, to ask their potential supporters for money. There is sometimes the thought that these people **should** give without being prompted and we shouldn't have to ask them. What we know is that if the school does not ask them, many who would give will not. After all, they **are** being asked by many other organizations and individuals, sometimes on a weekly basis, to contribute to many other worthy causes.

The Christian school needs philanthropic dollars. It is not a "love of money" that leads to asking for investment into the lives of children in the school. It is an appreciation of the needs that truly exist in the delivery of the school's mission. It is because the school can clearly and authentically identify a future-oriented need. It can be done with complete integrity and open accountability. It should be done transparently and without embarrassment.

The donor wants to give to causes they are passionate about. "The wicked borrow and do not repay, but the righteous give generously" (Psalm 37:21). It is natural (God's reality) for Christians not just to give, but to want to give, to be impelled by an inner energy to give. Indeed, being a Christian and not giving would be unimaginable. We are made in the image of God, the Creator of heaven and earth, the Giver of every good thing, and finally the One who gave Jesus, his only Son, as the Incarnate Word, to die for us who were guilty.

As Imago Dei, of course we want to give. And find great pleasure in it. Jesus makes a remarkable statement, as recorded by Luke: "You foolish people! Did not the one who made the outside make the inside also? But now as for what is inside you—be generous to the poor, and everything will be clean for you" (Luke 11:40-41).

The Christian gives because of Jesus; as a result, our internal motivation becomes exponential. This fits with the secular research that the first gift is never the largest – the secular explanation is that this is a test gift, to find out how you will steward it. That's correct. The Christian says, however, that the act of generosity multiplies on itself. Do it once, and it becomes easier to do it twice. Then it becomes a habit.

That's one of the two major purposes for the annual fund – to engage the heart and make the act of generosity habitual – to "clean" the inside. We don't have to worry about whether people want to give. The people of God want an excuse to give – you! Jesus reminds us earlier in Luke 11 that "because of your shameless audacity he will surely get up and give you as much as you need" (v. 8). We rely on our supporters being Imago Dei; we are shamelessly audacious in going to them and asking them to give.

The Ox Principle

The Mary Principle is built on the CSM Ox Principle. A school that has an operations surplus, limits / eliminates its debt, compensates its employees professionally, and has a reserve is a school that is positioned to succeed in raising money optimally. The school that manages its budget poorly, fails to charge tuition that pays the bills, goes into debt, and asks its employees to work "sacrificially," i.e., without sufficient income to raise their families, is positioned to fail in any meaningful philanthropy. These two principles work hand in hand. It is a seeming paradox that the school where tuition/fees pay for all operational expenses raises more money than the school that does not. The Mary Principle cannot work optimally without the Ox Principle (see the Appendix for the full Ox Principle).

Every Christian family that is involved with a Christian school wants to support it. The Mary Principle, and the Ox Principle that underlies it, give them every opportunity to do so. They will be eager and excited to see the miracles of what God has given them translate into the miracles that God will perform through their school. And done in a Christian fashion, our philanthropy will result in giving that we eventually will have to restrain. When Moses was building the Tabernacle, they did some serious fundraising that was so successful that Scripture tells us that people had to be "restrained" from giving any more.

"Moses instructed them to take his message throughout the camp, saying, "Let no man or woman do any more work for the offering for the sanctuary. So the people were restrained from bringing any more. Now the materials were more than enough for them to do all the work" (Exodus 36:6-7).

That is Christian philanthropy at its best and most inspiring!

Summary

- Giving is transformational for the donor as well as for the school.
- There are five operating principles for Christian philanthropy:

  1. Giving is in gratitude for what God has done for each one of us.
  2. Giving is done by people who are intimately involved with the action.
  3. Giving includes involvement, not just the act of giving itself.
  4. Giving galvanizes possibilities that otherwise could not be imagined.
  5. Giving is recognized and honored.

- The Mary Principle assures us that we are connected in our work to Jesus' own ministry.
- Donors want to give – donor burnout is caused by bad practices, not lack of generosity.
- Donors give more when the Ox Principle is in place, i.e., the school has an operations surplus, limits / eliminates its debt, compensates its employees professionally, and has a reserve.

MISSION

THIS SHORT CHAPTER STATES THE obvious: the school's mission is at the center of all philanthropic activity.

It is surprising that this truism is not always obvious in what schools do. The tyranny of the urgent overwhelms conversations so that fundraising desperation dominates: paying the bills or fixing the roof or providing underpaid teachers with a Christmas gift or "bonus." It is not unusual to be in schools where every Board meeting seems to be a crisis meeting. "Perfect love drives out fear" (1 John 4:18), but St. John points out that a lack of fear means being confident on the day of judgment (v. 17). Boards that are not confident in what they are doing are driven by fear. Here are four common fears:

- Fear that families will leave the school
- Fear that tuition will become too "expensive"
- Fear that a key teacher might leave
- Fear that the school may stray from its theological roots

Philanthropy must not be driven by fear. Instead, it needs to be inspired by the school's mission and point to a vibrant future. Deuteronomy 30 reads: "Now what I am commanding you today is not too difficult for you or beyond your reach. It is not up in heaven, so that you have to ask, 'Who will ascend into heaven to get it and proclaim it to us so we may obey it?' Nor is it beyond the sea, so that you have to ask, 'Who will cross the sea to get it and proclaim it to us so we may obey it?' No, the word is very near you; it is in your mouth and in your heart so you may obey it. See, I set before you today life and prosperity, death and destruction. For I command you today to love the Lord your God, to walk in obedience to him, and to keep his commands, decrees and laws; then you will live and increase, and the Lord your God will bless you in the land you are entering to possess" (vs. 11-16).

To take maybe a little liberty, Moses speaking to a Christian school would have talked about the obviousness of mission. In the language of the school, mission is not "too difficult for you or beyond your reach." CSM calls this The Kingdom Principle, that the school's task is to bring God's kingdom "on earth as it is in heaven" (Matthew 6:10). The way it accomplishes that is through the school's mission. The Board can, then, be confident as it moves forward if its actions are in support of the school's mission. The Board's responsibility in philanthropy is third in importance to supporting their Principal / Head of School and operating according to a Strategic Plan / Strategic Financial Management. Its actions in finding, nurturing and soliciting philanthropic dollars are crucial to next generational mission delivery.

The Christian school needs philanthropic dollars. It is not a "love of money" that leads to asking for investment into the lives of children in the school. It is an appreciation of the needs that truly exist in the delivery of the school's mission. It is because the school can clearly and authentically identify a future-oriented need. It is done with complete integrity and open accountability. It is done transparently and without embarrassment. When the Christian school takes its mission seriously, commits to its fulfillment at a level of excellence, identifies the philanthropic dollars that will best move it forward, it will provide God's children with a true experience of His Kingdom here on earth as it is in heaven.

Not only that, but a single-minded focus on the school's mission is what elicits inspirational giving. Dillon says in *Giving and Getting in the Kingdom*, "It is when the mission and passion of the organization match the mission and purpose of the giver that extraordinary giving happens" (p. 107). This is why the vast majority of the school's donors are current parents – they have an alignment of mission and purpose at this time in their lives as they love and provide the best they can for their children.

TRUE STORY – a parent heart connection!

My husband and I considered ourselves as enjoying a comfortable life. We did not consider ourselves as wealthy in terms of money, money we could afford to give away. One day that all changed. We did not earn more money, win the lottery, or borrow. We opened our hearts to what we had been given by our children's school.

Both our children attended for over 17 collective years. We were deeply moved by the experience of love for our children. Teachers who were available before and after school, a counselor who prioritized my child's anguish by staying in constant contact with him, his teachers and us. Celebrations of their accomplishments through writing comments and sharing stories that indicated the depth of understanding of each of our boys. A Head of School who was a fierce advocate for children.

These were the gifts given to us. We decided to give in return. We stretched, we pledged over five years to make the largest donation of our life. How did we feel? Elated, grateful, blessed.

It is certainly possible to motivate the parent out of self-interest. The child is on the baseball team and the team has a need. The parents support the team because it directly supports their child. They make a gift. Booster clubs are based on this premise of transaction – I give you something and I get something back. But this kind of giving does not fulfill the greater vision of what is at stake in Christian education. The child is not being prepared to play baseball, or go to college, or have a job, important as all those can be. The child is being prepared to take up an adult role in the Kingdom.

St. Matthew refers to this many, many times. For example, Matthew records Jesus saying "Not everyone who says to me, 'Lord, Lord,' will enter the kingdom of heaven, but only the one who does the will of my Father who is in heaven" (Matthew 7:21). How does a child know how to do the Father's will in their life's witness, in science, on social media, through communication, social studies, athletics, the arts? The Christian school teaches, demonstrates, models, encourages, and supports the child in their complete human development. To align the parent around that mission as it is carried out in the unique setting of each school is to unleash a passion far greater than transaction. The gift follows the passion.

As one parent put it in an interview, "Lord willing we are staying – I guess I would say he's being discipled in the Gospel well – he's being loved on really well (tears) – given what he needs to do well – with his unique challenges he's learning stuff – he's just really happy."

Summary

- Mission must be the prime motivator for the school's philanthropic efforts.
- Mission and the effect of excellent mission delivery will ultimately raise more money than other motivations.
- The Board has a front-seat role in philanthropy.
- The parent must be aligned around mission, not transaction.

CSM RELATIONAL PHILANTHROPY

CHRISTIAN SCHOOLS MUST MOVE WITH their donors into the 21st century. They will move from transactional fundraising to relational philanthropy. To be obvious, a transaction is where I give you a "gift," but actually my motivation is to get something you have in return. It might be the attempt to get something cheap at a silent auction; it might be to benefit my child on the baseball / softball team; it might be to buy access or influence; it might be to get my name in bright lights on the stadium. Humans like transactions, large and small. They are part of living. They are not necessarily immoral. They are the way in which we typically do business.

Transactional fundraising is not Christian philanthropy. It is not relational philanthropy.

Events, and even worse selling "stuff" (chocolates, poinsettias, Easter lilies, pizzas), doing raffles, are antithetical to philanthropy. Develop your philanthropy program on the basis of The CSM Mary Principle:

1. Giving is in gratitude for what God has done for each one of us.
2. Giving is done by people who are intimately involved with the action.
3. Giving includes involvement, not just the act of giving itself.
4. Giving galvanizes possibilities that otherwise could not be imagined.
5. Giving is recognized and honored.

There is nothing wrong with events – until we attach money to them. Events develop connections and relationships within the school community. They build community. They are excellent for inspiring fun. They provide safe opportunities for families to enjoy being with each other. They can raise money – but not optimally, not for the right reasons, and not in a way that can honor and transform the donor.

The donor wants to give to a cause/mission they are aligned with. The donor has no problem with giving, but wants to be asked. Donors want their philanthropy to be an excellent investment in the future and/or further the cause. They want to be asked within the context of a plan, to be included appropriately in the conversation, to be thanked, to be told that their gift was used as asked, and to be given evidence that children benefited as a result of the gift. When donors are treated in this way, they will want to be equally or more generous the following year. In this way, we develop loyal donors who will give to the end of their child's time at the school and then maybe even beyond and to death.

Their giving is not constrained by what they get. Their giving is not wasted because half the gift goes to a corporation (think chocolate bars) or to another donor (think the awful and ubiquitous 50/50!). Their giving is based on who, not what. Their giving changes who they are and brings them closer to shalom – the way things should be. Their giving brings them closer to God. "The generous will themselves be blessed (brought into relationship with God), for they share their food with the poor" (Proverbs 22:9). It is relational philanthropy.

We diagram relational philanthropy in the following way:

The CSM Relational Philanthropy Cycle

On the left of the Cycle is the donor. CSM knows with great justification from Scripture, research, and experience that donors have enormous hearts and want to give from what God has given them. In fact, you know the same thing in your own experience. You have received gifts small and large that you know came from the depth of the donor's heart and gratitude. The experience of receiving the gift was far more poignant than the gift itself. How can we bring all of those in the school's community to enjoy and relish the experience of giving and receiving?

Why should donors give? Simply, to ensure the child receives excellence in the school's mission delivery.

That's why the child is at the center of the Cycle. The child is the focus of the school's mission and is the place where the donor connects with the school. At a young age, the child is being formed and trained with and by Christian educators and within the love, mercy, peace, and justice of God. Almost every donor is motivated by children. Of course, for many, it begins with their own experience of the school's impact within their own children's lives.

The school is bringing the child to the point where, as an adolescent, the child is preparing to take the final steps toward making an impact for Christ as an adult within a culture that in all times and ages needs to know the faith, hope, and love promised to those who follow Jesus. Every donor lives in that same culture and is looking for the leadership of the next generation to take over as they retire and then die. The donor wants the child to be successful; wants the child's generation to be mature and living the life God desires; wants the children to be the next generation to impact their culture for the Lord. This is the reason that donors give.

Of course, that might be translated into a passion for the arts or athletics, a desire to provide buildings for a new time in education, a motivation to support children through financial aid, a foresight that will fund endowment for succeeding generations. The child is not abstract. The reason for giving is not abstract. The donor gives to help and even help transform the child's experience such that their impact will be even greater.

You might say that you know donors who are selfish donors. They are interested in their own child or children or grandchildren. We are, of course, interested in those whom we know best and love very dearly. That might mean that an initial gift is given from a heart that is thinking transactionally. The school's task is to help the donor move from transaction to relationship. It's not just about the school building a relationship with the donor. It's also about the school helping the donor mature into a relationship with the school and with God that helps the donor in their own faith walk. Henri Nouwen writes: "So if we ask for money from people who have money, we have to love them deeply. We do not need to worry about the money. Rather, we need to worry about whether, through the invitation we offer them and the relationship we develop with them, they will come closer to God" (A Spirituality of Fund-raising p. 41).

To the right of the diagram is the donor steward. This representative of the school might be the Principal, the Board President, a member of the Philanthropy Committee, the Athletic Director, a teacher, a parent. It is the personal conversation that draws the donor into a deeper relationship with the school. The donor Steward represents Mark 9:37 to the donor: "Whoever welcomes one of these little children in my name welcomes me; and whoever welcomes me does not welcome me but the one who sent me."

This is, of course, emotional. But it is much more than a mere engagement of surface emotion. It is a response to the call of Jesus; it is making Jesus welcome; it is making God the Father welcome. The donor Steward, through that personal conversation, reminds and represents the need of the child and invites the donor to respond.

The CSM Relational Philanthropy Cycle

© Christian School Management 2022

The response of the donor is at the top of the diagram. While almost anyone will give, the school seeks an inspired gift, one that maybe the donor did not even expect to make. This gift has the ability, on its own or with a great cloud of witnesses, to transform what happens in the life of the child. It also has the ability, solicited in the right way, with the invitational conversation, through relationship, to also transform the donor.

This double transformation is seen in Luke 8:3: "The Twelve were with him, and also some women who had been cured of evil spirits and diseases: Mary (called Magdalene) from whom seven demons had come out; Joanna the wife of Chuza, the manager of Herod's household; Susanna; and many others. These women were helping to support them out of their own means." Jesus' own Philanthropy Committee responded to transformation in their own lives by providing the means for transformation in everyone's life through Jesus' ministry. This provokes the inspired gift – the donor is invited to respond in the same way as Jesus' own followers did.

We always remember that even people who are not generous, nonetheless have the spark of generosity in them because they are made in the image of God. Almost all people will give when asked. The challenge is thus not whether the person makes a gift. The challenge is to obtain the inspired gift. The person who gives grudgingly, out of guilt, to get you away from them, to be able to say they gave, that person will give you $50.

When brought into relational philanthropy, that person will give for totally different reasons (even if the original reasons still echo in their minds). They will give because God first gave, because they love the school, because they want others to experience what they experienced, because they see a need and feel called to meet it, because they are grateful for what has happened in the life of their child. Giving will flow from each donor feeling encouraged and hopeful. They will give inspirationally. A $50 gift will turn into $500. The donor will give unexpectedly – unexpectedly in their **own** minds. "I never imagined I would ever give at this level. I am so privileged to be able to do so."

TRUE STORY – a grandparent heart connection!

In 2010, I received a "cold call" on the phone from a grandparent whose two grandsons were playing middle school football for our school. It turns out that he owned a property where another local private school used to send its football team for summer camp. He wanted to give us an old blocking sled that "is old, and rusty, needs to be painted and new pads purchased." Believing that it is better to say yes to accepting most gifts, to create forward momentum, I agreed. He even delivered the sled to campus.

Not long after, we got a gift of $5,000, and every year since he has sent $10,000–$15,000 from his IRA as an undesignated gift. Every semester I call to check on him, and through the years we have gotten in the habit of sharing books that we like or sharing a meal. I report on the impact of his gift, brief him on the school's opportunities and threats, and bring him merch from the school store to wear to games! The relationship has grown to one in which he mentors me like a son and tells me confidential things. I've been to his home and farm for meals, and we rode four-wheelers to his favorite places to look at his favorite trees.

Now we are discussing his estate, since he is 90, and I am meeting with his financial advisor. It appears that we will get a $1.5 million+ estate gift to endow a teacher position. It is 2024, and we still have and use the blocking sled. His grandsons have graduated, but still value the time they spent at our Christian school.

The school has continued to be and do the very things that are core to our mission even after all these years and it is, I think, the continuity of our relationship that has allowed him to be comfortable enough to plan one of the two largest gifts he will give to charity at the end of his useful life.

The arrow at the bottom of the Cycle diagram identifies that the school / donor relationship is well-founded when it encompasses the mission of the school. We may not agree about everything – the amount of playing time my kid received, the book you are using in eighth grade social studies, whether the entrance way should be gray or rose – but we agree that the school's mission is uniting everyone in the community on behalf of the child. That mission points us to the reason for the school and the Person who inspires, blesses, rejoices in that reason.

The word "relationship" means that the donor is not doing their act of charity **for** the school but **with** the school. This reflects a deep truth, that God came as the incarnate Son to be with us: "The virgin will conceive and give birth to a son, and they will call him Immanuel" (which means God with us)" (Matthew 1:23). The donor has moved from being an outsider looking in to being a participant in the action. It's a simple arrow, not simplistic. It's the heart of great philanthropy.

The CSM Relational Philanthropy Cycle

© Christian School Management 2022

Relational philanthropy is a cycle. We don't know where the beginning or the end is. We can't remember how that conversation began. We are amazed at the depth of the relationship. We are humbled by the inspired gift. We just know that each and every day the school must engage with and touch the heart of each member of its community. Relational philanthropy is astonishingly simple and outstandingly courageous. Jesus stands next to us in each part of the Cycle and knocks at the door. Both donor and donor steward respond to the knock of Jesus in their hearts and to the vision of Jesus in the life of each child. In Mark 9:37, Jesus says: "Whoever welcomes one of these little children in my name welcomes me; and whoever welcomes me does not welcome me but the one who sent me." Welcoming takes many forms – philanthropy is one of them.

CSM calls this The Golden Rule Cycle.

Summary

- The CSM Relational Philanthropy Cycle diagrams the school's relationship to the donor.
- The school engages the donor with the child as the reason for the relationship.
- The message is about excellent mission delivery.
- The donor response becomes more and more inspired as the relationship grow.
- It is the school's responsibility to steward each donor as a personal relationship.
- The donor moves from being an outsider to being a participant in the action.

THE GOLDEN RULE CYCLE: THE ACTIONS OF THE DONOR STEWARD

Lᴇᴛ's ᴅɪɢ ᴍᴏʀᴇ ᴅᴇᴇᴘʟʏ ɪɴᴛᴏ what the donor steward does in the Relational Philanthropy Cycle.

THE GOLDEN RULE CYCLE

©2024 Christian School Management

Stewardship

Stewardship is the profound inner heart of the approach. Whether it is carried out by a professional – the Philanthropy Director or Principal, for example – or whether it is carried out by a volunteer – a member of the Philanthropy Committee or the Annual Fund Cabinet, for example – stewardship is a way of living relationship. When stewardship becomes a series of techniques, we are back in the secular land of cleverness but without wisdom. The donor steward is the one who practices stewardship of the donor on behalf of the school and in service to the children through the school's mission delivery.

If stewardship is the inner heart and, at the same time, surrounds the entire enterprise of relationship, what does the Bible say about it? Here is St. Peter: "Above all, love each other deeply, because love covers over a multitude of sins. Offer hospitality to one another without grumbling. Each of you should use whatever gift you have received to serve others, as good stewards of God's grace in its various forms. If anyone speaks, they should do so as one who speaks the very words of God. If anyone serves, they should do so with the strength God provides, so that in all things God may be praised through Jesus Christ. To him be the glory and the power for ever and ever. Amen" (1 Peter 4:8-11).

We note that the word steward is next to the word good (καλοὶ οἰκονόμοι). *Strong's Concordance* offers the following meaning of the word good: beautiful, as an outward sign of the inward good, noble, honorable character; good, worthy, honorable, noble, and seen to be so. This is who stewards are. They are fitted to their task; they are seen to be honorable.

When we think of the donor steward as a member of the Philanthropy Committee, or as the professional Director of Philanthropy and the Principal / Head of School, we are not thinking primarily of a technical way of carrying out a task. We are thinking primarily about a relationship carried out by someone who demonstrates an "honorable character." Notice that this is in a section beginning "Above all, love each other deeply, because love covers over a multitude of sins."

The list following is predicated on loving each other deeply. Being a good donor steward is in the use of God's gifts given and passed on in love. The end of the 1 Peter section encourages the donor steward that, through this service, they are leaning on the "strength God provides." As donor stewards then:

1. We are seen to be honorable.
2. We are fitted to our task.
3. We use the gifts God has given us.
4. We lean on God's strength to serve in love.

Notice that outward appearance (seen to be honorable) is intrinsic to this Scriptural / Greek use of the word good. Paul emphasizes this in Romans 12:17: "Be careful to do what is right (καλὰ) in the eyes of everyone." The donor steward cannot be seen to engage in deceitfulness, artifice, manipulation. This is in antithesis to the steward in Luke 16 who squandered his master's goods. The outcome of this steward's actions was a loss of trust between the master and the steward, resulting in him being fired.

The four characteristics of the donor steward infuse the task of stewardship as we apply it to philanthropy. Stewarding a donor is an honorable task carried out by people who themselves are honorable. Their relationship to the donor is carried out in a way that honors the gifts given by God to the donor steward. Everything occurs through the prism of love – which is good because although we try to do the right thing, we often do the wrong thing (cf. Romans 7:15-20). Love helps the donor to see what I mean to do, even if I don't do it well. And so God's name is blessed.

The donor steward asks the donor to decide which of these three questions is the most appropriate:

- What do I want to do with my possessions?
- What do I want to do with God's possessions – what God has given me?
- What does God want me to do with what he has given me?

We realize that donors are at various points in their spiritual journeys. The steward may have to discern where the donor is and make a judgment call as to where to begin.

For some, the first question is the appropriate one. They are going to give but aren't sure whether Christian schools are going to be a prime beneficiary. *Giving USA 2023* provides insight into the challenge stewarding such donors might be:

FAITH-BASED CHARITIES

	None	Less	Same Amount	More	Unsure
Gen Z	26%	9%	26%	31%	9%
Millennials	26%	8%	36%	21%	9%
Gen X	37%	5%	34%	13%	11%
Boomers	38%	2%	48%	4%	8%

©2023 Giving USA Foundation and Dunham+Company

Generationally, boomers either are or aren't going to give and, if they are already giving to your school, only a few might consider giving at a higher level. On the other hand, with all other generations, there are potentially between 24 percent and 40 percent of donors who might consider giving more. How do we as relational stewards best help our clients answer the following question – What do I, as a faithful steward, do with my possessions?

Most mature Christian believers in the USA answer the first two questions for themselves using scripture. They understand that everything they have is from God (cf. David's prayer in 1 Chronicles 29:13-14). *Nonprofits Source* reported in 2023 that Christians give 2.5 percent of their income, and that is less than during the Great Depression (3.3 percent). It is not clear that Christians in North America, even when they know that all they have comes from God, translate that into generosity. The same report said, even more surprisingly, that 37 percent of churchgoers, including evangelicals, don't even give to the church they are attending. It is obvious how important the job of the steward is in connecting the heart of the donor to the mission of the school. According to *GivingUSA*, the younger generation may have a better understanding of this second question. At the very least, younger donors are more likely to go to church!

Since 2016, Millennials are the only generation to have increased attendance at worship services.

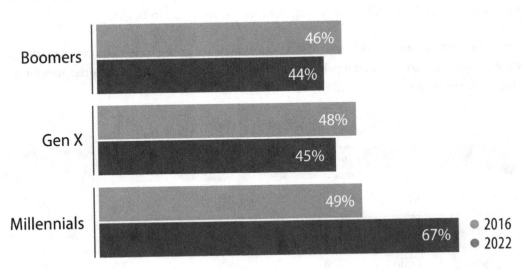

Percentage of donors who say they attend church at least a few times per month (2022 includes both virtual and in-person).

©2023 Giving USA Foundation and Dunham+Company

The most motivated donors, and the ones who will give most generously, are those who are ready for the third question – not what do I want to do with my possessions, but what does God want me to do with what he has given me? According to the *2023 Bank of America Study of Philanthropy: Charitable Giving by Affluent Households*, 85.1 percent gave and 36.8 percent volunteered their time. Affluent is characterized as households with income over $200,000 or net worth of $1 million+, not including their primary residence. Interestingly, those who volunteered time gave three times as much as those who didn't, on average. But this group is becoming less generous.

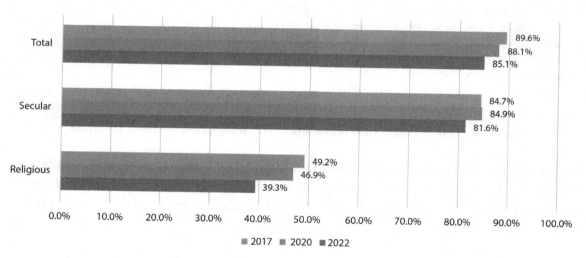

AFFLUENT HOUSEHOLDS REPORTING GIVING TO ANY CHARITY IN 2017, 2020, AND 2022

©2023 2023 Bank of America Study of Philanthropy: Charitable Giving by Affluent Households

If we can steward them through to the third question, we know we will find a generous heart for the school's mission. The task of the donor steward is a serious one – over half of these donors gave to less than five charities. How can the school be, remain, or become one of them? We can see that K–12 Christian schools attract a disproportionate amount of funding – which is a morale booster for us.

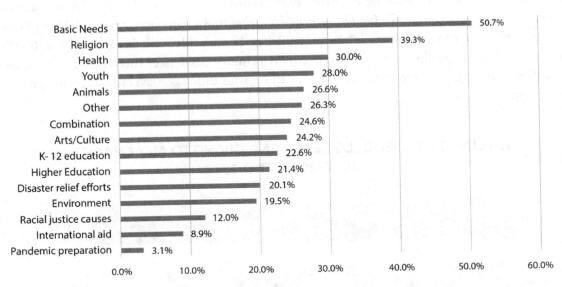

AFFLUENT HOUSEHOLDS REPORTING GIVING TO CHARITABLE CATEGORIES

©2023 2023 Bank of America Study of Philanthropy: Charitable Giving by Affluent Households

Stewardship is at the heart of and embraces the Golden Rule Cycle. donor stewards exhibit four Scriptural characteristics and understand the three questions that donors move through on the journey to spiritual maturity. Being able to discern and guide the donor is the stewardship task.

The Child

THE GOLDEN RULE CYCLE

©2024 Christian School Management

Mark 9, beginning at verse 33, portrays Jesus schooling his disciples about the nature of the Kingdom. It goes like this: "They came to Capernaum. When he was in the house, he asked them, 'What were you arguing about on the road?' But they kept quiet because on the way they had argued about who was the greatest. Sitting down, Jesus called the Twelve and said, 'Anyone who wants to be first must be the very last, and the servant of all.' He took a little child whom he placed among them. Taking the child in his arms, he said to them, 'Whoever welcomes one of these little children in my name welcomes me; and whoever welcomes me does not welcome me but the one who sent me'" (Mark 9:33-37). The child is at the center of the Golden Rule Cycle and is its focus. Placing the child at the center of stewardship is not to glorify the child. The child is in reality the mission or cause of the school. In philanthropy, this means is to acknowledge that the gift "welcomes" the child in the name of Jesus.

In the Golden Rule Cycle, the child at the center of stewardship drives two ideas:

1. In its stewardship of donors, the school understands that the motivation for the donor in its outward form is the school's mission. The result of the gift is to enhance mission delivery, i.e., improve the mission-driven education the child will receive.

    It is easy for the school to become adult-centered rather than child-centered. CSM consistently warns against such an orientation and provides counsel to influence the school to move in the child's direction. There are Philanthropy Officers in our schools who rarely, and almost never meaningfully, spend time in the presence of children. They don't sit at lunch with them. They never go on a field trip. If they are in the pickup or drop-off line, it is primarily to meet the actual or potential donor rather than to interact with the child. Thankfully, there are many more who delight in visiting classrooms, empowering the child to make the video, participating in the chapel service, and learning each child's name.

2. The donor understands that the gift enhancing mission delivery is in service to the child, not for driving special interests. Maybe oddly, it is easier to direct a donor in a child-centered way than it is to direct the school. With the donor, the objectives of the annual fund and capital campaign are presented by the school with the child as the point – more classrooms to accommodate enrollment growth; another gym so all children can play and practices don't have to go beyond 8 p.m.; HVAC for the Kindergarten so kids enjoy learning through every season. Rarely, though not never, do we find Christian donors adult-centered in their approach.

3. Both of these ideas derive from Jesus' teaching about service. Christians are not here to lord it over one another, including children. Matthew tells a parallel service in chapter 20: "Then the mother of Zebedee's sons came to Jesus with her sons and, kneeling down, asked a favor of him. 'What is it you want?' he asked. She said, 'Grant that one of these two sons of mine may sit at your right and the other at your left in your kingdom.' 'You don't know what you are asking,' Jesus said to them. 'Can you drink the cup I am going to drink?' 'We can,' they answered. Jesus said to them, 'You will indeed drink from my cup, but to sit at my right or left is not for me to grant. These places belong to those for whom they have been prepared by my Father.' When the ten heard about this, they were indignant with the two brothers. Jesus called them together and said, 'You know that the rulers of the Gentiles lord it over them, and their high officials exercise authority over them. Not so with you. Instead, whoever wants to become great among you must be your servant, and whoever wants to be first must be your slave – just as the Son of Man did not come to be served, but to serve, and to give his life as a ransom for many'" (Matthew 20:21-28).

TRUE STORY – keeping the focus on the child!

A CSM consultant was being given a tour of the school he was partnering with. It was early in the morning and there were no children present. Teachers and staff were busy setting up for the day. The school was making many efforts to improve its "look," and was rightfully pleased with the direction of its efforts.

Near the end of the tour, the guide swung into the elementary dining room. The consultant paused, rather puzzled. "This is the elementary lunch room?" he asked. "Yes," the guide replied. It was not much to look at – very traditional and somewhat dark.

But that wasn't the consultant's question. "How do the children get up on the chairs?" he asked. "Do they have ladders?" The tables and chairs were clearly far too large for elementary children! Without a hint of irony, the guide nonchalantly said, "We use it for donor receptions too."

Needless to say, the first recommendation was to replace the elementary lunchroom furniture. And it was accompanied by the admonition that donations would increase if donors had to sit in children's furniture – they would be "charmed" and inspired by the idea of giving to children. The school was adult-centered, worrying how to impress the donor. The donor is child-centered, concerned with how to benefit children.

CSM's Child Principle notes that child-centeredness asks us to leave behind our own adult selfishness (which scripturally is always attached to ambition (cf. 2 Corinthians 12:20; Galatians 5:20; Philippians 2:3; James 3:14). It asks us to come toward the child within the child's own context and in a way that makes sense to the child. And it asks us to exercise authority in order to serve the child, not to dominate the child.

In our schools, that means actually paying deep attention to what we **say** we are doing and what we are **actually** doing; to recognizing our missions as being almost exclusively and correctly about helping the child; to asking children their thoughts, fears, dreams, and aspirations, finding them of value, and acting on them; to beginning each conversation with the admonition to keep the child at the center; to coming to decisions and asking the question as to whom the decision primarily benefits; to running meetings that focus on mission delivery to the child, whatever the topic of conversation.

In our stewardship of donors, we are wise to point always to the child. At age 3 and 5 and 7, they inspire our donors through their joy and vulnerability and obvious dependence. At age 9 and 11 and

13, they inspire through their questions, desire, and burgeoning independence. At age 15 and 17 and 19, they inspire through their character, leadership and contribution. We point to our alumni as the Portrait of the Child in action, acting as lights on a hill and spreading the Good News within their own spheres of influence. Indwelt by the Holy Spirit, the Christian donor is fundamentally willing and even excited to give because of the child.

Prayer

©2024 Christian School Management

The Golden Rule Cycle places prayer at the top of the Cycle deliberately. The communication between God and the donor steward (professional and / or volunteer) is key to honest success. The ability to listen to God as well as advocate to God for others is both a Christian requirement and a philanthropic must.

One: Pray for your own heart

The Bible records 25 instances of Jesus praying during his time on earth. One of those times, in particular, is relevant to our vocation in philanthropy. In Luke's account, at the Last Supper, Jesus shares his body and blood with them. After this, they immediately turn to wondering which of them would betray Jesus, and that "naturally" morphed into an argument about who was greatest among them.

Jesus turns specifically to Simon Peter and says to him: "Simon, Simon, Satan has asked to sift all of you as wheat. But I have prayed for you, Simon, that your faith may not fail. And when you have turned back, strengthen your brothers" (Luke 22:31-32). Peter declares that his faith is strong. Jesus gently tells him that he will deny Jesus three times. Satan will test him. We know the end of the story. Peter, the rock on which Jesus declared the church would be built (Matthew 16:18), weeps bitterly and turns from his betrayal and strengthens the new church springing up from the Good News of resurrection and new life.

The steward is to be a good steward. It is easy to be led into temptation (cf. Matthew 6) and begin to act in a clever but not holy way. Winning is not the point. Money is not the point. Relationship is the point. Generosity springs from relationship. The steward must pray that he or she will not fall into temptation, even as we recognize that Satan sifts us. We are encouraged and strengthened by the fact that Jesus prays for us (cf. John 17) and that the Father wants all good things for us (cf. 2 Corinthians 9:8).

Proverbs 4 puts it this way: "Above all else, guard your heart, for everything you do flows from it. Keep your mouth free of perversity; keep corrupt talk far from your lips. Let your eyes look straight ahead; fix your gaze directly before you. Give careful thought to the paths for your feet and be steadfast in all your ways. Do not turn to the right or the left; keep your foot from evil (Proverbs 4:23-27).

What magnificent advice for the donor steward, whether you are professional or amateur, first time doing it or hundredth! Pray for your heart because everything you say comes from that heart. "A good man brings good things out of the good stored up in him, and an evil man brings evil things out of the evil stored up in him" (Matthew 12:35). So your words, your focus, your choices, your steadfastness, your integrity, all these are part of great stewardship. Who we **are** matters!

Two: Pray for the right hands

Stewardship seeks the right people to do the job. It is instructive that when Samuel went to pour the horn of oil on Israel's second king, Samuel had to ask Jesse if there was anyone else in his family because the seven sons, despite their outward appearance, had not been chosen by God for the task. The answer is also instructive: "There is still the youngest tending the sheep" (1 Samuel 16).

When we think about our next campaign, we need to know that God has already called donors to provide the funds for its success. Now apparently David (and his father Jesse), with oil running down his head, didn't know what to do and went back to working with the sheep. It was only later that God called him through Saul to action. Your donor may not know God's call, or may not be responding to it. It is for the donor steward to pray for discernment as the relationship grows in prodding the donor to examine their heart and find out what God intends. 1 Peter tells us that we are a chosen race, i.e., we are all called or chosen (1 Peter 2:9). But each of us has specific choices to make as well – ways in which God wants me to respond in a particular way as a member of God's people.

The donor steward's worst nightmare is the story of Ananias and Sapphira (Acts 5). These were not stewarded well to make a gift to benefit the community. They wanted to look good. They wanted to be appreciated for their generosity. They wanted esteem. They wanted to get much more than they wanted to give. As Peter said to them, what you owned truly belonged to you. You could do with it as you wished. You could have kept it or given it away. Why lie about it? Oh, that they had a donor steward to pray for their "hands"! This does not mean that, in our schools, as human beings, we are to attempt to read the donor's heart ourselves. Trying to understand, let alone judge, motivations is not our place. We are not Peter.

At the same time, we have an obligation to our donors to help them be like the Corinthians about whom Paul boasted (2 Corinthians 9:2), not like Ananias and Sapphira. We do this by:

- Praying with them (and for them)
- Educating them about the "project" but, maybe more importantly about the way/s in which they can steward their wealth to give glory to Gods
- Insisting that they give with a full heart

Three: Pray for the resources needed

We should be bold in asking for the resources – money, in particular – that we need. Praying for resources assumes that first, the school is:

- Planning strategically, i.e., within the context of a plan that understands not only the immediate need but how that need fits into future needs
- Planning sustainably, i.e., as part of strategic thinking, knowing how the gift outcome (building, endowment, renovation, program) will be sustained over time
- Budgeting responsibly, i.e., the school is running right-sized and balanced budgets

Taking responsibility for the current operations is a moral obligation before asking the donor to contribute to the future life of the school. Christian schools have for too long prayed for resources that maintain and support poor practices. We must ensure that our own house is in order. This might mean that we have taken steps to move the school along the right path, creating a virtuous vector. It might mean that the school has accomplished those steps. What matters is that the school has acknowledged and undertaken to use effective practices within which each donor's gift will have the ability to thrive.

In Luke 14, Jesus asks a question: "Suppose one of you wants to build a tower. Won't you first sit down and estimate the cost to see if you have enough money to complete it? For if you lay the foundation and are not able to finish it, everyone who sees it will ridicule you, saying, 'This person began to build and wasn't able to finish'" (Luke 14:28-30). Of course, he is using an example from real life to illustrate a spiritual truth. That doesn't take away from the real-life example. We pray for what we need, and that prayer is effective most commonly in circumstances when we have taken responsibility for what is ours to do.

The reality for our Christian schools is that the resources are there. We are surrounded by wealth. We pray that we can find the donors who are already there and build a relationship with them. We pray that we can inspire them (and listen to them) in order to identify those projects that will have the greatest impact on the school's witness and the child's success. We pray that we have enough to achieve excellence and not so much that we achieve arrogance. Pray that our success is holy and brings us peace / shalom.

God himself told us the kind of prayer we should have: "The Lord bless you and keep you; the Lord make his face shine on you and be gracious to you; the Lord turn his face toward you and give you peace" (Numbers 6:24).

Thank

THE GOLDEN RULE CYCLE

©2024 Christian School Management

Thankfulness comes next to prayer. Being thankful is another aspect of prayer. When we receive a gift, we thank God and we thank the donor whom God inspired. Without the thanks, the gift becomes dangerous. Deuteronomy 8 warns that failing to give thanks leads to pride and thus the idea that maybe all this money, this successful campaign, this wonderful relationship with the donor, was all the product of "my" work and "my" effort. "Otherwise, when you eat and are satisfied, when you build fine houses and settle down, and when your herds and flocks grow large and your silver and gold increase and all you have is multiplied, then your heart will become proud and you will forget the Lord your God, who brought you out of Egypt, out of the land of slavery" (Deuteronomy 8:12-14).

All of our efforts are founded in God's love for us that he made us and he redeems us. While God blesses our efforts and gives us our gifts to use, we are always to remember that we are but dust, i.e., that we should be humble (Psalm 103:14). Thanks, then, is an act of humility. We are humbled by the act of God through the donor to the school for the child.

When we live in Christ, we live in thankfulness, and that does not depend on circumstance. As the traditional wedding vow states, thankfulness is in all conditions: to have and to hold from this day forward, for better, for worse, for richer, for poorer, in sickness and in health. Thankfulness does not depend on success as the world sees it. How much more so should we be thankful when God has blessed our efforts and provided us with donors who want to bless our school with their increase. "So then, just as you received Christ Jesus as Lord, continue to live your lives in him, rooted and built up in him, strengthened in the faith as you were taught, and overflowing with thankfulness" (Colossians 2:6-7).

In the book *Donor-Centered Fundraising* by Penelope Burk, there is this poignant paragraph: "Have you ever said something kind to someone and regretted it? Probably not. Do you think that personal contact with donors is a good thing? If you are a fundraiser, I'm sure the answer is yes. Why, then, is it not automatic for fundraisers, their colleagues, their bosses and their volunteers to pick up the phone and say thank-you to donors as soon as their gifts are received? What is it that holds us back from responding to donors' generosity in such a natural way?" (p. 98). Burk then speaks of a research test that she carried out to see what happened when people were thanked. On average, their giving was 42 percent higher than those who were not. Four percent expressed interest in making a major gift.

When Jesus gave thanks at meals, or in the feeding of the 5,000, he probably used a standard formula:

BA-RUCH A-TAH A-DO-NOI ELO-HAI-NU ME-LECH HA-O-LAM,
Blessed are You, L-rd our G-d, King of the Universe (chabad.org)

Thanking is the "same" as blessing! When we thank God, we bless him. One commentator suggests that to bless literally means to kneel to.

There are four quasi rules for thanking. The donor steward must be:

1. Quick! While thanking late is probably better than not thanking at all (we have no data to support either position), thanking once the gift is received is highly effective. Donors universally are surprised, and then pleased when they pick up the phone or listen to a voicemail and hear a simple thank-you from the donor steward. Thanking quickly avoids the concern of the donor that the phone call, beginning with thank-you, is actually a cover to ask again. Thanking quickly makes the likelihood of the person giving again – in due season – very high.

We strongly recommend that the first thank-you is by phone and within 48 hours of the receipt of the gift. Life hasn't stopped if it's later. <u>And</u> every donor steward must have a sense of urgency about this simple act of thanks in response to generosity.

2. Sincere! We should take this for granted. However, thanking and sincerity are not easy to combine. A phone call is almost always or always sincere. It is one human communicating with another human on an individual basis. Other forms of thank-you are, however, not so simple.

    A form letter, sent to everyone and starting with Dear Donor, is clearly a duty to be performed and does not pass the sincerity smell test. A beautiful, heart-wrenching personal story that totally engages you the first year, totally loses its shine if you receive the same story two years in a row. A thank-you accompanied by a gift actually inspires a reverse response of dislike or even anger: Why did you waste my money giving me something I don't want?

    It's a lot of work to be sincere – is each donor worth it? Of course! When the donor steward takes the time to pen a unique personal note that acknowledges the gift, it says that I sincerely appreciate your generosity.

3. Warm! The initial phone call by the donor steward is great. The follow-up letter is important too. And so is the receipt that comes out in January or February. Notice that warmth is needed whether the interaction is direct to the donor (phone and letter) or Business Office to donor (tax receipt). The Business Office letter is often neglected. It is going to be a generic letter AND it can be thought through and prayed over in its creation as much as any other important communication. The donor steward should ask to have a copy of the Business Office letter to assure that it is "warm" as well.

4. Content rich! Our messaging has meaning. The letter to the Colossians advises: "Be wise in the way you act toward outsiders; make the most of every opportunity. Let your conversation be always full of grace, seasoned with salt, so that you may know how to answer everyone" (Colossians 4:5-6). Our communications are to be "full of grace, seasoned with salt," i.e., very tasty!!

Report

THE GOLDEN RULE CYCLE

©2024 Christian School Management

The school will have official ways of communicating with the whole community, whether donors or not. The donor steward acts intentionally in reporting back to the donor about the use and impact of the gift made. Why does that matter? Christian donors have been demotivated by Christian schools. Their gifts have been spent on objectives other than those promised, they have disappeared down a black hole and not accounted for, they have been solicited for crisis reasons way more than once, they have not been appreciated. Donors want and expect accountability.

The donor steward, then, is an accountability agent. The intent of reporting is firstly to assure the donor that their money was spent

- Ethically, i.e., on the matter promised in the solicitation
- In moving the school forward, i.e., not so the school could just survive another year
- In a way that mattered, i.e., that it had impact

Accountability leads to motivation leads to excitement – and leads to even more significant, or repeated, gifts in the years to come. When, by our behavior, we create this relational chain reaction, a donor will feel safe about continuing to generously support your school's mission and the lives of children. Giving will not be a one-off but one aspect of the developing relationship – to continue as long as the relationship continues.

Because the donor steward knows the donor well, knows why they give, what they primarily interested in, the reporting back will:

- Recognize the scope of the school's objectives and focus on the area of the donor's interest.
- Identify the stages of the objective's progress from beginning to end.
- See the gift's ongoing power, not just in the attainment of the immediate objective, but in its longer lasting impact.
- Point to what might still be accomplished through the school's ongoing and strategic thinking.

TRUE STORY – a lead donor heart connection!

A school we have been involved with for many years asked leadership donors to frontload a campaign that would open a new high school campus. Donor stewards spent three years providing a "picture" of the vision, the power of extending K–8 to high school, the dream of obtaining 40 acres, and the way that would be transformed into a wonderful new opportunity.

The donors bought into the vision and the land was purchased. Donors were taken on tours of the virgin property and the next phase was imagined together with them. Funds were constantly accounted for, pictures taken, students interviewed, tours taken, appreciation events held.

The school is now in the fifth phase, and most of the original donors are still with them over a decade later. At the time of writing, they are leading the construction of the STEAM wing.

Reporting might include the following, for example:

- A phone call update
- An invite to an event
- Texting a picture of the progress
- Facilitating a tour of the outcome with a child

Typically, reporting can assume that the donor will be on the school's mailing list and will receive the school's regular newsletters and digital updates, along with invites to the school's website to experience what is going on. The donor steward's job is to make that personal and specific to the donor.

The donor steward is willing to be accountable to the donor relationship by reporting back accurately, consistently, and with the donor's interests at heart. The strategic impact of that reporting is to ensure a healthy relationship. Remember always that relational philanthropy is about the relationship. Generosity flows from the relationship. A healthy relationship will continue on through the current endeavor to the next and to the next and the next.

Celebrate

THE GOLDEN RULE CYCLE

©2024 Christian School Management

Celebration is interesting. We might think that we come together to celebrate the donor. We want to honor the donors, for sure. The donor stewards and the school might organize a reception to honor them all. Or they might be mentioned on a plaque. Or the donors might have the seats of honor at the opening of the new building. These may or may not be appropriate to your community and culture. These kinds of celebration are common in the secular world where bringing glory to the leader is an acknowledged and expected sign of respect. Certainly, honoring those who made something possible has much biblical precedent – from honoring your father and mother (Exodus 20:12), to being crowned with glory and honor by God (Psalm 8:5).

But CSM is thinking about celebration rather differently. We don't bring the donor in to celebrate the donor. We invite the donor in to celebrate what God has, is, and will accomplish in the lives of children by working his good will through our generous and willing behavior.

Celebration is always an entire community affair. It's the BBQ before the beginning of school where we get together to reconnect after the summer, but also to celebrate our hopes and dreams for the new year. It's the ribbon cutting and enormous cake when we come together as a community to thank God for his blessings (to remember) and to look forward to what will be possible in the future (to anticipate).

This is the pattern of celebration – remembering and anticipating. Jesus' story in Luke 15 that we know as The Prodigal Son lays enormous stress on the word celebrate, mentioning it four times. Celebration is thus a remembering of the school's story to this point, a recognition that this is a turning point of some kind, and an anticipation of something better, foreshadowing the great celebration and feast at the Second Coming. Within that context, it is certainly appropriate to honor those who brought us to this point and those who are enabling us to move forward, in both great and small ways.

In celebration:

- The children are the stars.
- Accomplishment is the remembrance.
- Future growth is the anticipation.
- The supporting, praying, giving, rejoicing community is the context.

In 1 Thessalonians 5, these four things are put together: "Rejoice always, pray continually, give thanks in all circumstances." A celebration is a special time of rejoicing, praying together, giving thanks. We commend the thought that celebration implies the inclusion of these elements:

1. The participation of children
   Note: participation means as leaders. Too often, participation is more as the side show to the real thing – the choir gets up to sing and then leaves, for example. Participation means being an integral part of the action, from serving the meal to making the speech opening the field house to saying the closing prayer.

2. The reading of Scripture
   Note: we would recommend a psalm here. The Hebrew name for the book of Psalms is Praises (tehillim). Psalms 146-150 are obvious choices but there are many others. There are also "psalms" in other books of the Bible, notably Luke 1 in Mary's and Zechariahs' songs (the Magnificat and Benedictus).

3. Prayer
Note: here is an example of celebratory prayer:

Loving God. You are a generous God and we thank you for giving us the gift of Jesus, your Son. We are amazed that you give us so much. You reign forever and ever. Who is like you, majestic in holiness, awesome in glory, working wonders?

Lord, in this project, we have given a little back to you. Thank you for the opportunity to serve you in this way. We give thanks and rejoice in the hard work, fun, and fellowship that we have enjoyed during this campaign. We are so grateful for our children, donors, teachers, volunteers, and all those unknown to us who each played their roles in making this accomplishment such a wonderful experience for us.

Thank-you for the amazing gifts you have given each one of us. May we find gladness and satisfaction and humility in all of our successes. May we be strengthened by the Spirit through this experience of planning, courage, teamwork and focus. May we deepen our commitment to our mission to serve the children of this school. Grant all of us rest and renewal in the coming days so that we may continue to serve you faithfully and without ceasing. We ask this in the name of Jesus, your Son. Amen.

To put it bluntly, this is not another solicitation to God but rather a hymn of thanksgiving (cf. Exodus 15:1-18).

4. Food and drink
Note: breaking bread together has always had enormous significance. In the ancient world, "hospitality" was practiced out of fear of the stranger. In the Christian world, hospitality, the breaking of bread, is "in remembrance" (cf. Luke 22) of what Christ, a stranger in the world (cf. Hebrews 13), has done for us. Food and drink therefore always have a quasi-sacramental aspect to them. Celebration is symbolized in the breaking of the bread and the sharing of the cup.

Research is adamant that donors certainly want to be privately thanked for their contributions. They definitely want reports about what the school is doing to fulfill the promises made during your appeal process. But the vast majority have little interest in being publicly praised. And Penelope Burk reports that public recognition does not influence their future giving. In fact, the vast majority of our donors are living out their Christian commitment to participate in the life of the Christian community. They see their contributions as a response to God.

The school should not try to throw them off track by publishing lists of donors with giving levels, or providing opportunities for them to do what the Pharisees did through their ostentatious giving. "Woe to you Pharisees, because you give God a tenth of your mint, rue and all other kinds of garden herbs, but you neglect justice and the love of God. You should have practiced the latter without leaving the former undone. Woe to you Pharisees, because you love the most important seats in the synagogues and respectful greetings in the marketplaces" (Luke 11:42-43).

It would be terrible if, in the desire to respect the donor, we actually led them into sin! Celebrate as a community. Celebrate God's goodness. Thank him for our ability to give. Thank him for the children on whose behalf we give. Praise him for his great goodness.

Ask

THE GOLDEN RULE CYCLE

©2024 Christian School Management

Henri Nouwen speaks in *A Spirituality of Fundraising* (pp. 16-20): "From the perspective of the gospel, fundraising is not a response to a crisis. Fundraising is, first and foremost, a form of ministry. It is a way of announcing our vision and inviting other people into our mission… We are inviting people into a new way of relating to their resources … we want them to experience that they will in fact benefit by making their resources available to us. We truly believe that if their gift is good only for us who receive, it is not fundraising in the spiritual sense … we are calling them to an experience of conversion …. We can confidently declare with the Apostle Paul: 'You will be enriched in every way so that you can be generous on every occasion, and through us your generosity will result in thanksgiving to God'" (2 Corinthians 9: 11).

Asking is, then, an act of invitation. If it is not an invitation, it is a mere transaction and there is no relationship in the midst. The invitation is not just between the solicitor and the solicited, the one who needs and the one who has, but the invitation "meets on the common ground of God's love" (Nouwen p. 22). While asking has all kinds of negative emotions attached to it – fear of rejection, embarrassment, concern about the relationship – and those are very real, it is also an opportunity for both solicitor and solicited to grow and change. It is maybe not a surprise that the word 'worth' speaks to dual meanings of personal and financial well-being.

The relationship between the donor steward and the donor contributes to, is part of, and extends community. This community in the Christian school's context is about Kingdom building and bringing God's Kingdom "on earth as it is in heaven" (Matthew 6:10). It is the importance of what we are doing in the invitation that gives us the confidence to proceed. CSM has met many leaders, professional and volunteer, who really love talking with their donors and inviting them into a partnership on behalf of the Kingdom (the school's vision of the future, today). Most Board members, even Philanthropy Committee members, members of staff, parents lack even the most basic confidence for making this invitation. We can all become at least a little more comfortable knowing that we are taking this step for God, to bring about God's Kingdom, to make a difference in the life of each child at our school.

The request process becomes concrete and very personal as we connect it to the school's children. Both the donor steward and the donor are adults. We connect on behalf of children. The impact of the gift is not in the lives of adults but in the lives of children. Those children are grateful to God. While one may give $1 million and another the widow's mite (cf. Mark 12), we always look to God to multiply the loaves and fish to feed the 5,000 (cf. Matthew 14). It is not about our wisdom but God's power (1 Corinthians 2:5).

At the same time, we are to be wise, a word used 56 times in Proverbs: the wise listen to advice (12:15); the tongue of the wise brings healing (12:18); the tongue of the wise adorns knowledge (15:2); the wise in heart are called discerning, and gracious words promote instruction (16:21). The wise donor steward has, throughout the Golden Rule Cycle, understood better and discerned carefully what the donor is motivated by and will be most excited to invest in. When the invitation / ask comes, the donor steward is wise to be already attuned to the donor's heart knowing what the response will be.

The invitation to invest, the ask, is best done on the donor's own turf. It is a confidential conversation about money, an intrinsically private issue for most people. Whether at the donor's office or in their home, respecting the donor's choice of meeting venue is part of the deep honor we have in nurturing this relationship. The conversation flows naturally and, at the same time, is well planned:

- Affiliate: don't waste time – be personal but not for too long. The donor should know why you are here.
- Listen: ask the donor to think about your relationship.
  o The reasons they are connected to the school
  o The mission of the school
  o The "project/s" you've been discussing
  o The problems those projects are designed to solve
  o The impact the project/s will have in the lives of children

- Speak: share about the campaign
  o Where the campaign is now
  o What it needs

- Invitation: where do you see yourself?
  o Ways to give
  o Time to give
  o Accountability for the gift
  o Amount of the gift

- Wrap-up: thanks
  o Next contact with this donor

Summary

The Golden Rule Cycle teaches what the donor steward's job is:

- Prayer
- Thank
- Report
- Celebrate
- Ask

IN CHRISTIAN PHILANTHROPY, THE DONOR IS TRANSFORMED

Wʜᴀᴛ ʜᴀᴘᴘᴇɴꜱ ɪɴ ᴛʜᴇ ᴀᴄᴛ of generosity? What happens when the Golden Rule Cycle is followed? Is there any precedent in Scripture for what we are imagining can happen in the heart of the donor? If philanthropy is relational, then the relationship should make a difference.

What happened in the hearts of the Israelites as they brought their gifts for the building of the Tabernacle, as they saw it take place (Exodus 36), as they made the Ark, the table, the altar, the lampstand (Exodus 37), as they made the courtyard and the curtain for the courtyard (Exodus 38)? The first thing we know is that God was pleased: "Then the cloud covered the tent of meeting and the glory of the Lord filled the tabernacle" (Exodus 40:34). The second thing we know is that, through Aaron, God blessed the people (Leviticus 9:23). The third thing we know is that the people "shouted for joy and fell facedown." Giving in accord with God's pleasure results in joy for the giver and exuberant praise to God.

We find the same thing when David collects materials in preparation for his son Solomon to build the Temple. David shows leadership by giving first: "I now give my personal treasures of gold and silver for the temple of my God, over and above everything I have provided for this holy temple" (1 Chronicles 29:3). He gave as King, and then he gave as an individual. There's a parallel here with giving as the owner of a business, and then giving again as a private person.

Once David had demonstrated generosity, the next level of leadership followed: "Then the leaders of families, the officers of the tribes of Israel, the commanders of thousands and commanders of hundreds, and the officials in charge of the king's work gave willingly" (1 Chronicles 29:6). Leadership is inspirational – and it flows from the largest gifts to the smallest gifts. The next level giving was recognized by everyone else: "The people rejoiced at the willing response of their leaders, for they had given freely and wholeheartedly to the Lord" (1 Chronicles 29:9). This rejoicing, although it is not explicit in the text, seems obviously to have included the people's gifts as well since David reflects that in his prayer. It is worth quoting this prayer at length because it is so powerful in showing the impact of giving on the donor. David prays:

"But who am I, and who are my people, that we should be able to give as generously as this? Everything comes from you, and we have given you only what comes from your hand. We are foreigners and strangers in your sight, as were all our ancestors. Our days on earth are like a shadow, without hope. Lord our God, all this abundance that we have provided for building you a temple for your Holy Name comes from your hand, and all of it belongs to you. I know, my God, that you test the heart and are pleased with integrity. All these things I have given willingly and with honest intent. And now I have seen with joy how willingly your people who are here have given to you. Lord, the God of our fathers Abraham, Isaac and Israel, keep these desires and thoughts in the hearts of your people forever, and keep their hearts loyal to you. And give my son Solomon the wholehearted devotion to keep your commands, statutes and decrees and to do everything to build the palatial structure for which I have provided" (1 Chronicles 29:14-19).

What wonderful words to remind us that we give in response to God's great generosity! That we must give with willingness, with eagerness in that response! That we give with integrity and that God searches our heart to ensure that we gave for the right reasons! That what we gave must be used to the purpose for which it was given!

We are accustomed to talking about the effect of a gift on the children of the school – the ability to further an objective, such as building a new facility or renovating an old one, and so on. In the Christian gift, however, the transformation should be in both directions. The children should be blessed and so should the donor.

In *Giving and Getting in the Kingdom: A Field Guide*, Mark Dillon writes: "A gatherer in the kingdom should have the capacity and desire to grow the giver. That honors the giver and deepens their joy and resolve to invest generously and strategically in the kingdom" (p. 116). Penelope Burk in *Donor-Centered Fundraising* (Cygnus Applied Research 2018) speaks about donors this way: "Giving is a rush. It is an emotional act as well as an intellectual decision that may be the culmination of many years of thinking about giving. When a donor sits down to write a check, she is feeling the excitement that comes with doing something for others and she is certainly wondering whether her gift will have a positive impact on your work" (p. 26). Are your donors increasing their joy in giving? Is the donor transformed by their relationship with your children, your mission, your school?

Biblical authority stands behind philanthropy and the idea that those who give are blessed by their giving. The Torah is clear that the people of Israel were to exercise the habit of giving and giving in a way that God would honor.

Leviticus 27 speaks to the initial tithe to support the Levites: "A tithe of everything from the land, whether grain from the soil or fruit from the trees, belongs to the Lord; it is holy to the Lord. ... Every tithe of the herd and flock – every tenth animal that passes under the shepherd's rod – will be holy to the Lord. No one may pick out the good from the bad or make any substitution."

Deuteronomy 14 speaks of a second tithe (up to 20 percent!) that is required in order to rejoice in the Lord and worship in his holy Temple: "Be sure to set aside a tenth of all that your fields produce each year. Eat the tithe of your grain, new wine and olive oil, and the firstborn of your herds and flocks in the presence of the Lord your God at the place he will choose as a dwelling for his Name, so that you may learn to revere the Lord your God always. But if that place is too distant and you have been blessed by the Lord your God and cannot carry your tithe (because the place where the Lord will choose to put his Name is so far away), then exchange your tithe for silver, and take the silver with you and go to the place the Lord your God will choose. Use the silver to buy whatever you like: cattle, sheep, wine or other fermented drink, or anything you wish. Then you and your household shall eat there in the presence of the Lord your God and rejoice." A tithe to support the Levites and a tithe to party including going to the liquor store!

The passage even goes further and speaks of a third tithe (up to 30 percent) that was to be given every third year to support those who had little: "At the end of every three years, bring all the tithes of that year's produce and store it in your towns, so that the Levites (who have no allotment or inheritance of their own) and the foreigners, the fatherless and the widows who live in your towns may come and eat and be satisfied."

If we were to literally translate that into our times, it would be 10 percent of total income to support the Pastor/Priest and Christian teachers; 10 percent to party at Christmas, Easter, Transfiguration, Ascension, and Pentecost; 10 percent every third year to support the poor. And there is a "so that": "so that the Lord your God may bless you in all the work of your hands" (Deuteronomy 14:29). Giving changes the giver because God is able to bless the giver who has offered freely.

The Law is echoed many times in the Hebrew Scriptures as well as in the New Testament. The most famous is undoubtedly 2 Corinthians 9, but we need to read more than just the most often quoted passage. We need to read the whole piece:

"Remember this: Whoever sows sparingly will also reap sparingly, and whoever sows generously will also reap generously. Each of you should give what you have decided in your heart to give, not reluctantly or under compulsion, for God loves a cheerful giver. And God is able to bless you abundantly, so that in all things at all times, having all that you need, you will abound in every good work. As it is written:

> "They have freely scattered their gifts to the poor;
> their righteousness endures forever. [Psalm 112]

"Now he who supplies seed to the sower and bread for food will also supply and increase your store of seed and will enlarge the harvest of your righteousness. You will be enriched in every way so that you can be generous on every occasion, and through us your generosity will result in thanksgiving to God."

The reference to Psalm 112 is instructive because the actions of the righteous in giving freely have highly beneficial results for the giver who is transformed:

> "Their children will be mighty in the land;
> the generation of the upright will be blessed.
> Wealth and riches are in their houses,
> and their righteousness endures forever.
> Even in darkness light dawns for the upright,
> for those who are gracious and compassionate and righteous.
> Good will come to those who are generous and lend freely,
> who conduct their affairs with justice."

Not so with those who are the opposite. They are the wicked and they are totally frustrated at what makes no sense to them. How can generosity result in riches?

> "The wicked will see and be vexed,
> they will gnash their teeth and waste away;
> the longings of the wicked will come to nothing."

The paradox of generosity is that it allows God to be even more generous to his people. The giver is transformed by the gift. As Jesus says in Matthew 16: "For whoever wants to save their life will lose it, but whoever loses their life for me will find it. What good will it be for someone to gain the whole world, yet forfeit their soul? Or what can anyone give in exchange for their soul? For the Son of Man is going to come in his Father's glory with his angels, and then he will reward each person according to what they have done."

The joy of giving is that it multiplies until there is too much. Imagine (remember Exodus 26?) a building project where your vision was so inspiring that the building contractors had to come and tell you to stop bringing materials because they couldn't use them!

It is critical for us in philanthropy to understand that philanthropy is not just about the impact in the lives of the children, although that is the vision to inspire giving; it is also about the impact in the life of the giver, the one whose heart is changed by the act of generosity. Giving reminds us of God, the first Giver. The CSM Mary Principle relies on this sequence of being thankful to the first Giver, recognizing that we are stewards of what God has given us, and knowing that God honors the gift freely given.

We ask some obvious questions in our philanthropy: Did we make our goal? Did our cup run over?

Let's ask the equally important question: In what way did our campaign bless our donors and help them be transformed through their participation?

Note: The following material is from Andrews University, Berrien Springs, MI, and printed by permission from their website.

The Benefits of Giving

Research has shown that giving has many benefits for both the giver and the receiver, including increased happiness, reduced stress, improved physical health, and stronger social connections.

- Increased happiness and well-being
  Numerous studies have shown that giving, whether it be through donating money, volunteering time, or simply helping others in small ways, can boost our mood and improve our outlook on life. Research published in *The Journal of Positive Psychology* found that people who spent money on others experienced greater happiness and satisfaction. Similarly, a study published in *The Journal of Happiness Studies* found that even under the most conservative measures, volunteering is causally linked to increased happiness.

- Reduced stress and anxiety
  One of the lesser-known benefits of charitable giving is its ability to reduce stress and anxiety. Studies have shown that when individuals give to charitable causes, they experience a sense of purpose and fulfillment that can have a positive impact on their mental health.

  Charitable giving can help individuals put their own problems and concerns into perspective. By focusing on the needs of others and contributing to causes they care about, individuals can shift their attention away from their own worries and stressors. This can lead to a sense of empowerment and control, as individuals recognize the positive impact they can have on the world around them.

- Improved physical health and longevity
One study published in the journal *BMC Public Health* found that individuals who volunteered regularly had a lower risk of mortality than those who did not volunteer. The study followed a group of adults over the age of 50 for five years and found that those who volunteered at least once a week had a 44% lower risk of dying during the study period than those who did not volunteer.

Charitable giving has also been linked to lower levels of inflammation in the body, which is a key factor in a range of chronic health conditions. A study published in the *American Journal of Preventive Medicine* found that individuals who engaged in regular volunteering had lower levels of inflammation than those who did not volunteer.

Furthermore, charitable giving can provide a sense of purpose and fulfillment, which can contribute to a higher quality of life and greater life satisfaction. This sense of purpose and fulfillment can also help individuals maintain a healthier lifestyle, as they are more likely to engage in activities that promote their physical and mental health.

- Stronger social connections and a sense of community
Charitable giving can also lead to stronger social connections and a sense of community. When individuals donate to charitable causes, they are often supporting organizations or initiatives that align with their values and beliefs. This shared sense of purpose and commitment can help create a sense of community among donors, volunteers, and those benefiting from the charitable work.

Additionally, charitable giving can provide opportunities for individuals to meet and connect with others who share their interests and passions. For example, volunteering at a local food bank or participating in a fundraising event can allow individuals to meet like-minded individuals and form new relationships.

Research has shown that social connections and a sense of community can have a positive impact on mental health and well-being. Strong social connections have been linked to reduced rates of depression and anxiety, as well as a greater sense of purpose and fulfillment in life. Additionally, individuals with strong social connections are more likely to engage in healthy behaviors, such as exercising regularly and maintaining a healthy lifestyle.

- Spiritual growth and transformation
  Charitable giving can be an important part of our spiritual journey. It can be a way to express our values and beliefs and to put them into action in the world. When we give to causes that align with our spiritual beliefs, we are living out our faith and making a positive impact on the world.

When we give to others, we are acknowledging that we are part of a larger community and that we have a responsibility to contribute to the well-being of others. This can help us feel more connected to those around us and can enhance our sense of connection to God.

Charitable giving can also help us cultivate a sense of gratitude and abundance. When we give freely to others, we are acknowledging that we have enough to share and that we are blessed with resources that we can use to make a difference in the lives of others. This can lead to a greater appreciation for what we have, and a deeper sense of contentment and fulfillment.

The Joy of Giving: How Giving Can Improve Your Own Well-Being: Andrews University. Andrews University. https://www.andrews.edu/services/development/annual/the-joy-of-giving/index.html

Summary

- In the relationship, the donor is impacted by giving.
- Giving in accord with God's pleasure results in joy for the giver and exuberant praise to God.
- God blesses the giver who gives freely.
- The paradox of generosity is that God multiplies.

THE BOARD'S OBLIGATION TO GIVE

IT IS POSSIBLE TO HEAR volunteers tell schools that they give their time and their wisdom – don't ask for their money as well. They have the right to say that. But what about the Board? Can Board members claim that time and wisdom are sufficient? We have been to a number of schools where not every Board member gives each year.

Some Boards have a requirement that Board members must give a certain amount. We have seen stipulations of $1,500 and more. When they are recruited, the Board members are told upfront what the expectation is, and that if they can give more they should. Is it good practice to "require" Board members to give in this way?

If you don't have clarity in this area, it can lead to significant awkwardness. Christians are notoriously uncomfortable talking about money. Many strands of Christianity have an ascetic side to them, seeing money as a constant enticement away from the truth. We are sobered by Jesus' encounter with the rich man who "went away sad because he had great wealth" (Mark 10:21). They pull from St. Paul who said: "For the love of money is a root of all kinds of evil. Some people, eager for money, have wandered from the faith and pierced themselves with many griefs" (1 Timothy 6:10).

But that same St. Paul spent much time in his ministry fundraising for the church in Jerusalem, and a good portion of his travel was dedicated to collecting donations. And Jesus was the baby in the manger who received gifts of "gold, frankincense, and myrrh" (Matthew 2:11). That was undoubtedly incredibly helpful to the young couple who had to flee to Egypt! Jesus was not uncomfortable about money at all. Eleven of his 40 parables include money as illustration, and it was sometimes the main point. He taught life lessons as he pointed out the "poor widow" (Mark 12:42) and took action to protect his Father's house (John 2:13-17).

In addition, in our work with Boards and school leaders, we comment that we know the school's mission as we examine two documents: the budget and the schedule. Each provides a deep insight into what is really happening, whatever the public relations efforts of the school say. The budget tells us all about priorities and what the real investment of money in mission delivery is. It tells us about the delivery of program that may have little to do with the school's mission. The schedule tells us about the school's approach to sacred time and its allocation of time to mission and non-mission elements. Money and time: the two great resources we have!

So what should we say to potential new Board members? Should we back off and make no financial requests? Should we lean in and be really specific about how much we expect them to give? How do we rethink our current Board approach? We suggest four elements:

1. The Board member serves because the school's mission is part of his or her heart. Jesus told a whole set of stories in Luke 12 showing the importance of his followers understanding that outward actions must follow inward motivations ending with "For where your treasure is, there your heart will be also" (Luke 12:34). This has become a trite saying often used to make people feel guilty. That wasn't Jesus' point. Luke puts together a series of stories illustrating the importance of Jesus' teaching about being "rich toward God" (v. 21), a God who does not forget a single "sparrow" (v. 6). That was his point. What is the Board member's mission and is it aligned with the school's? If it is, the Board member will give time, wisdom, AND treasure. Not because she has to but because it is natural to – in accord with being rich toward God.

2. Board members truly love what is happening in the lives of children. In John 15, Jesus calls his disciples friends (v. 15) and takes away the servant / slave descriptor. Jesus has shared everything with us and thus welcomes us into a relationship with him, the Son of God, that is close and loving. In that relationship we have passed from "death to life" (1 John 3:14). St. Paul talks about the outflow of that in giving: "their overflowing joy and their extreme poverty welled up in rich generosity. For I testify that they gave as much as they were able, and even beyond their ability" (2 Corinthians 8:2-3). Is the Board member going to experience joy in serving the school as a Trustee? If they do, they will be generous, giving as much as they are able and even beyond their own expectation.

3. The Board Member has an awesome responsibility. It is legal, moral, and strategic. The Trustee is held accountable in the secular courts for good stewardship. The Trustee is the keeper of the mission in the bylaws. The Trustee is the creator of the school's Strategic Plan designed to ensure the school is there for the next generations of children. Under Jesus, the Trustee understands the school as the treasure of God. CSM therefore states that the school

should be one of the Trustee's top three gifts in each year they serve. Not to do so does not make you, the Trustee, a bad person; it does make you a bad Trustee. This is important and easy to communicate when talking with potential Trustees about their obligations. There is an expectation that you will assign your school one of your top three gifts each year you serve as a Trustee. The amount is not the key; the priority is.

4. The Board member always gives first – before anyone else in the community is solicited. Remember David? First David, then the leaders of the people, then the people. Any request to the community must include this immortal phrase: please join the Board in supporting …. So the Trustee gives first as a leader in and of the community.

There is a concomitant responsibility that the Board President has. Following the Mary Principle and the idea that each donor is treated with honor and respect, each Trustee should be solicited personally each year by the Board President (and maybe a colleague).

It is too easy to assume that Trustees will give and make the ask a generic one. During one Board meeting we attended, the President made a generic ask and included the quasi "threat" that anyone who failed to make a gift by the end of the coming weekend would receive a phone call from his secretary! The President certainly understood the obligation of each Trustee. Maybe there was a lack of understanding in terms of both honor and respect. While each Trustee knows the responsibility is there, it should still never be assumed. The Trustee is not a checkbook. The relationship with the Trustee – which leads to the gift and the transformation of the Trustee in the giving – is to be nurtured and honored and developed. If there is no conversation, there is no relationship.

This personal ask also allows the Trustee to bring up issues and questions that they may feel uncomfortable bringing up at a Board meeting. This may be because the issues are personal to the Trustee and family, rather than strategic and thus appropriately talked about at the meeting. It may be because they want to explore other options and would rather have a sense of privacy in that conversation. It may be because their gift is smaller or larger than others may expect, and thus confidentiality is important. It may be that their gift will be a family gift including both children and grandparents, and so the solicitation will include all members of the family.

It also allows the Trustee (and family) to discuss ways in which the gift could be given, and specific objectives the Trustee is particularly inspired by. Ways to give and options for directing the gift can lead to a larger, even significantly larger, gift than the Trustee had imagined.

- Make it a matter of routine that the Board President sits down with each Trustee (and spouse / family) each August. This will lead to a gift that supports the school's annual fund that year. Of course, it may be a comprehensive gift encompassing both the Annual Fund and Capital / Endowment Campaigns. It may be to set up a three-year pledge. It may be to appreciate the fulfillment of a pledge.

- It can be a simple meeting for 15 minutes at the end of a meeting, a lunch that lasts for an hour, an informal or formal meeting in the home. The length or place is not nearly as important as the fact that it is personal. It should never be casual but highly intentional with solicitation as the focus. It should be, whenever humanly possible, with both Trustee and spouse (if the person is not single). While the Board relationship is with the Trustee, the donor relationship acknowledges the importance of unity in the home.

- Ensure that the same processes are carried out here as with any other donor – a phone call of thanks within 48 hours of the gift being made, a follow-up note of thanks within two weeks. These phone calls and notes are made by the Board President.

- Ensure that Trustees are treated as leadership donors irrespective of the amount given. Their gift is amplified by their service as a Trustee and thus they are always invited to all leadership events.

Our care for our Trustees means that we should never take them for granted. We know that "neglect" is not intentional. That doesn't excuse it. We should take the time for a Trustee and ensure they understand the depth of our appreciation for their service (including the gift), and the depth of our concern that they are also cared for as human beings within the love and grace of God.

Summary

- Board members aligned with the school's mission will give time, wisdom, and treasure.
- Giving is in line with capacity.
- The gift is one the Board member's top three philanthropic gifts.
- The Board gives first before anyone is asked. It leads.
- Each Board member is solicited personally by the Board President and Principal.
- A Board member is a leadership donor irrespective of the size of gift.
- A Board donor is treated as well as any other donor.

THE RULE OF THREE ASKS

ASK PARENTS FOR MONEY ONLY three times in any given year.

- Ask One: tuition / fees
- Ask Two: the school's annual fund as part of annual giving
- Ask Three: an opportunity to give to annual giving through an event / experience

The reality is that the vast majority of our donors are parents and / or people connected to them, such as grandparents. A few of our donors are parents of graduates and a few are the graduates themselves. We have very few donors from the general population – except for schools that have a traditional church sponsoring community. Even in the latter case, the generation of churchgoers that routinely gave to the school is dying and giving way to a generation that doesn't think the same way.

If this is your reality, that parents are the vast majority group of your donors, then we have to consider what treating them with honor and respect (The Mary Principle) means. What we have learned over the years is that our parents truly dislike / hate being nickel-and-dimed to death. They want to know what the cost of tuition is upfront: "Don't constantly send me a bill for this fee and that fee as we go through the year." They want to know that they won't be asked for a donation over and over again.

Whether in tuition or in philanthropy, 99 percent of parents want to be approached as few times as possible, and they want to know how that works from the start of their relationship with the school. Too many schools fail to address philanthropy in the admission process; too many schools fail to create a total "tuition" cost that literally includes everything the parent will have to pay. Ensure the admission process includes the fact of these two 'asks'. And only two (or three) asks.

Why do parents want to know? It's obvious. Our parents have an annual income, an annual budget, and an annual budget line for their giving. Let's imagine that a family has a median household income – $74,580 in 2022 for the USA (census.gov) and $66,800 in 2020 in Canada (2020 Census statcan.gc.ca). And let's suppose that this Christian family tithes or gives 10 percent of its gross income to charity, an amount a little over $6,000. They have made a decision to pay their mortgage, their utilities, to put food on the table and clothing on their children, to take one holiday, and to send their children to a Christian school. They have also decided upfront how much they are going to give of what God has given them to their church, their school, and probably one to three other charities that they support.

What's the point? It doesn't matter how many times you ask them for money, they will still give you the amount they decided upon at the beginning of their financial year. When you ask repeatedly, they don't become more generous – they become more irritated. Once they've figured out how many times you are going to ask them for money, they just split up their gift into that many pieces. Asking them once means that you are being respectful of their budget process; spending far more time on celebrating what is happening in the life of their child than in asking constantly for money; and appreciating that their relationship with the school is about their child, not about the money they give you.

In working with schools, when we create a calendar together, we typically find 30–80+ asks in every school year.

Take the following steps:

Step One

Make a list of all the times you ask parents for money. Think of the following: tuition, annual fund appeal, golf tournament, auction. But then go further. Think of examples such as these: fee for the class retreat, yearbook cost, school photos, tissue for the classroom, Christmas gift for the teachers, fee for an after-school sport, the envelope in the annual report, the speech at Back to School Night, Giving Tuesday, donation for the food bank, Booster Club events, pizza night for the choir, three binders for this semester, library book sale, special Board appeal for scholarships, the Friday cupcakes for the senior trip, etc.

Step Two

Split all the asks into:

- What is programmatic
- What is annual giving

- What is student philanthropy
- What is a legitimate parent expense

Step Three

Programmatic asks: bundle everything together with tuition and charge as a single number (even if you identify and split out the fees to make them clear). A simple example is to charge everyone for a yearbook. Notice that eliminating separate collections also eliminates significant time and focus the Business Office or teachers should profitably be putting elsewhere. Several schools we have worked with asked teachers to "collect" funds and signed forms for everything from photographs to the cost of the field day. What a waste of teachers' time! Their job is to attend to their children's growth, not manage the bureaucracy of the school. Make everyone's life easier and your teachers' focus clearer. Ask once and once only for anything relating to the education of the child.

Annual giving asks: educate your families from the admission process onward that they will receive a request for a donation to provide those things tuition cannot. Assure them it will not be to fund the "gap," as if telling your parents that no donations means the school will close in April is a powerful motivator! Assure them instead that the school is well run and that donations will be spent in very specific ways, such as helping families attend the school, investing in the science program, upgrading the scoreboard, providing professional growth for teachers, etc. And they will be asked respectfully once in the fall – and invited to an annual giving event in the spring.

Children and Philanthropy: never ever use children to raise money for the school. If they raise money at all, it should point them to the needs of others, not their own needs. Ideally, children doing service is not about money but about time and commitment. This is explored further in the chapter on children and philanthropy.

Legitimate parent expenses: these might be identified as idiosyncratic expenses that are specific to their own children. Examples might include AP exam fees, a voluntary trip over Easter, participation in an after-school program. If it is during the school day, it must be included in the tuition.

Step Four

Strategically and tactically, over time move toward only talking with parents three times a year about money. Remember always that money is the one argument you can never win with parents. Sending children to a Christian school is expensive and is not affordable. Parents choose to give their children this opportunity as an incredible investment in their lives. Each of the four areas above can be approached in a different way and on a separate timeline. Over time, though, they should all align so that every family will clearly and succinctly understand what the school is asking them to do. Take every opportunity to reinforce the opportunity these asks will provide for them, for their children, and for every child at the school, as well as the blessings they will provide for future generations as well.

Summary

- Ask parents for money a maximum of three times a year, including tuition.
- Identify all the asks your school makes in a single year.
- Reduce the asks to three
  - Bundle all mission-delivery items into tuition.
  - Bundle all philanthropic asks into annual giving (that may have two stages).
- Remember that children do not raise money for the school or themselves.

EVENT-BASED FUNDRAISING: MOVING TO HEALTHY RELATIONSHIPS

CHRISTIAN SCHOOLS ARE STILL LARGELY mired in the idea that philanthropy is fundraising in the 20th century model i.e. let's do some fund-raisers. Here's a list of fundraisers we have come across over the time since CSM was founded:

- Raffles
- Dinners
- Auctions
- Golf tournaments
- Poinsettia sales
- Chocolate bar sales
- Sales of children's "baskets" of their creations
- Picture day
- Pizza night
- Etc.

They are all predicated on this idea – support the school and receive a benefit. This is 20th century transactional fundraising. It has no basis in Scripture, in research, and in experience. (There are exceptions – we know of one school where the annual auction is the major form of annual giving.)

Scripture and Relationship

It is very clear that Scriptural philanthropy is about relationships.

Exodus 25 highlights God himself as the chief development officer: "The Lord said to Moses, 'Tell the Israelites to bring me an offering. You are to receive the offering for me from everyone whose heart prompts them to give."' We note immediately that giving was not based on a return on investment (a round of golf with friends, a plant to take home, winning the 50/50) but on a heart response. Why would the Israelites' hearts move them? Because of their relationship with the God of Abraham, Isaac, and Jacob who had brought them out of Egypt. We find the outcome in Exodus 35 where we find their donations called a 'freewill offering.'

In 1 Chronicles 29, we find a similar situation with David, who was soliciting donations for the temple that his son Solomon was going to build. First David gives himself, and he is clear why he is doing it: "Everything comes from you, and we have given you only what comes from your hand. We are foreigners and strangers in your sight, as were all our ancestors. Our days on earth are like a shadow, without hope. Lord our God, all this abundance that we have provided for building you a temple for your Holy Name comes from your hand, and all of it belongs to you. I know, my God, that you test the heart and are pleased with integrity. All these things I have given willingly and with honest intent."

In liturgical churches, the offering is brought to the altar and the congregation prays with David: All things come of thee, O Lord, and of thine own have we given thee. David wants to inspire others to give and he leads with his own wealth. It is clear that others give for the same reason. The next thing David says in verse 17 is "And now I have seen with joy how willingly your people who are here have given to you." Once again, people give out of their relationship with God and, here, out of their relationship with David.

Jesus had advice for philanthropists as well. In Matthew 6, he explicitly says: "So when you give to the needy, do not announce it with trumpets, as the hypocrites do in the synagogues and on the streets, to be honored by others. Truly I tell you, they have received their reward in full. But when you give to the needy, do not let your left hand know what your right hand is doing, so that your giving may be in secret. Then your Father, who sees what is done in secret, will reward you." It's not about some kind of reciprocity where you take home the outcome of your giving. No, giving is considered righteousness by the Father who rewards in secret, not in public.

Indeed, Jesus had his own Philanthropy Committee. Luke records in chapter 8 that Jesus went around preaching and healing with others: "The Twelve were with him, and also some women who had been cured of evil spirits and diseases: Mary (called Magdalene) from whom seven demons had come out; Joanna the wife of Chuza, the manager of Herod's household; Susanna; and many others. These women were helping to support them out of their own means," i.e., he took with him the disciples and his Philanthropy Committee to make sure they didn't run out of food, lodging, sandals, clothing. How practical! They didn't sell cactuses – they gave in gratitude to God, asking nothing in return.

Research and Relationship

Penelope Burk, author of *Donor-Centered Fundraising* and the leading researcher and practitioner in North America, doesn't speak to events at all. The research just doesn't support them. But she spends some time in consideration of recognition gifts, another form of transaction – we are grateful for your gift and will give you something back for it. This is as far from Scriptural precepts as you can get! This isn't about a heartfelt, thoughtful, and personal thank-you. This is about getting address labels, T-shirts, pens or, at the higher end, clocks, briefcases, executive toys. What do donors say about such transactional fundraising?

"All of these items have to be purchased and that is money that could be used to fund grants and research," she comments (p. 205).

She also says (p. 206): "Most of the time, gifts call into question what paid staff are doing with their time, how they are spending donors' contributions, and whether they understand what donors are trying to accomplish. Donors say that when they receive a gift after making a donation, they wonder whether they supported the right cause. Our research findings on this subject are very one-sided, reflecting a level of irritation not found anywhere else in our surveys."

On a scale of 1 to 7, 7 being strongly agree, donors rated the following statement 5.8: I do not wish to receive token gifts from any not-for-profit I support because I want as much of my gift as possible to be directed to the purpose for which I am giving.

The relationship between the donor and the charity supported is not based on weak and money-wasting transactional efforts but on the mission of the charity and the power of the charity to effect change. The 2023 Bank of America study of giving by affluent households showed that their donors' top three motivations were:

- Because you believe in the mission of the organization – 60.3% (always); 36.4% (sometimes); 4% (never)
- When you believe that your gift can make a difference – 39.5% (always); 54.0% (sometimes); 6.5% (never)
- For personal satisfaction, enjoyment, or fulfillment – 30.5% (always); 55.6% (sometimes); 14.0% (never)

Interestingly, the fourth was:

- In order to give back to your community – 28.2% (always); 60.9% (sometimes); 10.9% (never)

Research is adamant that donors are interested in developing a relationship and that trying to buy their donation or to thank through trinkets is not just a waste of money but actually takes away from the relationship. Interestingly, 80.8 percent sometimes give "when you are asked" – it just takes an act of relationship, please give, for generosity to be unplugged.

Experience

This fits in well with experience. What does it take to do transactional philanthropy? How long does it take to put on a well-run event? How much does it cost to set up and take down? And organize? And market? And administrate? The answer, of course, varies depending on what "transaction" you are trying to carry out. However, the generic answer is that the vast majority of volunteers, when asked whether it was worth it, typically say how much they enjoyed the social nature of the affair – but in terms of fundraising, for the 35 hours they put into it, would have rather written a check for $200.

In other words, our exclusive finding when it comes to events, to the actions of parent organizations, booster clubs, is that our parents love getting together and enjoying each other's company. The moment money enters the equation (outside paying $7 for the pancake breakfast to cover costs), the enjoyment begins to diminish.

TRUE STORY – a donor's gift based on relationship!

At a training session for the annual fund, several parents were sharing why they gave and to whom. The CSM facilitator mentioned that donors are giving larger amounts to fewer charities than in the past. A couple immediately reflected on their giving experience: "We used to give to 10 to 15 charities a year. About two years ago, the phone rang, and it was one of the charities that we had contributed to. They had not called to ask us for more money. They asked us why we gave to them. Among other things, we mentioned that we were particularly interested in Sierra Leone. They thanked us and that was the end of the conversation. But six months later, the phone rang again, and it was the same charity wanting to tell us what was happening in Sierra Leone. My wife and I sat down and rethought our giving – we gave to fewer charities, and we gave the same amount, or more. And this charity became a major charity for us." Donors are giving more money to fewer charities – and the decision about which charities depends on how the charity is creating a relationship with the donor.

The other experiential finding is that transactional fundraising does not develop loyalty or commitment to the school's mission. Instead, it tends to result in a loyalty to their child's athletic team or their child's mission trip or their child's new rug in the classroom, i.e., the loyalty is to their child, as it always has been. There's nothing wrong with that, but it does not lead to inspirational giving. That only happens once we have connected the heart of the donor to the mission of the school and where the donor's gaze includes their own child or grandchild but broadens generously to include all children / grandchildren.

Thinking About Events

Christian schools must move with their donors into the 21st century. There is everything right in running events that develop connections and relationships within the school community. They are excellent for having fun and providing safe opportunities for families to enjoy being with each other.

Events – and even worse selling "stuff" and carrying out raffles – are antithetical to excellent relationship-building and exceptional philanthropy. We reiterate, develop your philanthropy program on the basis of the CSM Mary Principle:

1. Giving is in gratitude for what God has done for each one of us.
2. Giving is done by people who are intimately involved with the action.
3. Giving includes involvement, not just the act of giving itself.
4. Giving galvanizes possibilities that otherwise could not be imagined.
5. Giving is recognized and honored.

The donor wants to give. The donor has no problem with giving, but wants to be asked. Donors want their philanthropy to be an excellent investment in the future. They want to be asked within the context of a plan, to be included appropriately in the conversation, to be thanked, to be told that their gift was used as asked, and to be given evidence that children benefited as a result of the gift. When donors are treated in this way, they will want to be equally or more generous the following year. In this way, we develop loyal donors who will give to the end of their child's time at the school and then maybe even beyond and to death.

Summary

- Transactional fundraising has no basis in Scripture, research, or experience.
- Donors are not motivated to generosity by receiving something in return.
- Raising money through "transaction" is inefficient, wasting resources.

- Giving is transformed through the relationship.
- Loyal donors want:
  - To give within the context of a plan
  - To be thanked
  - To be shown that their gift mattered
  - To contribute to the conversation

PHILANTHROPY AND STRATEGIC / OPERATIONS: HIRING THE PROFESSIONAL TEAM

THE TIMING FOR HIRING THE professional team is different for each school, depending where they are on the life cycle. It is also, partly, a function of size. Clearly, a school of 180 children is going to look very differently administratively than a school of 750. Nonetheless, the following sections will outline best practice when it comes to thinking about the Philanthropy Team.

Remember that when there is no professional member of the team, the job doesn't go away. It has to be carried out by one or more volunteers. If you read this and know you will not be hiring everyone here, then think how this can be embodied through Board and community volunteers. If you are large enough and at the point where hiring all these positions makes sense, then consider what part your volunteers will play now supported, trained, and inspired by the professional team. Professionals don't replace volunteers; they enhance and magnify their impact. For most schools, if you are able to hire one or two positions to support the Principal, that will be a great achievement.

The following table gives very rough approximations of what schools that are operating within CSM's tuition levels can typically afford. It is meant to be helpful, not prescriptive. You may be able to do more or less in your own situation. However, CSM's position is always to hire as close to the child as possible. We would not want the philanthropy role at any of our schools to outstrip support of children, for example, in providing resources for a counselor. Always first consider the needs of children, and then balance that with the resource outcome expected from philanthropy hires.

Size of School	Positions Hired
<100	Principal
100-200	add Database Manager
200-300	add Annual Fund Manager
300-750	add Philanthropy Director
750+	consider adding Planned Giving Officer and then the Alumni Relations Coordinator

Principal / Head of School

The Principal / Head of School embodies the mission, vision, and values of the school. Therefore, he or she must lead courageously, inviting others into the process of doing that which will drive the school forward toward its goals. This includes envisioning, planning, and articulating the philanthropic vision (the why) for the school to thrive for its children, and actively inviting other stakeholders into its service. There are three primary stakeholders.

1. The Board is the Principal's employer and co-leader in the philanthropic function. Since many of our Boards have still not embraced their philanthropy role, the Principal's leadership in inviting them into this key Board responsibility is vital.

2. Leadership donors will typically have a door open to the Principal. Their relationship is also of vital importance to the success of any significant endeavor requiring funding outside the operations budget. The Principal's relationship to a good number of leadership donors (and, in many schools, the vast majority), is the difference-maker between success and failure.

3. Parents include both leadership donors and support donors. The Principal's job in developing and maintaining a healthy parent community is the environment within which leadership giving thrives.

Every school has a Principal. Every Principal has this function.

The Principal has a unique position in philanthropy. The Principal knows everyone, can talk to everyone, can ask anyone for anything. The role of the Principal includes the willingness to:

- Know and clearly articulate the why.

- Develop an organized relationship building plan.
  - o A communications calendar
  - o A calendar of events for the whole community to gather, learn, and celebrate
  - o A calendar of group gatherings, large and small, for discussion and commitment-building

- Communicate the plan.
- Have and utilize a set of desired outcomes.
- Expand the number of people that understand and own the plan, such as Trustees and key staff.
- Free up to 25 percent of their own schedule to meet with key constituents to pray, thank, report, and celebrate the good work that is being done (cf. the Golden Rule Cycle).
- During comprehensive campaigns, understand that their time spent in philanthropy will increase to 50 percent.

When the school is smaller and / or doesn't yet have the resources to make the following hires, the Principal has to embody or find the volunteer who will act in these roles.

The Database Manager

When you are in a position to hire someone to assist in the school's philanthropy, the **order of hiring** is as follows:

1. Database Manager (DM)
2. Annual Fund Manager (AFM)
3. Philanthropy Director (PD)
4. Planned Giving Officer (PGO)
5. Alumni Relations Coordinator (ARC)

Philanthropy is not a task for well-meaning amateurs. It is a relationship business where a wrong move can set a school back for a generation. It is a fundraising business where the ability of the school to raise money every year and through economic downturns and lockdowns can determine the viability of the school. It is a data-driven business where respecting and honoring the donor depends on the accuracy and utility of the database.

Philanthropy is a "professional" task irrespective of how many paid professionals you have. For small schools with no paid staff at all, the Philanthropy Committee must act in a totally professional manner and have the training in their various roles to ensure they can serve effectively. Other volunteers need their roles defined and need training to carry them out. If your school does have a staff and even a large staff, it is unwise to assume that they have experience in the Christian school industry and that they are up-to-date in the trends of giving.

This brings us to the question about how to look after data. If the annual fund is the base and basis of all excellent fundraising at the school, then the database is the veins and arteries that make it possible. A Database Clerk who essentially carries out data entry does not provide the level of service that the school needs. CSM advises that a school that is going to hire their first employee in philanthropy should invest in a Database Manager BEFORE hiring a Philanthropy Director. The Principal / Head of School, together with the Chair of the Philanthropy Committee, can carry out the overall strategic coordination of the school's fundraising. What neither has the time or skills to do is to manage the data.

To illustrate, here is one school's description (slightly edited) of the DM's responsibilities:

> *The Database Manager is responsible for coordinating database activities that serve the needs of current and prospect families, current and prospective donors, and various other constituencies. Particular responsibilities include: (1) the oversight of strategic plans for database utilization and optimization (serving admission, philanthropy, and family relations); (2) the provision of donor and constituent research (for both current and prospective donors); (3) the integration and optimization of the school's multiple databases, including the school's Student Information System; and (4) the stewardship of all constituents.*

This is a position that has requires the tactical skills of data maintenance as well as the strategic skills of coordination and foresight. The person is not only doing fundraising. The school must acknowledge that data is largely about the same person – the parent. While the school segments the functions of the school into its component parts, the parent is unitary.

	School	Who
Tuition Request	Business Office	Parent pays
Communications	Teachers	Parent receives
Annual Fund Request	Philanthropy Director and / or the Philanthropy Committee	Parent gives
Event Invitation	Arts, athletics, Principal	Parent goes
Yearbook and School Photos	School receptionist	Parent gives children cash

The school has a hard time remembering that, while many people are in contact with the parent, from the parent's point of view, the school needs to coordinate and ensure the right hand and left hand know what they are doing. The Database Manager is the conductor.

At the same time, when it comes to philanthropy itself, typically associated with data management, the DM enables both the Principal and the volunteers (and the philanthropy professionals if the school has them) to build relationships with leadership donors that are focused on a solid and deep understanding. The DM carries out research profiling the donor to ensure that the solicitor asks for an amount the leadership donor is excited / willing to give. The DM uncovers potential leadership donors by mining the annual fund data and providing reports that highlight opportunity. Another school put it this way:

> *The Database Manager is responsible for database management, advancement reporting, prospect management, gift recording, data integrity and data security. They are also responsible for the strategic execution and management of a comprehensive annual giving program, including the coordination and oversight of supporting initiatives in the areas of development services and donor relations. They will develop and implement data and gift-entry procedures, produce reports and mailing lists for departmental and schoolwide use, and provide database training when called upon.*

This work acts as the crucial foundation-building when your school moves into capital campaign mode. In the years while the campaign is running, the school not only needs the capital asset gift but also and still the annual fund gift to support the excellence of the ongoing mission delivery to the child. Knowing and understanding donor motivations allows the Philanthropy Committee and Principal (and Philanthropy Director) to engage in conversations, confident in the relations they already have. Not only that, but the DM provides reports before visits, allowing the solicitors to spend their time on the relationship itself and not on the "bureaucracy" behind it. This is particularly important for volunteers who have scarce time and don't appreciate it when they perceive it being wasted. One school put it this way in their job description:

1. *Develop, implement, and manage the internal systems of prospect identification, cultivation, solicitation, and stewardship, with strong emphasis on major gifts prospect management.*
2. *Ensure the Director of Community Development has efficient, effective tracking systems to support cultivation and solicitations.*
3. *Provide full services support for comprehensive campaigns including tracking next steps, pledge commitments, solicitation strategy management and reporting.*
4. *Develop donor prospect lists and analyze current donor prospect lists for cultivation and solicitation.*

5. *Manage a calendar of special events designed to cultivate and steward donors, as prioritized by the strategy.*
6. *Provide prospect research services for Institutional Advancement*
7. *Perform online and hard-copy research to evaluate giving potential and develop solicitation strategies.*

The job is not finished when the gift is given. There is considerable work to do in accepting the gift, processing it, and ensuring the follow-up is carried out. This requires complete coordination with the Business Office since the annual audit will look carefully at the management of these monies. There are legal requirements that must be followed, particularly for the increasing number of schools that are developing their endowment funds. The same school as above laid it out like this:

- *Interface with the finance department and general-ledger accounting staff regarding gift entry, gift posting, fund creation, gift restrictions and audit reporting.*
- *Enter and acknowledge gifts, assisting in account reconciliation, and producing regular reports as to the status of various fundraising efforts.*
- *Serve as departmental resource and liaison for Admissions, and the Records offices.*
- *Provide financial reports to the Foundation and School board when needed.*

And finally, the DM supports the school's enrollment and recruitment efforts. Another job description put it this way:

- *Admission and Enrollment Management – Records admission funnel data from inquiry to enrollment; maintains enrollment records; and maintains re-enrollment records*
- *Produces regular reports on enrollment activity*
- *Marketing Communications – runs reports, queries, and lists for targeted mailing – for all sectors of advancement*
- *Maintains re-enrollment records*
- *Produces regular reports tracking the performance of social media and web-based communications to aid the Director of Institutional Advancement, the Director of Admission and Enrollment Management, the Director of Development, and the HOS in Annual Strategic Advancement Planning and travel planning in service of both hard and soft incomes goals*

What kind of person does this kind of thing? Below is a composite from various job qualifications paragraphs (personal qualifications have been kept while pure technical requirements have been edited out):

- *Imbued with a deep sense of the school's mission and culture*
- *Has an unflagging commitment to accuracy*

- *Demonstrates extreme commitment to data privacy and donor confidentiality*
- *Loves "order"*
- *A "data hound" – i.e., enjoys collection, analysis, and manipulation of data to generate meaningful information for decision-making purposes*
- *Committed to recording both qualitative and quantitative data*
- *Proactive and is obsessed with the timely capture, recording, and retrieval of data*
- *Ability to investigate, analyze, and synthesize large quantities of data into a user-friendly and concise format for the use of the development team*
- *Strong analytical and problem-solving skills*
- *Provides excellent customer service to both internal and external customers*
- *Excellent written and oral communication skills, with the ability to work with both technical and non-technical users*
- *Committed to own professional growth and renewal*

Your school is not looking for a data clerk. Irrespective of the size of your school and its budget, the job of the Database Manager exists. If you don't have the funds to hire this person, then look into your volunteer base to find two or three people who can work together to do this. If you eventually find the funds to get someone either part-time or full-time, remember to hire this position BEFORE you hire the Philanthropy Director. Your Principal, your Philanthropy Committee Chair, and your parents will thank you!

Compensation: salary and benefits vary widely for this position. Remember, however, that you are looking for a high-functioning individual who can take on real responsibilities. Our recommendation is to think about compensation at the level of a teacher with 10 years' seniority.

Note: there is a generic job description in the appendices that you can use / edit as you will.

The Annual Fund Manager

Here is the second hire. We remind you of the order of hiring.

1. Database Manager
2. Annual Fund Manager
3. Philanthropy Director
4. Planned Giving Officer
5. Alumni Relations Coordinator

Of course, often schools move straight to the Philanthropy Director position. Whatever the title, the reality is that this person initially will be doing the job of the Annual Fund Manager (AFM) and the Database Manager (DM). But you will be paying them at a director's salary. Save yourself money and hire the right person at the right salary.

Once your school has a DM (always the first hire), your next philanthropy hire is the AFM. Unlike the DM, who has high technical skills, the AFM is not a technical position. Let's think about what the annual fund is: the annual fund is the way in which the school develops a culture of philanthropy. Through the annual fund, the next generation of leadership donors is found and stewarded.

The AFM is therefore not primarily a fundraiser. The AFM is a relationship builder, an inspirer, a trainer, an organizer, a culture builder. From the relationship comes generosity and from generosity comes giving. This means that the AFM does not have to have a vast technical knowledge of philanthropy, or the ability to solicit in person. Instead, as one school put it in their job description, the AFM must:

- *Recruit, train, lead, engage, and retain the Annual Giving Cabinet for peer-to-peer outreach, communicate updates and determine next steps*
- *Identify, cultivate, and strengthen relationships with potential donors*

Another school called this position the Donor and Parent Relations Coordinator. This is helpful since the primary focus of the Annual Fund is the current parent body. They are the most likely to give to the school and, given that their children will be with the school over 13 years or more, they are also donors who can give for a decade or more. Given that 64+ percent of gifts are one-time-only, i.e., a second gift is never made, longevity in giving is to be prized.

It is important that the AFM is someone whom parents trust – and whom you trust with parents. The annual fund is an intersection with retention and recruitment. Happy parents are motivated to support the school beyond tuition. The communications that the AFM carries out are a key part of the school's retention and recruitment strategies. Annual fund communication is a positive message about the school pouring excellence into the life of each child. It does actually support excellence and undergirds the school's mission promise. One school put it like this in their job description:

- *Strong interpersonal skills, i.e., oral and written communications, presentation skills, professional demeanor, judgment, and diplomacy*
- *Strong team builder*
- *The ability to establish strong and effective personal and professional relationships*

The AFM must understand the primacy of the school's mission and that the annual fund in the sense of fundraising is not for its own sake but to enhance mission delivery. Too many job descriptions that we see put too much emphasis on raising money – an indicator that the annual fund is probably a desperate effort to cover a tuition gap rather than an effort to support enhancements and growth.

Here's an example of a "bad side" descriptor: *The Director of Advancement is responsible to help raise funds ...*

We much prefer the understanding of this next school that begins with the spiritual attributes of the applicant.

Spiritual Leadership

- *Personally reflect the purpose of the school, which is to honor Christ in every class and in every activity.*
- *Maintain professional ethics as reflected in Scripture and the fund development profession, integrating the Christian worldview in all tasks.*
- *Provide spiritual leadership in garnering all resources (prayer, volunteer, and contributed support) for advancement of the school's mission.*

If you follow CSM's teaching, you will already know that the annual fund is one of only three asks made in any given year of parents. It is not a sequence of multiple asks in an array of communications and events.

Again, the bad side:

> *The Director of Development's principal charge is to create numerous, efficient, and compelling opportunities for donors to support an organization ...*

Ouch! Don't offer that job!

Rather, the AFM must be a persistent and persuasive logistical organizer whose job is to tell the story. Why should I volunteer? Let me tell you a story! What is philanthropy? Let me tell you a story! What difference does your school make? Let me tell you a story!

As one job description puts it:

> *Creates a Case for Giving connecting the donor with the school mission; finds the stories and tells them.*

Storytelling is allied to excellent logistics capacity. Look how many times the word "coordinates" appears in the following job description:

- *Coordinates planning and communications with Annual Giving Cabinet of volunteers*
- *Prepares appeals and publications; coordinates volunteer calling and thanking*
- *Coordinates the solicitation process for all constituent groups*
- *Responsible for donor acknowledgements and recognition*
- *Coordinates portfolio stewardship for leadership donors with the Philanthropy Committee*

The Annual Fund Manager is your second philanthropy hire – after the Database Manager. This is someone imbued with the school's mission, a relationship-builder, an excellent communicator, highly ethical, a storyteller, logistically superior. Find that person, develop your culture of philanthropy, uncover your next generation of leadership donors, and, by the way, raise more money than you have ever done in the school's history.

Compensation: this is a key position and it doesn't need high technical skills. Someone who is skilled at logistics, has a warm personality and can get along with parents, and is totally committed to the vision of the school is "ideal." Remember that the Principal and Philanthropy Committee are going to work with the leadership donors. This person is going to broaden the base of philanthropy and uncover the next generation of leadership donors. Think total compensation equivalent to one of your teachers with 0 to five years of experience.

The case for support is the central message of your campaign. It is designed to connect the donor's heart with the school's mission, inspiring the donor to give generously in return for all that God has provided.

Consider these examples of case for support letters.

A Letter "Case for Support" Example (from a Principal of a CSM school)

Dear Joseph and Maria:

Time off from school can be a blessed thing. God has used the summer break to teach me the importance of rest, which is vital since we will soon begin a year-long celebration of our 50th year as a school! This milestone is a testament to the faithfulness of God and the dedication of our community. Our mutual objective must be to continue honoring the Lord, building community, and preparing ourselves well to impact the next generation of Christian leaders. Our Leadership

Team is planning several celebratory events and initiatives throughout the year to commemorate this special occasion, and we look forward to your participation.

As you know, [name] Christian School is a ministry of [name] Bible Church, a partnership that has been steadfast since our inception in 1974. The church offers us their unwavering support and we are deeply grateful. They provide the building, maintenance, utilities, and other improvements, which lightens our financial burden, and we are thankful. This is an advantage that not many other schools enjoy.

Looking ahead, our vibrant school community must build on the church's kindness, by doing more for ourselves. We crave each parent, grandparent, and alum's ongoing prayer, volunteerism, testimony, and generosity during the journey. You will fuel the school's Five-year Strategic Plan, which you can read by clicking on [embedded link included in the letter]. The board and I are committed to elevating the total student experience and rewarding our faculty in morally responsible and competitive ways. As we go, you can trust that I will lay out the details of each step for transparency and accountability, but in general, our strategic vision compels us to take these steps:

- We will expand learning opportunities for children, helping them to grow in truth, kindness, and wisdom to impact the Kingdom.
- We will recruit and retain a world-class and Godly faculty by offering competitive compensation, benefits, and professional development. (We desire to underwrite 100% of our operational budget, including people, programs, and property.)
- We will add new and improved spaces for academics, the arts, and sports. (Tax-deductible charitable giving above and beyond tuition, with the church's ongoing partnership, will be the driving force.)

Let's use our 50th year to build on that which the Lord has already done, as examples of biblical generosity (Luke 6:38). To that end, after studying the best practices of peer institutions nationwide and gathering counsel from trusted advisors, we are launching the annual **Husky Fund** this fall. It will be the primary way by which our friends and families are invited into the school's ongoing improvement process through charitable giving. When communicating with you about the fund, our volunteer team and I will be specific about the objectives and celebrate the immediate impact when the fundraising goal is met.

Please respond joyfully to the best of your ability when a **Husky Fund** volunteer asks you to participate. Go Huskies!

Sincerely,
[Principal's name]

A Letter "Case for Support" Example (from the Receptionist of a CSM school)

I wanted to tell you a little story about [name] Christian School. My name is Michelle and I work in the office, and I really enjoy people, especially children. I sometimes wonder if this was the right job for me and the Lord always assures me that I am where I should be.

In the office we wear many hats and we've got children who need someone to tell them they are special. (I can do that.) We have usual suspects in the office daily for a temperature check or medication or just to complain. We have the occasional crier that will stop in the office to just cry and take a minute to pull themselves together before going back to class. We have the children who were sent to the office by the teacher to receive discipline. We get the tattletales, the fights on the playground, the sick kiddo going home and the sick at heart. You name it, we have it in the office.

Now we get to live out truth, wisdom, and kindness. We get to share the love of Jesus. We tell these children that God has a plan for their life, that God has a better way. We get to show the reality of how truth, wisdom, and kindness can make a difference in their own current situation, whatever it is. NOW we get to love on these children while they are at our school and try to guide them to their own personal relationship with Jesus.

If this sounds like a place that you would like to have your children attend school, please join me in giving to the Husky Fund so we can add more students that we can support, love and guide to a great future.

A Testimonial "Case for Support" Example (from the Board President of a CSM school)

In June of 2008, as the [name] River rose to engulf my town, water surrounded everything in my life – my city, my work, my home. In a metaphorical and literal sense, floodwaters washed away everything in my life, leaving me and my boys adrift. God, family, church, and community became the life rafts that we clung to. God provided tools and resources for us to rebuild our lives and people to build along with us – our family, our church family, and my future wife, Robin. Through Robin, God led us to the safety and warmth of the family at [name] Christian School.

My boys and I came into the school family recovering from deep trauma. The school family welcomed us in, gave us a place to belong, grace to heal, and space to serve. Over the next 10 years my boys got to see the Body of Christ in action. They grew with other children – succeeding, failing, doing wonderful things, and messing up spectacularly. Through all of it, teachers, staff, students, and other parents were there by their side. My boys were loved and served and learned to love and to serve. Now that they are out of school, they practice that love and service that they were shown and learned.

That is why I am committed to Christian education and to our Christian School in particular. My boys came to the school looking for a dry, safe place to land. They left stronger and with the tools they needed to lead others to the warmth and safety of Christ.

The Philanthropy Director

Your Philanthropy Director is the third of your philanthropy hires.

1. Database Manager
2. Annual Fund Manager
3. Philanthropy Director
4. Planned Giving Officer
5. Alumni Relations Coordinator

You are hiring into a high-level position, a director, to do three things:

1. Supervise the other two philanthropy positions (reduce the number of the Principal's direct reports).
2. Support the Principal (carry out high-level administrative tasks).
3. Support and advise the Philanthropy Committee (leading from below).

Supervision of the Database Manager and Annual Fund Manager

Let's remind ourselves that the DM is not a data clerk, although data entry is part of the responsibility. This person is a report generator, a researcher, and a coordinator / interpreter of the data relationship between family relations, philanthropy, and the Business Office. The AFM is the logistics person who coordinates the volunteers in delivering a peer-to-peer relationship program that drives the school's culture of philanthropy.

Supervising these positions means:

- Articulating the vision of the department and ensuring alignment in purpose; sharing the Director's own annual objectives
- Developing their annual objectives with the requisite calendar and metrics for success

- Supporting them to success and holding them accountable
- Assisting and sometimes interposing in conflict situations
- Being a servant leader in a willingness to get in the weeds when they need it
- Providing the resources needed to accomplish the task
- Recommending continuance (or not) to the Principal

Supporting the Principal

If there is no Philanthropy Director, then the Principal fills that role. Hiring a Philanthropy Director releases the Principal from many time-consuming jobs:

- Developing and maintaining the school's Strategic Philanthropy Plan
  - An annual giving plan
  - A leadership giving plan
  - A calendar
  - A communication plan including materials development
  - Identification of key strategies for each constituency: parents / caregivers, grandparents, alumni, community members, vendors, teachers, staff, friends of the school

- Maintaining a list of leadership donors
  - Reviewing the annual fund data with the Annual Fund Manager and uncovering potential new leadership donors
  - Developing a relationship plan for each donor
  - Accompanying the Principal on visits
  - Proactively visiting leadership donors on behalf of the school

- Dealing with the logistics of donor acknowledgement and gratitude
- Maintaining the giving section of the website.
- Coordinating activities and plans with the Philanthropy Committee
- Creating the formats for and producing all reports
- Providing regular news updates for the weekly calendars and newsletters
- Monitoring pledges outstanding with the Business Office
- Creating each year's annual report

Support and advise the Philanthropy Committee (leading from below)

The Board is responsible for the approval of and the success of all capital, endowment, and major gift campaigns. The logistics of such campaigns are handled by the school. But the effectiveness of any campaign is dependent on the Philanthropy Committee taking responsibility for the leadership donors.

This committee is one of the five mandatory Board committees, which also include Finance, Buildings and Grounds, Board Stewardship, and Head Stewardship. The committee accomplishes two very important goals. It provides access to talent for the Board to carry out its duties. Second, and equally importantly, it supports the work of the school both operationally and strategically without fear. It does this task in partnership with the professional leadership of the school represented by the Principal. As a Board committee, it is chaired by a Board member. It includes many at large members.

Typically, the members of the Philanthropy Committee (and Board) have little or no experience in philanthropy. The Philanthropy Director thus has the ongoing task of educating and training the committee (and Board) in relational philanthropy and the Golden Rule Cycle, helping and assisting them in the stewardship of the school's leadership donors.

The Philanthropy Committee is responsible for:

- Creating the case for support, the central message that will hopefully connect the heart of the donor with the mission of the school, engendering generosity
- Bringing the stories that illustrate impact and success
- Accompanying the committee members in executing the Golden Rule Cycle, including solicitation visits
- Being a lead solicitor for the school
- Training committee members in solicitation
- Bringing regular updates for any campaign and identifying the key metrics to watch
- Celebrating this enormously important group of volunteers
- Eliminating any drudgery tasks, coordinating appointments, providing the briefing papers, writing up the outcomes
- Connecting the Philanthropy Committee, the Principal, the Board President, and the Philanthropy Director

Note: because the Principal is ex officio a member of all Board committees (as is the Board President), the assumption in this section is that it automatically includes the Principal as well as the leadership volunteers.

The Christian Philanthropy Director: Qualifications

- Imbued with a deep sense of the school's mission and culture with deep faith.
- Five years' experience, at least, in philanthropy (preferably in Christian schools)
- Excellent communication, computer, and database skills
- Tact in dealing with people at all levels including a significant capacity for collaboration and team-building
- Excellent project management and follow-up skills (e.g., ability to take ownership of solicitation groups and develop lead donor strategies)
- Skilled at managing and motivating volunteers to meet goals
- Strong attention to detail; accuracy a must
- Flexibility in work schedule, available as needed (assumption of evening and weekend responsibilities)
- Exhibits an inherent zeal for exceeding goals (extremely competitive and self-motivated, with "fire in the belly" to excel on a daily basis)
- Meets deadlines and can work under pressure
- Assumes that "no" means "not yet"
- Implacably optimistic
- Communicates, inspires, and educates the community about the critical needs of the school and how donors can support the school through philanthropic investment
- Presents well in public (able to speak well and professional in appearance)
- Committed to his / her own professional growth and renewal
- Displays an innate ability to show respect for and to honor the dignity of all donors, regardless of gift level, and communicates with a loving / nonjudgmental perspective.

Compensation: this position is not an inexpensive one. The hierarchy of compensation goes from the Principal to the Business Manager / CFO and Philanthropy Director. Look at your current Business Manager / CFO and see where this job would fit in. People who are qualified for this position, while they can often stay at their schools for decades, constantly deepening the school's relationship to its donors, are as likely to leave after five to seven years. They are not Annual Fund Managers and are not highly motivated "just" to do that kind of work. They typically need challenges and the excitement of moving the school forward in dramatic ways. Excellent compensation helps.

As a Principal, your education curve should be steep so that you can effectively supervise your Philanthropy Director. Ensure that, while you may not have their depth of expertise (one of the reasons for hiring them), you do understand CSM Relational Philanthropy and the Golden Rule Cycle and can thus hold them accountable for their performance.

The Christian Planned Giving Officer

Even if you will never be in a position to hire someone in planned giving, every school should be connected to a financial services firm that can provide advice and counsel to members of the school community as they think about end-of-life estate planning. They can and will provide a brochure you can brand and that you can pass to people who have shown interest. There are also Christian organizations that provide support to Christian schools in this area including, for example, the Barnabas Foundation. While we do not officially endorse any particular organization, we point to them because you can lean on them for assistance even when you cannot provide high-level guidance yourself. In the USA, an umbrella organization is the National Association of Charitable Gift Planners; in Canada, it is the Canada Association of Gift Planners. Both have much useful material to scrutinize.

If you have already hired managers for the first three positions (Database, Annual Fund, and Philanthropy), and can consider adding a Planned Giving Officer, it's important to know why this matters. There are about 77 million boomers in the United States, and the 2021 Canada census counted over nine million. You can see in this Statistics Canada chart below how important that is.

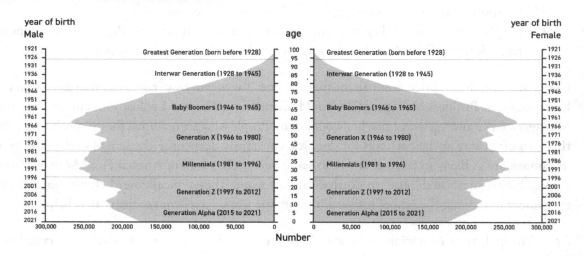

AGE PYRAMID OF THE CANADIAN POPULATION (2021)

Source(s): Census of Population, 2021 (3901).

THE CHRISTIAN SCHOOL AND PHILANTHROPY

In North America then, the boomers are nearing the point where they are all at retirement age (2030). According to the American Association of Retired Persons (AARP), 10,000 people in the USA are hitting the retirement age every day. They are inheriting over $15 trillion from their parents and, according to Cerulli Associates, will pass on about $53 trillion to their children. Sun Life Financial's research (reported in the *Financial Post* in November 2023) showed that the average inheritance would be $940,000. Those are big numbers.

And, again according to AARP, only 58 percent of boomers have estate-planning documents in place. This is an enormous opportunity.

Why is planned giving important? Simple answer: endowment. Endowment is an invested corpus of funds from which a "draw" of typically 4 percent to 6 percent income is derived. All Christian schools must have an endowment, also for a simple reason: financial aid. While there are many expenditures that an endowment draw might support, the primary one for our schools is to support families who would otherwise not be able to attend.

Over 95 percent of our schools provide an average of 20 percent of gross tuition in financial aid every year. But CSM metrics state that the school can only afford to give away 10 percent and still maintain a healthy budget. Of course, schools "balance" their budgets, but that is not the same as having a healthy budget where teachers are compensated well, classroom resources are universally excellent, and the facilities are beautifully maintained. An endowment is thus a third income stream to support the Christian school's desire for including all families in its community.

There are donors who have little to no interest in endowment. They do not want their money "tied up," but rather used now to have an immediate impact in the lives of children. We are always excited and motivated to listen to the donor and understand their motivations. We thus guide their gift to a need that is mission-appropriate, useful to the school, and meaningful to the donor. Such gifts can be transformational in their own right in their ability to move the school toward a strategic goal.

While the school's primary strategic focus is to support families through financial aid, other objectives are no less important. There is no hierarchy when we are stewarding the generosity of donors through their estates. It is good to remember that your school, if named in an estate plan, will be one of two or more recipients. Always assume you are not the only one!

Planned Giving Officer Form and Function

If you cannot afford a Planned Giving Officer (PGO), we reiterate that you must have a relationship with a (Christian-led) local financial services firm who will act as your PGO. You may only need to hire a part-time PGO and that may be enough for your size of school. Or a full-time PGO might become a strategic initiative as part of your strategic plan.

If you can hire, what does the PGO do?

1. Plans and implements programs designed to inform all school constituents about the advantages of estate and gift planning
2. Stewards, prays, thanks, reports, celebrates, asks donors for Planned Giving gifts
3. Supports and advises the Board Philanthropy Committee

The PGO reports to the Philanthropy Director. All activities are coordinated together to ensure that there is complete alignment of the work being carried out and that the donor is honored and respected.

PGO compensation, according to job advertisements at time of writing, ranges from $65,000 to $240,000. One reason is the high level of technical expertise required and the importance of constantly staying abreast of changing tax laws and rules and opportunities for estate vehicles.

Job qualifications might include the following (taken from a job placement advertisement for a Christian school):

- *Commitment to the mission of the school*
- *Minimum of 4 years frontline fundraising experience in a mission-driven nonprofit institution. A strong record of closing five- and six-figure gifts*
- *Excellent communication skills and a strong ability to inspire and engage a wide range of donors and build long-term relationships in order to close major and leadership gifts*
- *The ability to provide thoughtful insights and high-level strategic input in all areas of fundraising and prospect management*
- *A working knowledge of constituent management systems, Microsoft Windows and Google suites*
- *A solution-oriented mindset, a demonstrated sensitivity in handling confidential information, strong skills in diplomacy, communication, collaboration, and a sense of humor*
- *Some weekend and after-hours work required*

Maybe implicit in the commitment to mission is spiritual maturity. We would include the walk with Christ as a separate bullet point. At this level of philanthropy sophistication, the PGO is someone who is dealing with two difficult topics – death and money. That requires great maturity, understanding, empathy, and insight. Listening is a crucial skill and a qualification in most lists we looked at. One job description put it this way:

- *To succeed, this individual needs to have a mature faith and desire to disciple others along their journey with Christ*
- *Relationship-minded, Kingdom-driven, task-oriented servant leader, and generous giver.*
- *Ability to listen for understanding*

The notion that planned giving is discipleship is very powerful indeed and places this kind of giving in a very profound context. Along with that is the place of the school as an extension and extender of God's Kingdom. The PGO is an inspirer of the school's mission across generations. Whether it is a gift intended for endowment with multi-generational impacts, or a gift intended to have immediate impact, the outcome should be a stronger school that can continue to deliver its mission across decades of service.

The Christian School Alumni Relations Coordinator

Note: while we are talking here about the position of Alumni Relations Coordinator, the relationship between the Christian school and its alumni is a universal. The fact that most of our schools can't afford to hire a coordinator should not make the content of this section irrelevant. Instead, think about it from the point of view of a volunteer or several volunteers who each take on an aspect of the position in your own school. Like the PGO, this is also a position that can be hired part-time or full-time.

The topic of alumni is tricky because it feels very emotional – these are our children who are now making a difference in the world – and is also very practical – these are adults who can help the school move into the future. We need alumni for five very clear objectives:

1. To provide affirmation that the mission-in-action is worth the investment in a 13-year-long Christian school education
2. To bring their children to the school
3. To connect with and mentor current children at the school
4. To volunteer and, in particular, to volunteer on Board committees and at the Board level
5. To give

Here's a much more limited and philanthropy-focused role from a job description on the web:

> *The Alumni Relations Coordinator is responsible for building and maintaining positive relations with the Alumni community of [name] and coordinating all aspects of the Alumni program. The Alumni Relations Coordinator works closely with the Director of*

Philanthropy to ensure the school community remains connected and engaged, as well as raising the significant philanthropic contribution provided by the Alumni.

We have often heard that the only point with alumni is the money they bring and that, otherwise, they have no value to a school. This would certainly be a secular point of view. In Christian schools, with the high value we place on community, that would be an inappropriate single emphasis. We are equally interested in the other four CSM objectives and, based on relational philanthropy, believe that objective giving is an outcome of the other four. That's why we have placed it at the end. The other four can go in all kinds of order depending on the alumnus/a. But giving should always be an outcome.

Still, this position does report to the Philanthropy Director, so we do not want to minimize the giving aspect. Relational philanthropy does not suggest giving is somehow less important. It says that optimal giving, i.e., generosity, derives from a thankful heart, a desire to give back, to support what benefited the child all those years ago.

If I had a meaningful, even powerful experience that has informed my adult life, if I live close to my alma mater and send my children to the school I went to, if I am volunteering in the life of the school, if I am providing summer jobs to my school's juniors and seniors, I will also give. Develop the relationship and the money will follow. Indeed, our teaching of our alumni should lead their values in that direction. First seek the Kingdom of Heaven and then … (cf. Matthew 6). First put your heart / treasure in the right place and then … (cf. Matthew 6). We should implicitly and explicitly ensure that our values continue to be Jesus-centered as we move into a different kind of relationship with our children who have now become adults.

Here's a description of the "alumni activities" that the Coordinator supports in another job description that gives a wider flavor of the function:

- *Manage and coordinate the Alumni Ambassador Program as part of the overall Alumni Relations Program.*
  - o *Coordinate, plan, and execute alumni community building events, such as the Pigskins & Pints night.*
  - o *Facilitate efforts to increase alumni participation in all appropriate areas of the life of [school], such as invitations to and inclusion in homecoming and other athletic and extracurricular events.*
  - o *Organize, plan, and work in coordination with the Alumni Board for meetings.*
  - o *Organize, plan, and execute all homecoming events for alumni.*
  - o *Facilitate all alumni basketball league operations.*

- *Ensure current and accurate updates on all information on the alumni section of the website.*
- *Plan, organize, and create the monthly Alumni Newsletter in coordination with the director of marketing and communication.*
- *Manage, organize, and facilitate the Valentine's Day cards to alumni and birthday cards.*
- *Organize, plan, and execute the logistics of Christmas on [School] and the Easter Egg Hunt.*
- *In coordination with the director of development – organize, plan, and execute the logistics and fundraising efforts of all Alumni Class reunions and the golf outing.*

Note the reference to "Program," i.e., organization, in the first item above. This refers to community, to an alumni association, to a newsletter, to appreciation of their personal lives, to fun events at the school that involve them and their families, and of course to soliciting gifts.

The CSM five objectives provide focus for the Alumni Relations Coordinator. A CSM job description might include:

1. *Work with the Vocation, College, and Careers Counselor to get to know the junior and senior classes and connect them with potential alumni mentors, coaches, employers.*
2. *Act as school support and liaison with the Alumni Association. This group is a school-sponsored and alumni-directed organization run under the auspices and rules laid out by the school and alumni together.*
3. *Ensure the maintenance of an alumni connection and news page on the website and connected to appropriate social media.*
4. *Regularly communicate the news of the school and the news of alumni to the alumni. Where appropriate, communicate alumni news to the broader school community.*
5. *Invite alumni to school events.*
6. *Invite alumni to alumni events at the school.*
7. *Together with the Family Relations Director, invite alumni families to consider the school as a best choice educational opportunity for their children.*
8. *Together with the Principal, identify and bring closer to the school alumni who can volunteer their time on Board committees and, potentially, the Board.*
   Note: *alumni on the Board are a mixed blessing because their tendency is to look backwards. CSM has been with a number of Christian schools whose Board alumni members were barriers to the school moving forward. They must respect and honor the past but keep their eyes forward.*
9. *Together with the Principal and Philanthropy Director, identify visiting "tours" each year where particular alumni are engaged through personal visits.*
10. *Together with the Database Manager, ensure records are constantly updated.*
11. *Together with the Philanthropy Director, solicit testimony in written, digital, and in-person ways to clearly articulate the value of the education being provided.*

12. *Together with the Philanthropy Director, solicit class funds that will support the Board's Strategic Plan / Strategic Financial Management as well as specific-to-alumni projects such as endowment for financial aid.*

The Alumni Relations Coordinator is a connecting role. The person is mission-appropriate; likely an alumnus/a; in the first five to 10 years of their career and looking for an excellent place to hone skills and be mentored by a good professional; personable, well-organized, and an excellent organizer; easy to like, a team player; has a good memory for names. Their compensation is probably in the teacher one- to five-year range.

At a certain size of school (over 750), it will be impossible to have this kind of work carried out by volunteers. If the school is serious about their alumni, someone has to be hired to look after this task and support the school's Leadership Team in identifying and connecting alumni to the school to meet the five objectives. For small and smaller schools, the function of ARC can certainly be fulfilled by one or more volunteers. And at any size, volunteers will be necessary. Ensure always that the role remains one of coordination, not direction. In that way, the task remains tactical, even as it supports the strategic pathway of the school.

Summary

The order for hires in philanthropy is:

1. Database Manager
2. Annual Fund Manager
3. Philanthropy Director
4. Planned Giving Officer
5. Alumni Relations Coordinator

THE BOARD AND THE PRINCIPAL: WHO'S RESPONSIBLE FOR WHAT?

Your Board is Strategic; your Principal / Head of School is Operations. The Operations Team includes all those who report to the Principal / Head of School and who have leadership responsibilities.

What does that mean in philanthropy?

The simple, but not easy, answer is that the Board of Trustees is responsible for ensuring that Operations has the money / building and grounds / human capital necessary to deliver the mission with excellence.

This happens in two basic ways. The first is that the Board sets tuition each year that provides the basis for paying the Operations expenses of the school. Tuition and fees cover the operating expenses of the school in the Key Performance Indicator (KPI) ratio of 102 percent, i.e., ensuring that the school makes a profit in order to fund the Operations reserve. Even with that, there are many needs that tuition does not and cannot cover. The second is that the Board raises philanthropic dollars to meet those other needs. These may include significant renovations, new builds, enhancements to mission delivery, endowment.

You are, as Trustees, liable for the budget, for deficits, for potential bankruptcy, for the assets of the school. It's why the school purchases Directors and Officers (D&O) Liability Insurance. If there is a shortfall, it is ultimately your responsibility to fix. If there is a roof to replace, it is your responsibility to do that. So, for example, you can't pass a deficit budget without writing a check to cover the difference. For whatever reason you are raising money, you have the primary responsibility to ensure that it is successful.

Operations has the prime responsibility for mission delivery, for providing an education for each child in the school, for deploying those resources given by the Board for excellence. The Principal and the school's Leadership Team, whether in a small or large school, lead the community within the embrace of the mission, ensuring the values of the school are transmitted and lived throughout the community, and even symbiotically into the lives of its families. Operations spends the operating budget. It identifies needs for the Board to support.

The distinction of Strategic / Operations functions is crucial to understanding the role of the Board in philanthropy. Because Trustees are typically parents, it is easy for them to become far too interested in mission delivery (including hiring and curriculum) rather than in their philanthropic responsibilities, which are admittedly far less enticing. However, not understanding this distinction is the cause of enormous dysfunction. For example, when the Principal is fired for poor mission delivery (resource deployment), all too often, the reason is as the resources (tuition and philanthropy) were inadequate, and the Trustees failed to accept their resource responsibility.

But how does this work in practice? Doesn't Operations actually do the fundraising? The Board, after all, is a group of volunteers and doesn't have the time or the expertise to be the leaders in fundraising. So isn't the argument moot? It doesn't matter who is responsible in management / leadership theory, the Board doesn't have the time or expertise to do it and so Operations is going to have to.

Hopefully, that is not the attitude of your Board!

Fundraising, the outcome of philanthropy (relationship-building), comes in four ways:

1. Annual giving
2. Leadership giving
3. Capital and endowment campaigns
4. Planned giving (this focus is talked about elsewhere in the book)

Let's look at how this might happen in different sizes of Christian schools

	Annual Giving	Leadership Giving	Campaigns
Less than 150 Students	Principal / Annual Fund Cabinet	Board, Principal, and Philanthropy Committee	School Board and Principal

150–300 Students	Principal / Database Manager and Annual Fund Cabinet	Philanthropy Committee and Principal / Database Manager	Board supported by Philanthropy Committee and Operations leadership
More than 300 Students	Principal / Database Manager / Annual Fund Manager and Annual Fund Cabinet	Philanthropy Committee and Operations Team	Board supported by Philanthropy Committee and Operations Team

The difference is accounted for in the kind of resources that can be called upon at each level of school, i.e., the number of employees that Operations has.

	Operations Personnel (Philanthropy)
Less than 150 Students	Principal, Executive Assistant
150–300 Students	Principal, Executive Assistant, Database Manager, Annual Fund Manager
300–750 Students	Principal, Executive Assistant, Database Manager, Annual Fund Manager, Philanthropy Director
More than 750 Students	Principal, Executive Assistant, Database Manager, Annual Fund Manager, Philanthropy Director, Planned Giving Officer, Alumni Relations Coordinator

Let's look at each in turn.

Less than 150 Students

A school of this size with an average tuition of $7,500 can't afford philanthropy personnel.

- 150 students at $7,500 is $1.125 million.
- Financial aid at 15% is $168,750.
- Net tuition is $956,250.
- Compensation at 75 percent of total budget = $717,187.
- A staff of 10 teachers at $55,000 = $550,000.
- Principal, bookkeeper, janitor / custodian, receptionist, lunch person, etc., takes up the rest of the budget.

Since that is so, while the Principal can and must do something, the Principal's prime responsibility is providing support, direction, and growth to the teachers. This means that the Board has to take ownership of all forms of giving and, specifically, provide leadership for the Annual Giving Cabinet. This is probably why event fundraising has lasted as long as it has rather than moving to cultivation, stewardship, and solicitation, a more effective and mature philanthropy model.

Operations doesn't have time to develop the relationships; the Board members, as volunteers, don't necessarily understand that they have to do it. "Let's get some volunteers together and run a gala or golf tournament or sell a product or rely on scrip." It seems easier. And it's what everyone in our community is doing.

Maybe it is "easier," and even successful in the short run, but it is not a generational approach. Making philanthropy sustainable means moving from transactional to relationship philanthropy. The school cannot afford to have a down year – something most of your community groups experience. Every year has to be a winner or the children will not be served well.

Board leadership through the Annual Giving Cabinet drives the best use of volunteers and the maturing of fundraising into the relational philanthropy model. The Principal (together with the Board) is an integral partner for working with leadership donors, but simply does not have the professional time to run the details of an annual fund. We might add that it is very unlikely that this educational leader has any professional expertise to lead. Most Principals are recruited from the academic or business realms and have no training in philanthropy. Their philanthropic leadership is weak, although typically enthusiastic, and based on whatever experience they have – and whether they learned the right lessons from that experience! The Annual Giving Cabinet must take up the mantle of leadership.

Note that, at this size, the database is also run by a volunteer who loves that kind of detailed and important work. There are databases that make that possible. At the next size of school, this should be taken over by a professional to ensure that there is consistency, timeliness, and internal coordination within the school. There will be plenty for that detail-oriented volunteer to do!

150–300 Students

Economies of scale allow a richer mix of support professionals. The Principal, at this stage of growth, can hire a Database Manager and thus free up invaluable time to put effort into higher-level professional leadership. This hire – the Database Manager – should always be the first hire in philanthropy and supported through Strategic Planning / Strategic Financial Management by the Board. It is the best initial way in which the Principal can be supported.

Without data, philanthropy is lost, and data is the logistical support that allows the donor to be treated with honor and respect. Every family represents an additional unit of work and at this size of school, there are too many "units" for a volunteer to appropriately handle. The DM tends to data across the school, i.e., from admission through the Business Office to philanthropy. In this way the parent becomes unitary in the school's data management rather than being "split" between departments.

At this school size, Operations can become a true partner with the Annual Giving Cabinet. The Principal can devote personal / professional time along with support from the DM, who carries out research, organizes the calendar, runs reports from a software that can now be developed intentionally, and assists in cultivation / stewardship events. The Principal can partner in creating materials, soliciting leadership donors, advising and participating in the Annual Giving Committee (Cabinet) on a regular basis, acquiring expertise and demonstrating leadership. If and when there is a campaign (small or large), Operations can support it. Philanthropy beyond the annual fund requires the Board to direct the Philanthropy Committee toward leadership giving – the Annual Giving Cabinet becomes a subcommittee. As the school moves toward 300, an Annual Fund Manager becomes essential to handle that workload. Remember, every additional family is an additional unit of work!

Over 300 Students

Operations now staffs a Philanthropy Office, adding a Philanthropy Director to the Database Manager and Annual Fund Manager. Much larger schools will scale up hiring other personnel such as the Planned Giving Officer and Alumni Relations Coordinator. The onus for annual giving at this size of school is now the responsibility of Operations and the Annual Fund Cabinet, supported by the Philanthropy Committee for leadership donors.

The Philanthropy Committee's primary responsibility is to steward the leadership donors who will support the school's campaigns. The Annual Fund Cabinet carries out the nitty gritty of the annual giving basic operations – creating and sending out materials (case for support and solicitation), and handling clerical management, organization, thanking, and celebrating.

The Philanthropy Committee is able to focus exclusively on supporting Operations in raising leadership gifts for both annual and campaign efforts. Each member of the committee has a portfolio of donors that he or she is responsible for. In campaigns, there is now the ability of Operations to bring a fuller support to the table because there are just more people who can devote their time to it – and because any campaign must include annual giving in it.

Amount versus Scope of Work for the Board

While the size of the school makes a difference as to what Operations and Strategic do, the prime responsibility for raising funds still belongs to the Board. The **amount** of work is the same for the Board whatever the number of students. The **scope** of work changes, and changes dramatically, at different levels of enrollment. Operations takes on a greater and greater responsibility for basic functions. It is clear, though, that at low student numbers the Board must carry out the bureaucracy of fundraising — it cannot be handed off to the Principal. It should be delegated to the Annual Giving Cabinet, but the Board has the responsibility to ensure that such a committee is well led from the Board level. This goes away as the school is able to hire professionals to take over these responsibilities. The Board always has responsibility for stewarding leadership donors, first through their own example and modeling, and second through engagement with the school's leadership donors, following the Golden Rule Cycle.

Since neither the Board nor Operations is likely to have professional training in philanthropy, continual upgrading of knowledge and skills is mandatory so that donors are respected and honored in the right way. This is not a one-and-done but an ongoing process. The Stewardship Committee can take some responsibility for this through their education function at the annual retreat and at each Board meeting. A part of that education should include philanthropy. It would be wise for the Board to engage with professional consultants in this area, typically through executive coaching (rather than workshops). Such consulting provides ongoing support and question answering through a process allowing individuals to continually learn the right lessons from their experience and gain just-in-time advice and counsel. Those who might benefit from executive coaching include the Principal, the Database Manager, the Chair and members of the Philanthropy Committee, and the Philanthropy Director.

Most schools CSM works with are underperforming in their philanthropy for one or more of six reasons:

1. The Board does not accept their responsibility.
2. The Board does not provide the human resources.
3. Philanthropy remains at the event level of maturity.
4. Everyone is embarrassed to go out and actually make the ask.
5. Data collection and management is weak.
6. Leadership is weak because of lack of knowledge.

As the CSM Mary Principle shows, philanthropy has a long and honorable history in Scripture, from the building of the second Temple (funded by Babylon) to the support of Jesus' mission (funded, in part, by Herod!). Boards must embrace their primary role and enjoy the outcome — funds to support children and the extension of God's Kingdom.

Summary

- The Board has the primary role for provision of resources, supporting excellent mission delivery through tuition-setting and philanthropy.
- The school's professional staffing of philanthropy depends on the size of the school and the efficiencies that size brings.
- At less than 150 students, the Board is responsible, with the Principal, for all philanthropic outreach.
- Above 150 students, the Principal can be a true partner in supporting both annual and leadership giving.
- Above 300 students, the Principal takes on primary responsibility for annual giving while the Board and the Philanthropy Committee take on primary responsibility for any other campaigns, and for leadership giving (in both annual giving and campaigns).
- The amount of work the Board does is not very different from stage to stage; the difference is the move from operational responsibilities to becoming truly strategic in scope.
- Without the Board, philanthropy cannot be truly optimized.

THE PHILANTHROPY COMMITTEE

Schools are very different from other areas of philanthropy. Here are some major differences between the typical Christian school and many other nonprofit organizations.

	Christian School	Nonprofit
Potential Donors	A small body of potential donors, most of whom are current parents	The general public (e.g., United Way) or a large interest group (e.g., an orchestra or hospital)
Attrition	Can't afford any loss	50%+ attrition the first year
Professional Leader	None or one / two	Well-organized office
Data	May be the most recent, but no historical data	Significant data, past and present
Use of Technology	Amateur	Sophisticated use of database
Solicitation	Prefer events	Personal and specific (and events)
Board Involvement	Limited or none	Assumed primary role

The biggest issue for all our schools from small (under 100) to large (over 2,000) is that there are not enough professionals to do the work. This will always be true. Because we want the dollar to be as close to the child as possible and the school's budget is thus largely devoted to the child and the child's needs, there is not and never will be enough money to pay people to do the jobs that need to be done.

Philanthropy is a strategic role and each Board must embrace this as a significant part of their role. CSM finds that well over 50 percent of Christian school Boards see raising money as either not their job (I didn't come onto the Board to raise money) or just a minor role. We even see a tiny minority of Boards where not every Board member donates!

Let's repeat the point. The school does not and will not have enough money to pay for enough professionals to do the job. Even the office of three or four or five people at the largest schools is not nearly enough. Philanthropy is relational and every family is a unit of relationship that has to be stewarded. Add in the school's donors who are not current parents (alumni, grandparents, alumni parents, supporters) and the task looks superhuman. The Board must step in to play its leadership role in this area. The Board at their meetings is tasked with forwarding the strategic direction of the school and ensuring that the Strategic Plan / Strategic Financial Management is implemented. The Board is, further, responsible for raising money over and above operations income (maintaining) in order to move the school forward (next generation). The Board delegates the actual organization and leadership of philanthropy to the Philanthropy Committee.

Philanthropy is one of the five mandatory Board committees, which also include Finance, Buildings and Grounds, Board Stewardship, and Principal / Head of School Stewardship.

First, the Philanthropy Committee provides access to talent for the Board to carry out its duties i.e., it includes many non-Board members who supplement the skills on the Board and some of whom may eventually become Board members. Second, it supports the work of the school both operationally and strategically in raising annual, capital, endowment dollars. It does this task in partnership with the professional leadership of the school represented by the Principal and, based on the school's size, other professionals.

The vast majority of Principals have no professional training or background in philanthropy although they may have some experience. In many of our schools, they are often the only "professional" for the committee to work with. Even if there is another fundraising professional, it is quite likely that this person will also have no formal training in the practice of philanthropy in Christian schools. This is CSM's experience. Interestingly, our Christian Principals don't duck the work of philanthropy; they are eager to learn. Some are already skilled amateurs in the relationship-building that leads to generosity. And philanthropy is a professional undertaking. Whether paid or volunteer, the actions taken to inspire giving must be professional.

Getting Going: The Six Steps

How does the Board set up the Philanthropy Committee, and what happens next? Take these six steps.

Step One: Set up the Committee – the First Meeting

Begin with a small group of perhaps six people. The Chair of the Committee must be a Board member. Typically, in Strategic Planning / Strategic Financial Management, we look around the room and ask who would see themselves heading this committee. Someone is always willing to step forward. It is always someone who understands its importance and often someone who either enjoys asking for money (solicitation) or is willing to be coached in that role. So long as they feel they will be supported, we don't find it hard to recruit this person. Often, they have already been doing some of this work.

Think of the next five members in the following way:

- The Principal must take a leadership role.
- If there is a professional fundraising staff member, that person must be a member. If there is more than one, they can potentially all be members.
- Ask at least three other people to join the committee. They might be:
  - One of your leadership donors who is interested in seeing this done much more effectively and is willing to put the time in to help make that happen
  - Someone very interested in data who will look after the database
  - Someone who is experienced in or would like to find out about fundraising

Everyone on the committee must have a history of giving to the school.

Note: everyone on a Board committee has a vote. There are not two classes of committee members. This is safe because the committee only carries out the mandate of the Board and always recommends action to the Board for approval, i.e., the Board does not delegate away its power.

Step Two: Develop the Philanthropy Committee's Mission

Establish a Philanthropy Committee Mission Statement for the committee so that when you invite people onto it, you can show them the intent of the committee. The mission can be derived from the Three Promises the school makes to its donors:

Promise One: We promise to be grateful to God and to you for your generosity to the "family of believers" in the school, ask you for gifts that fit your own prosperity, and honor you as a giver.

Promise Two: We promise that asking you to invest in God's work at the school will be accompanied by the school's accountability in spending your money in the way you intended.

Promise Three: We promise that we will use your gift to move the school forward on behalf of the children, within the context of a plan showing excellent stewardship and financial sustainability.

Here is a suggested example:

> *The Philanthropy Committee is a partner with the school community in providing solicited resources to enhance and strategically forward the mission and benefit the children of the school for this and succeeding generations, acknowledging and being thankful to a generous God.*

There is one more important step. It is possible to carry out great philanthropy when the school's finances are appropriately stewarded. The Philanthropy Committee should endorse both their own mission and the CSM Mary Principle. They outline the committee's intent to:

- Raise money over and above operating income.
- Exercise and teach philanthropy.
- Develop a culture of philanthropy.
- Treat donors honorably and respectfully.
- Follow the highest ethical standards.

The first bullet point is crucial. The effective Philanthropy Committee is part of a whole-school financial endeavor. The Board agrees to move the school toward 102 percent income / expenses without the help of donations (a CSM KPI). Many of our schools have already achieved this – it is both believable and doable for 99.5 percent of Christian schools. That first bullet point then empowers the Philanthropy Committee to raise money "over and above operating income."

Step Three: The Second Meeting – the Charge

At the second meeting, examine three documents. This is the "what are we supposed to do and what do we know" meeting.

1. The first document is the charge given you by the Board Stewardship Committee, i.e., what the Board expects you to achieve in order to meet the objectives of the Strategic Plan / Strategic Financial Management. If there is no current Strategic Plan, create your own charge based on the following four criteria:

   - Annual giving objectives
   - Stewardship of leadership donors
   - Communication of giving impact
   - Preparing for the next campaign / running the current campaign

   Ensure that the charge is elaborated until there are due dates, report to the Board dates, assignment of tasks, meeting dates, measures of success, processes to create / follow.

2. The second is a copy of the Board's Strategic Plan and Strategic Financial Management. This should be included in each committee member's binder (digital and / or print). Ensure that it is considered once a year to understand the context for the charge. Where is the school going? Why are you doing what you are doing?

3. The third document is the record of giving over the previous decade. Of course, this may be a sequence of documents. If there is no or spotty data, agree that the committee and the school will collaborate to ensure that data is collected from here on. This is a list of basic data that should be collected on an ongoing basis about each donor:

   - Quantitative data about the donor – donor's name, relationship to the school (parent, former parent, grandparent, alumnus/a, faculty / staff, Board, student) – note that donors often fit into more than one category; each donor's gift/s; solicitation type, person who made the solicitation, solicitation objective, date given; date phone call made to thank, date thank-you note sent, date of tax receipt, date of recognition sent

   - Qualitative data about the donor – occupation, address, preferred mode of contact, likes and dislikes, hobbies, vacation destinations, other charitable interests, potential for giving, etc.

   - Notes made from contact with the donor – in person, through phone calls, responses in writing from the donor, casual interactions, meeting the donor at school events

Step Four: The Third Meeting – Annual Giving this Year

The third meeting is to discuss annual giving. (The annual fund is covered at length in another chapter.) Here, we identify the basis for the school's fundraising efforts – the annual opportunity to enrich the child's experience through exceptional philanthropy.

As schools inaugurate organized philanthropy and move from a transactional to a relational approach, some start with an Annual Fund Cabinet. They then "grow" a broader-based Philanthropy Committee as one or more members, having practiced their skills and leadership, become the nucleus of this new group. Others call their initial effort a Philanthropy Committee, although annual giving is the focus of its action. Eventually, the Annual Fund Cabinet is created to take care of annual giving with the school taking a leadership role.

Annual giving is the way in which the school:

- Broadens its philanthropic basis developing a culture of philanthropy
- Uncovers future leadership donors

Of course, it also raises money for the school's annual case for support.

At this session, discuss or create the annual fund case statement. The case statement identifies the needs of the school. It doesn't have to be particularly inspirational and definitely should not be fancy. Its appeal will be in its brevity, so that potential donors will read it and appreciate its clarity. A one-sided sheet of paper is sufficient. Five bullet points for needs is enough, so long as the need is aligned with the impact it will have on children.

The committee should then determine a communications calendar (including the method) for its outreach to donors. The calendar should include:

- Solicitation of leadership donors (August – October)
- Solicitation of school personnel (August / September)
- Solicitation of general population (October – December)
- Phone acknowledgement of gift (time elapsed from receipt of gift, e.g., 48 hours)
- Written acknowledgement of gift (time elapsed from receipt of gift, e.g., 14 days)
- Date tax receipts are mailed (typically January)
- Date campaign success is reported, including when the money is spent (January through August)
- Annual report publication date – the "impact" report (somewhere between June and September)

The calendar will include a subset dealing with leadership donors (however the school defines that) who will receive an in-person request for philanthropy. Every donor receives an in-person thank-you.

Step Five: Ongoing Work

This step is not a meeting but a delegation of jobs and a timeline for completion. Primarily, it involves the preparation of materials – solicitation letters, website updates, database checks to make sure all new parents are included.

Note: solicitations and information bulletins / newsletters are two separate kinds of communication. Don't mix them up. For example, some schools place an envelope for donations in the annual report. Don't do things like that! Keep information and solicitation completely separate.

In addition, the committee asks the school to identify its events throughout the year and ensure that philanthropy is not a part of them. For example, is the Back to School Night an appropriate time for the Principal or Chair of the Philanthropy Committee or the Philanthropy Director to stand up and talk about giving for the year? Is Grandparents Day an opportunity to solicit or to share? What about the Christmas carol service? Or the musical performances? Or graduation? (The correct answer is "No"!)

Solicitation and thanking / reporting should not be mixed up. This applies to events as well. Work hard to clean up the event calendar so that celebration, community-building activities, and children's performances are not hijacked. However, ensure the committee / school philanthropy staff are represented at all events to meet the community and develop relationships.

In the same light, eliminate from the calendar any philanthropy events that are about "sales." Examples might include wrapping paper at Christmas, lilies at Easter, chocolate bars at any time. Such attempts to raise money dilute the impact of solicitation and make philanthropy transactional rather than relational. You will actually lose money and goodwill doing these things because parents are frustrated by repeated asks and, at annual fund time, will feel that they've already donated to the school.

Step Six: The Fourth Meeting – Review / Establish Policies

In this step, done once and then reviewed every three years, the committee ensures that there is a Gift Acceptance Policy to illuminate the ways in which the school will accept and deal with donations. Donors give in a variety of ways and the school will find it helpful to be able to talk with a donor and have clear guidelines about accepting a gift and what will happen when the gift is accepted, e.g., in relation to stocks or real estate. The gift acceptance policy is a Board policy and must be taken to a Board meeting for approval.

The National Council of Nonprofits urges for a written gift policy for the following reasons (edited and adapted for Christian schools):

- It allows the donor to understand how the school treats gifts, and gives the committee and school staff guidance during solicitation or and receiving contributions.
- Not all gifts are mission-appropriate because they move the school away from its mission. There are times when a gift should be refused.
- Some gifts may place the school in a difficult legal situation such as the school that was offered a property in Florida with a $1million liability attached to it.
- Hard to imagine, but you may be offered a gift you have no idea what to do with, e.g., a painting that would need to be sold to realize its value – a task you are not able to do.
- It's a risk-management practice.
- In the USA, IRS Form 990 asks whether a nonprofit has a "gift acceptance policy" and requires nonprofits that respond "yes" to complete Schedule M, as well as report any non-cash contributions/in-kind gifts.

The committee creates or reviews the School Philanthropy Policy. Some examples of items follow:

- Any form of fundraising must be approved through the Philanthropy Committee (or the Philanthropy Director if and when that position is in place).
- Children may not be involved in fundraising for the school.
- Children can participate in drives, e.g., for the food bank or for clothing – they may not compete with each other.
- Only high school students are permitted to raise money and only for charities they are personally and actively involved with.
- Parent organizations may not solicit donations, e.g., booster clubs, parent associations, with some exceptions such as business sponsorships and then only with the direction / support of the Principal / Philanthropy Director. Parent organizations are focused on building community and providing volunteer support.
- All donations belong to the school, not to specific programs.
- Donors have the right to restrict their gifts to the objective of their choice, assuming this is part of the school's current case for support.

The committee creates or reviews the philanthropy ethics policy. The CSM Philanthropy Code of Ethics includes the following:

1. We promise to build a relationship with you as Jesus did with his own Philanthropy Committee (Luke 8:3).
2. We promise to cover our "ask" with a canopy of prayer.
3. We promise that we will use your gift to move the school forward on behalf of the children within the context of a plan showing excellent stewardship and financial sustainability.
4. We promise to strategically ensure that philanthropy dollars go to extending the mission in the life of the child and will not be diverted to running the operations budget except to support financial aid.
5. We promise not to show partiality to one over another because of the gifts they have or have not made.
6. We promise to accept only gifts that are mission-appropriate.
7. We promise to involve you, if you wish, as a partner with the school.
8. We promise that asking you to invest in God's work at the school will be accompanied by the school's accountability and good stewardship in spending your money in the way you intended.
9. We promise that we are paid a salary and not a commission.
10. We promise to be grateful to God and to you for your generosity to the "family of believers" in the school, ask you for gifts that fit your own prosperity, and honor you as a giver.

It also includes the Donor Bill of Rights (AFP – Association of Fundraising Professionals). Both of these documents are available on the CSM website at *https://christianschoolmanagement.org/csm-code-of-ethics/*

We invite all of our Christian schools to adopt this document (see Appendix).

Our experience is that, at least on the website, Christian schools make no ethical commitments of any kind as to how they will steward money, philanthropic or not. This is a serious gap in our relationship with the school's supporters. We recommend that these policies, once Board-approved, are public on the school's website and referenced in the school's published documents.

Note: all policies must be recommended to the Board for approval. The committee cannot decide policy on its own. Once approved, the committee follows what is now Board policy.

These six steps comprise the first year's task for a Philanthropy Committee. Of course, elements of these steps may already be in place, making the task easier. If not, these are the basics on which great philanthropy can be built.

Focusing the Philanthropy Committee on Leadership Donors

The Philanthropy Committee is a committee of the Board, chaired by a Board member, and focused on stewarding leadership donors. It is generational, i.e., it is intended to benefit the children and grandchildren of those currently at the school. While it might begin as the Annual Fund Cabinet, it must develop and grow into its prime generational task of stewarding the school's leadership donors.

The Annual Fund Cabinet is focused on broadening the base of philanthropy and uncovering leadership donors while raising immediate impact dollars. It is a subcommittee of the Philanthropy Committee. Annual giving is to benefit the current children at the school.

In its mature stage, the Philanthropy Committee supports annual giving through the lens of the leadership donors. Leadership donors give to the annual fund as an ongoing, almost maintenance, task. They are essential to the annual fund's success. Pareto's Distribution articulates that 20 percent give 80 percent (see Appendix). This 20 percent leads the community into a culture of philanthropy.

The six steps above are organizational in character. They are tasks that need to be done in order to set up the school's work of philanthropy for long-term success. However, they don't help in identifying what the Philanthropy Committee does in order to actually raise money. The whole point of the Philanthropy Committee is to pray for and with, thank, report to, celebrate with, and ask the school's leadership donors, i.e., to carry out the Golden Rule Cycle with each donor.

Focusing on the Leadership Donor

The Philanthropy Committee is focused on those in the school community who provide leadership gifts, gifts that are the backbone of any campaign (annual to capital to endowment) and without which any campaign will fail. Whether the Philanthropy Committee is in its early stages of development where it is looking after the annual fund (and stewarding the leadership donors toward that end), or engaged in comprehensive campaigns including annual, capital, and endowment giving, it is the leadership donor that is its singular focus. Effective philanthropy must, of course, have the involvement of the whole community. At the same time, philanthropy operates on the premise of leaders inspiring others. Successful campaigns begin with the largest gifts. Once they are gained, campaigns then move to the smaller gifts.

While we would love to treat all our donors in the same way, there just isn't time. Thankfully, donors realize this and don't expect it. Every donor, and we'll repeat this several times, does expect the following:

- A telephone thanks within 48 hours of the school's receiving the gift
- A thank-you note that arrives within two weeks of the gift being received
- Tax receipts (mailed by the end of January) with a warm note
- Report of use of money demonstrating that the school's promises were kept and showing the impact on the children
- Annual report – this can be digital and should be put out no more than two months after the end of the school's fiscal year; we note that it is not best practice any more to include a list of all donors, saving you immense amounts of time!

For our lead donors, we add three more elements:

- A stewardship visit at least once a year and potentially other touch points
- A solicitation visit once a year
- A thank-you reception once a year

Know Your Donor

Notice the singular. Know your donor. It is each member of the committee's responsibility and joy to truly know their portfolio of donors "personally." s

The Donor Portfolio

Every member of the committee (and every member of the Board whether they are on the committee or not) has a portfolio of one to three leadership donors that they are personally responsible for. Each person is responsible for the relationship with these donors. Why one to three? The number has to be believable for you as a volunteer. With the best will in the world, how many people can you keep and establish this kind of relationship with? Of course, if you truly do have more time, then three is not a "legal" number! But we don't want our volunteers overwhelmed by a task that is beyond them.

Stewardship Visit

This can be as formal as arranging to meet at the donor's home and spending significant time with them. It may be as casual as having coffee at Starbucks / Tim Hortons for 30 minutes. Try to avoid doing stewardship at the school unless you have a very strong relationship already. If there is a couple, always meet with the couple. Very occasionally, a donor will not want you to meet with both together. That is unusual. More often than not, the donor will be delighted to include the spouse in the conversation. You should know that gender roles in giving are very fluid. While there may be some conventionality around it (the male may write the check), the wife may actually be the decision-maker. Spectrem Group asked married investors, "Who makes the financial decisions in your household?" The answer was intriguing:

Household Wealth Net Worth	Women	Men
	(We make financial decisions jointly)	
$5–25 million in net worth	75%	36%
$1–5 million in net worth	74%	43%
$100,000–1 million	76%	50%

Whatever one might imagine from these answers, it is clear that it is wise for the school to try to work with the couple together.

The stewardship visit is designed to give the donor the respect of knowing where the school is headed and will include two or more of the following:

- Share the Board's Strategic Plan, including a simple handout to leave behind. Always share where the plan is and is going.
- Show how the money has been spent that was raised.
- Provide assurance that the school's budget is balanced and that future budgets will be as well.
- Share a story of transformation in a child's life.
- Verbally thank the donor for their gift.
- Find out what motivates the donor and if there are particular areas of the school that they are passionate about.

That's a very nice 30 minutes. Don't get bogged down in detail. If the donor wants more information, make sure it is available to share. Do not ask for a gift. Do not inquire about a gift. Do make notes after the visit and ensure it is handed to the person in charge of the database to update the donor profile.

The committee / Board member will know the donor's portfolio well enough to understand what kind of relationship the person or couple would like. Some are perfectly happy to be kept up-to-date with a special leadership donor email that the committee (or the school) puts out six times a year. Some like to go for coffee. All will be invited to at least one or two school-year events that correspond to their interests (are they into athletics or the arts or both?). Know what motivates them and meet them where they are.

Solicitation Visit

This visit is for the purpose of asking for a donation. When you call to set up the visit, make sure you say that you would like to meet with them in order to discuss with them their gift. There should be no surprises. Again, it doesn't have to be long. If appropriate, it can be followed up by a letter including the request. That will depend on where the conversation ends. Ensure that you:

- Know the donor's giving history, including what they gave last year.
- Carry out at least basic research to understand the donor's financial background – house, vehicle, occupation / salary, donations to other charities, as a start.
- Review the notes in the database / file.
- Know if there is a particular objective (financial aid, technology, outdoor garden) that the donor has expressed interest in.
- Think about the relationship you have with the donor.
- Pray for a pure heart and steadfast spirit (Psalm 51).
- Know how much you are going to ask for.

Plan for the conversation to be short – don't request more than 15 to 30 minutes. Anticipate that many conversations will last longer as you both enjoy talking about the progress of the school, reminiscing about how it used to be, and telling stories of student triumphs. Some meetings might be very short. The donor (individual or couple) should leave the meeting feeling enriched by the opportunity to give.

While you might do this visit on your own, it is more likely that you will go on a solicitation with the Principal or the Philanthropy Director or a Board member. You may not be the person comfortable or good with the actual words of solicitation. You may be opening the door for your companion to make the ask.

On the other hand, you may be perfectly comfortable making the ask but know that the donor would appreciate meeting the Principal or Board member or basketball coach or music teacher. As always, it's based on knowing the donor, understanding their interests, paying attention to the things they talk about, and meeting them where they are.

Thank-you Reception

Never give donors gifts unless it is for a very particular reason and the gift is highly personal. One school invited a donor to a recital where they played one of her compositions. Another gave the donor season tickets to all athletic events. These two examples highlight the specificity of the gift – they were aligned to the donor's interests and to the reason for giving. They were carefully thought through.

Schools have often given donors school clothing (caps, scarves, jackets) to memorialize an anniversary of some kind. They were special moments. Avoid cups, trinkets, junk that tells the donor you are spending their money on things they don't want rather than on the children. Gifts should be a rare occurrence. And random gifts should never happen at all. The donor wants to "know" their gift makes a difference, not that you spend their money on something they didn't ask for and didn't want.

A leadership donor reception is very important, however. A reception is a low-cost, high-impact event that brings donors of the same caliber together and makes thanking them both personal and corporate. While some donors have large egos that need stroking, most say they don't want thanks (which isn't true) and certainly don't want to be exposed on their own (which is true). Give them the cover of a crowd, offer them simple refreshments, i.e., not a dinner but rather wine and cheese, or tea / coffee with a nice cake, and keep it short. They are busy people!

Some won't come – don't worry about it. They will appreciate having been invited. Others will come and leave. Some will stay and talk all night. They will enjoy seeing and meeting each other, knowing they are not the only donor and appreciating the way in which the community is supporting the children. For all, it will be a meaningful gesture. The Philanthropy Committee, the Board, the Principal, the school's development professional (if you have one) will all be at the reception. Many in that group are also leadership donors, in which case they are both being honored and playing the host. Note that while this is a low-cost event, the reception should be very high class and tasteful. Don't get cheap coffee and plastic cups. Get good coffee and china mugs. Show that you have put thought and effort into it.

Notes on Organization

The Philanthropy Committee self-organizes together with the Principal, the Database Manager, and the Philanthropy Director (if the school has one). Develop an annual calendar to ensure that the wheel is not being reinvented each year. Add detail as time goes by. The calendar is not just a list of dates but a "memory" of the 5W1H questions – who, what, when, where, why, how.

Meet regularly as a group. You will, of course, transact business. These sessions are also an opportunity to celebrate with each other, to give each other encouragement, to know that you are not in this alone. Philanthropy is hard work and work that takes a lot of time. It may be two or three years of stewardship before a donor gives an optimal gift. Sustaining enthusiasm over time requires being part of a community.

In formal meetings, ensure good minutes are taken that include important discussion points as well as decisions. To be able to look back and see why a decision was made can be very important in philanthropy. It is easy, a year or two later, to change direction without understanding the reasons for the original decision.

Summary

- The Philanthropy Committee's prime responsibility is stewarding leadership donors according to the Golden Rule Cycle.
- The committee is essential because the school can never hire enough professionals to do the work that needs to be done.
- There are six initial steps for the committee to carry out:
  o Set up the committee, including non-Board members.
  o Develop a Philanthropy Committee Mission Statement.
  o Understand the committee charge.
  o Organize annual giving.
  o Delegate jobs and create a timeline; establish the calendar of money asks and determine a strategy to reduce them to three.
  o Develop policy, including an ethics policy.

- Focus on the leadership donor.
  o Understand and adopt the concept of the leadership portfolio.

- Set the date for and attend the annual leadership donor reception.

WHO IS A LEADERSHIP DONOR?

IDENTIFY LEADERSHIP DONORS. THIS PROCESS is straightforward but has some complexity to it as well. Let's begin with your giving pyramid.

The Giving Pyramid

Step One: Create the List

List all the money gifts in the previous financial year from largest to smallest Where a donor has made several gifts during the year – for example, to the annual fund, through participation in a fundraising event such as an auction or golf tournament, and through an unsolicited check to support a student going on the eighth-grade trip – aggregate the amounts into a single total. Similarly, a donor may give monthly or through a payroll deduction – aggregate the gifts into an annual amount. In other words, the metric is dependent on the total giving within a school year.

In the example of a giving list below, note that this is a very short list. You hopefully will have several hundred names in your list of donors.

Name	Gift	Name	Gift	Name	Gift
Dobson	$100	Stevens	$150	Jenks	$50
Adams	$1,500	Reilly	$35	Chen	$100
Kim	$75	Thoelke	$750	Jeynes	$350
Patel	$574	Gabriel	$125	Phelps	$5,500

DeJonge	$150	Fischer	$240	Cronin	$5,000
Scharlach	$1,000	Chang	$240	McKay	$1,500
Junge	$150	Malter	$150	Kresge	$800
Smith J.	$50	Smith K.	$50	Park	$50

Step Two: Order the List

The objective of this step is to identify ranges of gifts in order to create a giving pyramid. Take the list of donors and organize them by size of gift. This is where Excel spreadsheets come in very handy if you don't have a database. Use the "sort" function to get instant results! Using the above example, the outcome is:

Gift	No.	Gift	No.	Gift	No.	Gift	No.
$5,500	1	$800	1	$240	2	$100	2
$5,000	1	$750	1	$150	4	$75	1
$1,500	2	$574	1	$125	1	$50	4
$1,000	1	$350	3	$100	2	$35	many

Step Three: Create the Giving Pyramid

With this information in hand, you can develop a giving pyramid that splits gifts into standard ranges that fit the way your donors currently operate. The following chart provides both an example and a simple spreadsheet format to do this. The levels are fairly typical – adapt them to fit the giving patterns in your school.

Level	Number of Gifts
$5,000 and up	2
$1,000 – $4,999	3
$500 – $999	3
$100 – $499	10
$0 – $99	Many

In this example, there is a natural break between those who give $499 and less and those who give $500 or more. So, for this school, leadership donors can now be identified as those who give $500 or more each year.

Remember that each school's giving pyramid will look different, and the breakpoints will be in different places. Many schools have that natural break at $1,000. We know some schools where the break is at $2,500 or $5,000. Certainly, the number is pushing upward. It's a practical matter. At what point does it become unwieldy to do in-depth stewarding of donors who fall into your school's "leadership" category?

If you think of it in terms of percentages, you are looking for the giving level that includes 10 percent to 20 percent of your total donor community. Or you can think about it as those donors whose giving supplies 80 percent to 90 percent of the school's philanthropic funding. Either or both metrics should give you a list of donors that it is practical for the Philanthropy Committee and Board to steward through their donor portfolios.

TRUE STORY - from a parent survey!

The chart below was created for a CSM client K–12 school. It's not a big school with 247 respondents to a parent survey (response was about 50 percent). The range of incomes, however, is telling. The school knew that it had families with means in its community – but the level of wealth was not known until the school asked and the families answered. Note that CSM does not ask for a specific income in surveys but, rather, what range of income correlating to segments of wealth.

Your range of incomes will look different. It depends on where the school is located, how many students are enrolled, how established it is, how wide a geographic reach it has, etc. However, the general spread of your families' income will be very similar, in most cases. In other words, a small number of families exist at the bottom of the wealth ladder; most are above the $75,000 household income level; some will be truly wealthy and in the top 10 percent.

Only a couple of our schools do not have significant philanthropic potential. These are schools that exercise their mission in low-income areas and are predominantly reliant on community donors for support. Everyone else has a range of incomes – and those incomes are mostly above average.

Levels of Income	Number	Percentage
Under $40,000	4	1.6%
$40,000 – $75,000	10	4.0%
$75,001 – $100,000	12	4.9%
$100,001 – $125,000	18	7.3%
$125,001 – $150,000	19	7.7%
$150,001 – $175,000	9	3.6%
$175,001 – $225,000	18	7.3%
$225,001 – $275,000	18	7.3%
$275,001 – $325,000	25	10.1%
$325,001 – $375,000	11	4.5%
$375,001 – $425,000	14	5.7%
$425,001 – $500,000	23	9.3%
$500,001 – $750,000	22	8.9%
$750,001 – $1 million	23	9.3%
>$1 million	4	1.6%

Leadership Through Longevity

While leadership donors are typically identified by the size of their gift, there is one other important category of leadership donor. We want to honor and celebrate those who give over an extended period of time.

We recommend that seven years be used as the turning point when a donor, irrespective of amount, becomes part of the leadership group and is treated with the same personal stewardship. In other words, if a donor has given to the school for seven consecutive years, clearly they are committed to the school and its mission. It is more than likely that the donor also holds the school in their prayers, talks about the school to others, and comes to the school for events.

Why seven? In one sense it is an arbitrary number. You can pick your own longevity period. Some schools we know use a decade as their number. For CSM, seven is an important Biblical number. It is the number mentioned most often in the Bible (735 times). It is important at the beginning of the Bible when it is identified as the number of the days of Creation. It is the day God rested. Jesus is ascribed seven titles in Hebrews. Jesus performed seven miracles on the Sabbath. There are many other interesting uses of the number seven! It is, of course, also the number of perfection and the year of Jubilee is the 50th year after seven times seven years (49). You choose the number and stick with it. It should not be less than seven and not more than 12. Any number in that range is a good number to recognize a donor within the leadership category.

For schools that are K–12, many parents might become leadership donors just because of their children's stay at the school. If so, that is a good thing and might well be an additional help to keeping them as donors once their children have graduated.

Giving Circles

Knowing your giving pyramid enables you now to develop giving circles. Philanthropy operates from the inside out. It always begins with the biggest gift first. This is a Biblical practice. In 1 Chronicles 29, David gives first from his personal bank account: "Now, to show my commitment to the temple of my God, I donate my personal treasure of gold and silver to the temple of my God, in addition to all that I have already supplied for this holy temple." Then the other leaders give generously, inspired by David: "The leaders of the families, the leaders of the Israelite tribes, the commanders of units of a thousand and a hundred, and the supervisors of the king's work contributed willingly." And everyone was inspired: "The people rejoiced at the willing response of their leaders, for they had given freely and wholeheartedly to the Lord."

As Paul puts it in his letter to Timothy: "Command those who are rich in this world's goods not to be haughty or to set their hope on riches, which are uncertain, but on God who richly provides us with all things for our enjoyment. Tell them to do good, to be rich in good deeds, to be generous givers, sharing with others."

It doesn't always work that the largest gift comes first. St. Paul had this problem with the churches – the poorest seemed to give more, much more, than the richest. He was not happy about that! The reality is that while God undoubtedly blesses the $5 gift (and James reminds us not to show partiality when it comes to riches), optimal philanthropy occurs when King David gives first and others follow.

Those with wealth know this. They perfectly understand that their gift has to make a big dent in the giving target so that the small gift can also be a difference-maker in finishing the effort. At the beginning of your $150,000 campaign, $5 doesn't seem to matter much. But when you have raised $149,500, $5 is a great contribution.

So we raise money from the inside out. Once you have your giving pyramid in place, you can create your giving circles:

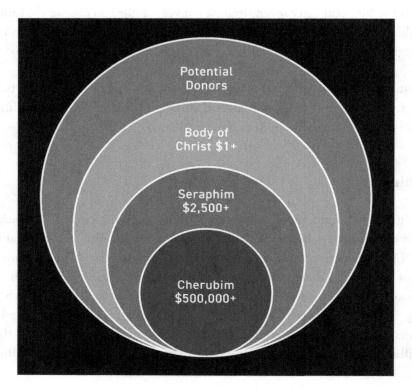

This is an example and yours may differ. Note that while there is a leadership circle, there may be other categories as well. Some schools have a whole list of categories. For CSM, four circles would be fine – Cherubim (transformational), Seraphim (leadership), Body of Christ (supporting), and potential donors. If you think that you will inspire different levels of giving through a larger number of circles, don't hesitate. Some Philanthropy Directors believe that some donors are motivated to reach particular levels and will increase their gift to achieve that. We have no opinion about that.

Notice that this also means that your school's efforts should be focused first on those who have given. Occasionally, conversations begin to wander into fantasy land – there's a philanthropist in town, I wonder if he or she would give; there's a foundation, maybe we could ask them; there's a big corporation / employer, surely they would support us?

The answer to any of these questions is that it is highly unlikely that anyone will provide support who is not already part of your community. Your sweat equity is only worth spending on those who already know you and have experienced your benefits in the lives of children.

This relates to the inside-out principle too. Relational philanthropy speaks to, well, relationships. If you don't have a relationship, it is highly unlikely that you will receive a gift. If you have a relationship, it is hard work to develop that relationship to include money – almost 40 percent of those who call themselves "Christian" in surveys don't give to charity. Fortunately, over 90 percent of churchgoers do give!

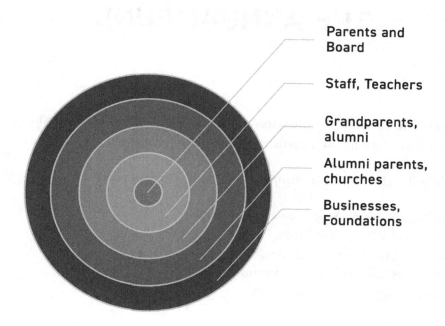

Parents and Board

Staff, Teachers

Grandparents, alumni

Alumni parents, churches

Businesses, Foundations

The inside-out story tells us that we should spend all of our time on the inside circle first – our school's parents. As time allows, we can move outward from that. As we move away from the center circle, the intrinsic commitment is less than that which a parent experiences when their child is receiving such a great benefit – and one that is visible and constantly growing. Only if (stress on only) there is time left, can you afford to spend it on potential relationships with people / institutions that have a tenuous link to the school.

Summary

- Know your data – who's on the list?
- Establish a giving pyramid.
- Understand the concept of giving circles – the inside-out principle.
- It's not about the gift, it's about the relationship. No relationship = no gift.

THE ANNUAL FUND

ALL CHRISTIAN SCHOOLS DO FUNDRAISING. They almost all do it every year. Most do it because otherwise their budget would not be balanced. There is a better way.

The CSM Mary Principle on Philanthropy states that it is very important to:

- Raise money over and above operating income.
- Exercise and teach philanthropy.
- Develop a culture of philanthropy.
- Treat donors honorably and respectfully.
- Follow the highest ethical standards.

The Budget Paradox

Strategically, you will improve your annual fund outcomes by improving your school's financial situation. If you did nothing differently in your annual fund but relied less and less on that money to balance the budget, your fundraising dollars would increase. Simply, donors are more motivated to move the school ahead than they are to see the school just keep on doing the same thing. When your annual fund moves the school ahead, the donor is more motivated and gives more. It is a paradox to say that by raising tuition to cover expenses, parents who pay tuition will give more. And it is true – particularly with your leadership donors. And, of course, donors who are not parents are far more motivated.

How do you get to the place where the annual fund can support the purposes above, i.e., where the operating budget appropriately funds compensation, classroom resources, fixed costs (these are the three expense buckets) as well as providing financial aid? The answer is to boldly raise your tuition by .5 percent or 1.0 percent a year above the usual tuition rise to cover more of your operations budget. Your goal is a 102 percent ratio.

Each year you do that, you will free up the same amount in the annual fund – each dollar in tuition frees a dollar in donations. Over time, all your philanthropic dollars will go to grow the school, not just maintain the Operations budget. CSM advocates for this consistently – where schools do it, their quality of education improves and enrollment grows. When the budget is funded well and mission delivery needs are met, philanthropic annual fund dollars can go to enhance the child's education, the experience improves, and enrollment is enhanced, i.e., more money in the budget, more money to spend on the child's experience, more children in the classrooms, resulting in higher income and a better budget. It is a self-reinforcing virtuous cycle.

Tuition Is not Connected to Enrollment

Further, tuition increases do not impact enrollment, except to the positive because the school is finally able to provide excellent mission delivery. Quality and enrollment strength go together. This is another paradox. We know that people in other situations are greatly affected by price – the grocery store, airline tickets, computer purchases. It makes complete sense that schools are price sensitive too. To be the most expensive school in the area, or to raise tuition more than a competitor, or to go over $10,000 or $15,000 seems like an elementary mistake in marketing.

It is not.

A study was carried out in 2016 by three reputable organizations: Independent School Management (ISM), the National Business Officers' Association (NBOA), and Measuring Success (MS). Their study was put up on the NBOA website for everyone to see. They wanted to test whether tuition and enrollment were connected. This study followed two similar studies that had been carried out in 2006 (MS) and 2011 (ISM and MS). It included virtually every kind of school at every price point and grade structure. Their findings were as follows:

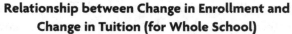

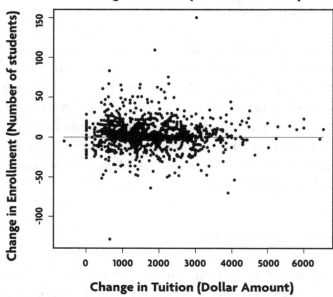

Relationship between Change in Enrollment and Change in Tuition (for Whole School)

Their commentary read as follows: "The vertical axis represents enrollment changes, and the horizontal axis represents tuition changes. The line of best fit is flat. While we show a simple scatter plot, we conducted a sophisticated time-series regression controlling for many factors both in and outside a school's control to see if we could explain what drove enrollment change. If there were a relationship between these two variables, the line of best fit would be at an angle to indicate a positive or negative relationship. Therefore, the data suggests results that are consistent with previous studies: enrollment and changes in tuition share no significant relationship. To further test our hypothesis, we analyzed this data across all divisions, and across whole dollar and percentage dollar changes. All regressions reflected similar results: the line of best fit was flat" (p. 4).

Counterintuitive as it may seem, our schools are not price sensitive based on tuition increases. What is true is that our schools are price sensitive based on perceived value. If your families believe that you are not delivering what you promised, enrollment will fall. On their way out the door, families will complain about the price. But that's not the issue. The issue is perceived mediocrity. Funding your budget and using annual philanthropic dollars to improve mission delivery is what parents want – not cheaper education.

This leads to an important insight – what donors give is variable. You may be grateful for any gift and think about them in the aggregate. For example, this year we raised $5,000 more in total than last year – a success. However, when we break it down to the individual donor level, we might come to a very different conclusion. This individual donor gave $100 but we know they are capable of doing better. This individual donor gave $100 and we know they are capable of giving at least $1,000. This donor gave $5 a month and we know that is a stretch gift. We need to motivate our donors to give optimally and even beyond what they thought they were going to give.

If we improve our school's financial situation by pointing fundraising toward moving the school ahead and balancing the budget with tuition and fees, we can think about our annual fund and how that can be improved as well. In this book, we go back again and again to the need to move to Christian philanthropy, i.e., relational philanthropy rather than transactional fundraising. The latter is largely event-based fundraising. The former is driven through the annual fund.

Let's summarize so far:

- Raising money by any method is improved when that money is not needed to support the school's operating budget.
- We approach philanthropy by considering each individual donor rather than donors in aggregate.
- Raising money is best done through Christian philanthropy – building relationships.
- The annual fund is the mechanism by which relationship-building leads to optimal giving.

Annual Fund Outcomes

The annual fund has two clear outcomes:

1. To widen the donor base, which develops a culture of philanthropy.

   We go to schools where only 20 percent of parents are donors to the school. And we go to schools where 70+ percent are. The difference is the annual fund.

   Teaching about philanthropy begins in the admission process – we cover our budget with tuition and we provide enhancements through the annual fund. Then it continues through building a personal relationship with each donor in a sequence of prayer, thanks, reporting, celebrating, and asking on an annual cycle. Reporting shows that the money made a difference.

   In this scenario, most parents will participate in the annual fund. It is a matter of persistence in developing relationships that gets the school to 75 percent parent participation (75 percent is the CSM participation metric for parents).

This creates a culture where philanthropy is a norm; it is part of the culture. First comes the relationship. The gift is the outcome of involvement in and buy-in to the school's mission and its outworking in the lives of the child / children. The annual fund makes that obvious. Annual fund donations are spent in the year and / or year following each campaign. It is not money to be put in the bank. It is instant gratification money. We raise it. We spend it. The donor doesn't have to wait to see the impact. The money is spent as directly as possible on the children of the school.

This is clearly visible such as when we use annual funds to improve science resources. It is also invisible such as when we use annual funds to support financial aid – but it's still directly into the life of the child. When we identify what we want annual funds for and when we report on expenditures of annual funding, we always point to the child as the recipient. The relationship points to the child, leads to the gift, identifies the impact on the child, strengthens the relationship.

It is important that everyone is honored irrespective of the size of the gift. The celebration of the community (the culture) is crucial so that people feel honored and respected as people, not as checkbooks.

Philanthropy is holistic. The gift is the evidence that philanthropy is in place. Participation rates are thus a sign that the school's connection to its parents (and grandparents and alumni) is strong and that the community understands the school's message about the power and importance of the school's mission. The annual nature of this philanthropy means that mission messaging never stops and that the community is continuously engaged in the story of the mission at work as the school continues to grow and adapt and mature in an ever-changing world. And that continuous engagement is what we call a culture of philanthropy.

2. To uncover potential leadership donors.

In their annual fund participation, donors reveal their giving potential. While annual giving is about the culture of philanthropy, our schools need significant gifts that can move us from one place to another. Leadership gifts in capital and endowment campaigns are crucial generational investments. We need leadership gifts, six- and seven-figure gifts, that can build us classrooms to accommodate enrollment growth; we need leadership gifts to take a building built in the 1950s and make it useful to children in the 21st century; we need leadership gifts to buy the property next door in order to create an oasis in the city; we need leadership gifts to keep the school relevant; we need leadership gifts to create endowment that will support the school generationally; we need gifts that will support any family to come and thus make the school a true reflection of the Body of Christ (cf. 1 Corinthians 12:27; Ephesians 4:12).

Annual giving is here today and gone tomorrow. But annual giving provides an opportunity for potential philanthropy leaders to make themselves known. Those giving leaders are in our communities and the annual fund gives them an opportunity to declare themselves. In one Christian school, a new family gave $1,500 to the annual fund. That's making yourself visible. After conversation with the Principal and Philanthropy Director, one of the parents became a member of the Board that January. By the following summer, the couple chaired the $5 million comprehensive campaign and gave one of the leadership gifts.

No one would have known without the annual fund.

Every year, the school brings in a group of new families. At the very least, an entire new class of the youngest students comes in. Typically, 5 percent to 10 percent of families leave / graduate and 5 percent to 10 percent of new families come in, sometimes more as the school fills its classrooms. The annual fund provides a mechanism to build relationships with them and get them involved immediately – and uncover maybe one or two families each year who can provide leadership gifts.

The Annual Fund Cabinet

The Philanthropy Committee is a committee of the Board of Trustees with a Board member as Chair. The Annual Fund Cabinet is a subcommittee of the Philanthropy Committee. If you currently have no committee at all and/or are doing transactional / event-based fundraising rather than relational fundraising, then we typically recommend that schools begin with the Philanthropy Committee operating as the initial Annual Fund Cabinet. The order of creation doesn't matter.

The Annual Fund Cabinet is the mechanism for engaging many volunteers whose job is relational philanthropy, translated as peer-to-peer relationships. There are two key principles for thinking about involvement in philanthropy at the annual fund level:

1. Peer-to peer-relationship building

    When we say that Christian philanthropy is based on building relationships, those relationships are almost always peer-to-peer. In the general world of peer-to-peer fundraising, it is usually attached to events where you invite your friends and relations to come and participate, such as a 5K run or selling Girl Scout cookies. In Christian philanthropy, peer-to-peer has a different presentation.

It's an invitation to invest alongside "me." It is from me to you. It is highly personal. You have met me. Maybe it was on the bleachers at the gym where our daughters were playing volleyball. Maybe it was when I helped you because I am also a room parent. Maybe it was when our children had sleepovers at your house. Maybe it was a casual hello at Back to School Night. But you know me.

There's intimacy in that. When I use your name, it's not just a jumble of letters but a real connection. The power of naming that God gave Adam(ah) in Genesis says a lot about relationship – Adam named all the animals but none of them was a suitable helper. God then made him a helper. For us, the naming of the donor is identifying a person, not a crowd or group, and identifying that the person really is a suitable helper in philanthropy (Genesis 2:18-20).

In the annual fund, I invite you to join me in something I am already deeply engaged in. I believe in what the school is doing because of its evidence in the lives of children – it is likely that I am a parent and that I see the evidence in the lives of my own children! I am grateful and want to help, so I have given to the annual fund. When I come to you, I ask you to do what I have already done. It's a through-the- glass-darkly reflection of us loving God because God loved us first (1 John 4:19).

TRUE STORY – peer to peer!

In CSM Annual Fund Training with volunteer parents, we provide time for the volunteers to partner up to practice writing short, engaging text messages of no more than 15 words. The texts encourage class parents who have not yet given. Most volunteers have very close relationships with fellow parents and can come up with funny reminders as you can see below (you really have to know your people to send these!):

- 96 kids; 17 teachers; 1 God; 0 money
- The chickens are hungry – they need feeding!
- $ with 7 digits: send now!
- Dude, you need me to come over and collect?

2. Immediacy

The second key principle is that it is in real time. The annual fund is a hurry-up kind of philanthropy. Each campaign only takes four months. The interactions we have as volunteer and donor are instantaneous. The reason for giving is a "now" reason. The monies that come in are a "now" income that becomes a "now" expenditure almost immediately.

Immediacy means that there is follow-up identifying what happened, what is happening, what will happen. In construction projects, there is often a camera where you can watch the progress in real time. Each change can be captured. The annual fund is the same. We watch it in real time, experience it in real time, and feel a part of whatever is going on.

This means that those who are part of the annual fund as volunteers (supported by the school's professionals and the Philanthropy Committee) are going to be those directly involved in the action. The volunteers are people who like to see things happen now, like the action, like to see the fruits of their labor. They are peers and their work and involvement are immediate, as is the outcome in the lives of children.

Who Is on the Annual Fund Cabinet?

If you have never put an Annual Cabinet together, start simple. Think about your first committee having the following peers on it:

Board member (from the Philanthropy Committee if you have one)	1
School representative	1
At least two representatives from each division of the school	Early Childhood – 2 Elementary – 2 Middle – 2 High School – 2
Data person – professional or volunteer	1
Total	11

Many hands make light work! The Cabinet is going to get much bigger but, for committees, it is already pretty large with 11 people. Most schools that we work with have Cabinets with four to six people on them and that's too small. This Cabinet starts its life with seven to 11 and it needs all of them. They are going to run an operation that is highly personal, individualized, that appreciates the importance of intimacy at every stage of the process.

As the committee continues to develop, it will eventually include the following groups, with at least two representing each group except the Board (one member):

- Board
- School staff
- Parents from every grade level, maybe even each classroom
- Grandparents
- Alumni
- Teachers / staff
- Leadership

Work out what that looks like in your school. For a K–12 school, the Annual Fund Cabinet might include:

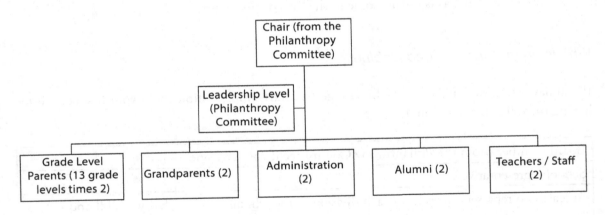

That's a committee of 35! Note that the Leadership Level is off to one side. These are donors who will be assigned to the Philanthropy Committee. The Annual Fund Cabinet, in other words, works with the wide base of smaller gift donors. Identified leadership donors are passed back to the Philanthropy Committee. As potential leadership donors are uncovered through the annual fund process, they are also segmented out and passed to the Philanthropy Committee. In schools where the Annual Fund Cabinet is the first one created (and there is no Philanthropy Committee), those leadership donors are passed to the Principal and Board for stewardship and solicitation.

Stewarding the Annual Fund Cabinet

There is increasing research showing the importance of involving the donor directly in the organization. The 2021 Bank of America Study of Philanthropy found that affluent individuals who volunteered gave twice as much as those who didn't. The committee work and the personalized peer-to-peer relationship-building drives philanthropic giving, in part, because it involves the donor in more than just asking for a check. Your Cabinet are all donors who are volunteers as well. How you look after them matters.

Involving volunteers is an intentional process that must be well thought through. Every Christian is a volunteer. St. Paul is maybe the most interesting example of this. There are times where he is totally on as the evangelist. In Acts 18, he "devoted himself exclusively to preaching" (v. 5) once he had the support of Silas and Timothy. But in that same chapter, it is clear that, when he was staying at the house of Aquila and Priscilla, he helped them in the workshops since they had the same trade of tent-making: "because he was a tentmaker as they were, he stayed and worked with them" (v. 3).

Paul was actually determined to act as a volunteer and not be a burden to any with whom he stayed. In 2 Thessalonians he writes: "We were not idle when we were with you, nor did we eat anyone's food without paying for it. On the contrary, we worked night and day, laboring and toiling so that we would not be a burden to any of you. We did this, not because we do not have the right to such help, but in order to offer ourselves as a model for you to imitate" (3:7-9). The model might be described as the call to serve, to not be a burden, and thus to work when necessary in order to make volunteering possible.

N.T. Wright in *Paul, A Biography* (2018, p. 68) notes that before Paul sets out on his journeying, he probably spent the decade of 36CE to 46CE in Tarsus tentmaking. There's nothing wrong with paying the professional. The example of the Levites in the Hebrew Scriptures and Paul's own statement that it wasn't because he shouldn't be supported by others show that the professional is worthy of his hire (cf. 1 Timothy 5:18). But he modeled the actions of a volunteer, practicing his own craft to support himself.

As we think about the action of the volunteer, we recognize that work / volunteering is a spiritual activity reflecting the image of God who works, and works in us "to do good works" (Ephesians 2:10). It is worth quoting John Paul II at length in this regard from his encyclical Laborem Exercens: *The word of God's revelation is profoundly marked by the fundamental truth that man, created in the image of God, shares by his work in the activity of the Creator and that, within the limits of his own human capabilities, man in a sense continues to develop that activity, and perfects it as he advances further and further in the discovery of the resources and values contained in the whole of creation. We find this truth at the very beginning of Sacred Scripture, in the Book of Genesis, where the creation activity itself is presented in the form of 'work' done by God during 'six days,' 'resting' on the seventh day. Besides, the last book of Sacred Scripture echoes the same respect for what God has done through his creative 'work' when it proclaims: 'Great and wonderful are your deeds, O Lord God the Almighty'; this is similar to the Book of Genesis, which concludes the description of each day of creation with the statement: 'And God saw that it was good'* (p. 35).

Stewarding these important volunteers is not a mechanical, instrumental task but a spiritual, invitational task that incorporates the volunteer into the community of the school. As we consider training the Annual Fund Cabinet, whether they spend an hour or seemingly all their waking hours in service to the school, and thus to the school's children, they all deserve the following:

1. Prayer

   The model here is Jesus, who prayed for his disciples in those amazing passages in John: "I pray for them. I am not praying for the world, but for those you have given me, for they are yours" (John 17:9). Paul underlines this attitude when he writes to Timothy: "I urge, then, first of all, that petitions, prayers, intercession and thanksgiving be made for all people" (1 Timothy 2:1).

   The best examples we have seen for this are prayer groups that come together each week to pray for the children, of course, and also for the leaders of the school and the volunteers from Board members to committee members to those doing the ordinary everyday tasks.

   However prayer and intercession is done, it must be done. We need our volunteers under a cloud of prayer. They are typically doing their work on top of caring for their families, carrying out their paid vocations, helping in their own churches, and even taking care of themselves (!). Without them, the school literally cannot operate. They need God's grace continually prayed over them. Intentionally and regularly.

2. Training

   Jesus spent three years training his disciples and followers before commissioning them (cf. Matthew 28) and sending them out. This included opportunities to try it out for themselves (cf. Matthew 10:25 and Luke 10:1) and coming back for a debrief and reflection.

   Well, we don't have three years and, of course, the tasks we ask the Annual Fund Cabinet to carry out are much simpler than those of the disciples. Whatever task we ask our volunteers to do requires training. The training needs to be organized, pertinent, intentional. There's nothing a volunteer hates more than to have their time wasted and their talents misused. A training session as CSM carries it out is 2.5–3 hours long. We cover:

- Why are we doing this? (the case for support for this year)
- What is the job? (signing letters, making thank-you calls, writing thank-you notes, reminding)
- How long will it take? (10 hours total from September through December)
- When can I do it? (at a time convenient to you)
- Are there deadlines? (yes, absolutely!)
- What is your own experience of giving – what made it good or bad?
- What is the research?
- What is the plan?

3. Feedback

"I came and signed letters for two hours on a Thursday morning. I did that several times during the annual fund season. I never found out whether what I did mattered. There are many things I could have been doing with that time. I was glad to help. I would so like to know that it made a difference." Feedback can be very simple. At the end of the annual fund season, the Annual Fund Cabinet sends a one-page synopsis that includes:

- Hours spent by all volunteers
- Dollars raised
- Impact on the children – carrying out the case for support
- Without them, "this" would not have been possible
- Heartfelt thanks

Volunteers don't get burned out by the amount of work they do. They get burned out by the assumption that they will do it and the lack of feedback as to their importance. It's not about ego. It's about the desire to make an impact. In the negative, it's the desire to know their time was not wasted. Tell the volunteers that what they did mattered.

4. Thanks

Then thank them for it. As Paul said: "I always thank my God for you because of his grace given you in Christ Jesus" (1 Corinthians 1:4). Notice the word always. Don't list the names of volunteers in printed materials. It's not what they are looking for. The job of the Principal / Philanthropy Committee, at the end of the season, to sit down and write the thank-you notes to each member of the Cabinet. Include an invitation to a January volunteer reception where everyone can celebrate together. You can also highlight volunteers in the e-letters. Maybe there's someone who's in their fifth year of volunteering. Or someone who is a grandparent and school alumna. Do it consistently. This implies good data collection! If you don't have time to thank your volunteers, you don't have time to have volunteers.

5. To be held accountable

Oddly, maybe, volunteers need to be held accountable for what they do, just as professionals who are paid should be held accountable. You need each volunteer to know that their efforts should be wholehearted, done with as much skill as they have, and in a timely fashion. As Proverbs 27:17 says, "iron sharpens iron." Those who don't want to be held accountable, and there are always one or two who think they are doing you a favor rather than serving the Lord, should be counseled out of volunteering. The volunteer has to come with the right spirit. Work is spiritual as well as manual.

Training The Annual Fund Cabinet

Whether it is the Principal, the Annual Fund Manager, a consultant, a previous Cabinet member, the volunteers for the Annual Fund Cabinet are invited to a 3 hour training. Typically, not everyone is able to attend. That's not a problem. Just as long as you have someone from the Board/Philanthropy Committee and a smattering of the peer-to-peer folks, they will take the enthusiasm from the training and carry it out to their fellow volunteers. They will also have a handbook to take with them to share with their fellow Cabinet members.

Here is a suggested outline for your training session. It should take no more than three hours. At the end of it, your Cabinet members should understand the tasks, be aware of the time commitment, and have increased their enthusiasm for what lies ahead. Typically, in trainings that CSM undertakes, we ask volunteers to come without commitment, i.e., they will not be asked to commit to being on the Annual Fund Cabinet until they know exactly what is expected of them. This will generate interest and curiosity. Today, volunteers will no longer make open-ended commitments. The respect you show them in inviting them "behind the curtain" will engender confidence.

Hour One

Efficiently review the Mary Principle and the Three Promises we make to all donors.

1. Promise One (Giver): We promise to be grateful to God and to you for your generosity to the "family of believers" in the school, ask you for gifts that fit your own prosperity, and honor you as a giver.
2. Promise Two (Money): We promise that asking you to invest in God's work at the school will be accompanied by the school's accountability in spending your money in the way you intended.
3. Promise Three (Child): We promise that we will use your gift to move the school forward on behalf of the children within the context of a plan showing excellent stewardship and financial sustainability.

Spend a little time on what Penelope Burk says all donors are looking for:

1. Prompt, meaningful acknowledgement whenever they make a gift
2. Confirmation that each gift, regardless of its value, will be assigned to a project, program, or initiative narrower in scope than the mission as a whole
3. A report on the measurable results achieved to date in the program or project they are funding before they are asked for another gift

Ask them to share their own experiences of giving money – how many charities do they give to, how many have they given to more than once, how many are they currently giving to and have donated for over five years. Typically, expect your volunteers to reflect the research saying that donors rarely give more than once to the same charity, and even more rarely more than twice. Ask them what about charities makes them more willing to repeat and increase their gift.

One couple in a CSM volunteer training session said they had given to six or seven charities. One day, they received a call from one of their charities, not asking for a gift, but seeking to understand why they gave. They responded that they were particularly interested in Sierra Leone. The caller thanked them for sharing.

Six months later, they were contacted again and the caller this time wanted to tell them about what the charity was accomplishing in Sierra Leone. The couple said that, as a result of these interactions, they were currently reducing the number of charities they were giving to and were planning on significantly increasing their gift to this charity serving Sierra Leone – without even having been asked to. Their experience was a direct parallel to Burk's three points.

Tell your volunteers how important they are. There are several reasons for this that link together:

- They believe in the school's mission and understand that the work of the annual fund is to further the mission of the school in the lives of children.
- They inspire by their example. Leadership inspires the actions of followers. Without leaders there cannot be followers.
- They build confidence because of their own commitment. Everyone in the room is a current annual fund donor. They are giving of their treasure and of their time. That says to the person on the outside that, because you believe in it, they can as well.
- They act authentically and with great integrity. As people look at their example, they can appreciate the honesty of the enterprise.
- They can act in a way and with a different kind of authority than a school professional. They are not "paid" to be enthusiastic.

Hour Two

Identify exactly what you are asking them to do and the time commitment involved. All examples given here were used in a Christian school.

1. Personally give

2. Sign letters to their peer group (60 minutes)

   The peer group is a school class, e.g., grade 1 or grade 11. It might be grandparents or volunteers. Leadership donors are taken out of any individual segment and will be personally solicited. The volunteer does not do face-to-face solicitation. The school prepares the annual fund letter asking for support, personalizes it, creates the envelope and stamps it. The volunteer comes into the office, signs the letter and stuffs the envelopes. Ideally, there would not be more than 20–30 letters for any one volunteer. Here's an example of a letter that might go to a new family to the school:

   To a new family (kindergarten family)

   Dear Simon and Carolynn,

   I am thrilled to welcome you as a new family. It's a year of stories – you are part of a growing school, now 300 families strong, "more than we can ask or imagine" (Ephesians 3:20). Every day, the teachers are working to equip the minds and disciple the hearts of every child. What a thrill after our year of COVID!

Now, acknowledging God's goodness, we are continuing to imagine and to plan. I am writing to ask you to join me in supporting the annual fund. Your tuition pays for the school's operations. The fund invests in extensions to the children's learning that will enrich and extend possibilities.

Last year, the annual fund successfully filled classrooms with innovation furniture; supported families in giving their children scholarships for their Christian education; provided major upgrades for music, band, and equipment for the new cafe and for the dining room. It was amazing!

This year, we intend and hope to raise $250,000 in order to:

- *Provide scholarships ($100,000)*
- *Extend "fitness" with a new gym curtain and outdoor playground ($72,500)*
- *Enrich technology in the theater and innovation / science labs ($22,500)*
- *Foster innovation K–12 and teacher professional growth ($25,000)*
- *Provide real-world learning experiences K–12 ($30,000)*

Join me and inspire each of our students with your support! I would be happy to talk with you if you would like before adding your gift to our school's story.

Miranda (Kindergarten parent)

Note: 10 percent of all fundraising goes to the school's endowment to support financial aid.

We strongly recommend that part of the training includes asking the volunteers to participate by actually writing *the letters*. They can contribute to the message in profound ways – and stop you making big mistakes in approaching parents! Schools tend to write in a very academic fashion and this one-pager needs to be direct, clear, and specific. Letters will be tailored to the different audiences – families (new to the school as well as current), alumni, grandparents, and so on.

3. Reminder texts to their peer group (60 minutes)

In the past, schools used to do telethons where everyone would gather and make follow-up phone calls. Some schools are still doing these. We recommend the practice of sending a short text, less than 15 words, instead. Families are less willing to answer the phone and calling can be a frustrating, time-consuming exercise. Texts seem to work much better. Here are a couple of examples:

- *Hi, it's Miranda. 15 percent annual fund goal still to achieve! Please join!*
- *Brian, it's me, Miranda. We've completed 65 percent of our annual fund goal. Will you help us finish strong?*
- *Reminder – the annual fund is elevating the student experience. Please consider sending your gift today.*
- *We're almost there. We just need your support to make a difference.*

Volunteers like the examples, in turn, want to send texts that sound very personal from them – messages the recipient would read and say: Oh yes, that's definitely from Miranda. While the letters are standard / adapted to each group, the texts are highly personal. Volunteers enjoy practicing them, and there is often laughter at the idiosyncratic way different people in the group communicate. All this involvement builds an esprit de corps. It is very rare for an attendee not to become an official volunteer once they have participated in this experience.

4. Thank-you phone calls to those from their group who are giving (three hours)

Once the gift is received by the school, the school's responsibility is to get that information to the volunteer on a daily basis so that the thank-you call can be made within 48 hours of receipt. This immediacy is crucial. The phone call doesn't have to directly connect. If no one answers, the job is to leave a message and send a text to tell the family to listen to the message. It is one phone call and it follows a script. Here is one example from a school:

This is Miranda calling. I am so happy that you joined me in making a gift to the annual fund this year. Thank you very much. You have made a difference to the lives of the children at our school. If you want to get back to me, please phone or text me at [number].

If the family actually does pick up, the initial conversation is also scripted for the volunteer. For example:

Hi, this is Miranda. I am calling to personally thank you for your gift that came in this week. I am so glad that you joined me in the annual fund.

The donor will either say thank-you and hang up – or you will have an inspirational conversation where they talk about what the school means to them and why they gave. Your job is to listen, make notes, and pass the notes on to the school for addition to the database.

Many will just say, okay, in a somewhat surprised tone since they've rarely been thanked for a gift before. But several will engage you because they genuinely want to share what the school means to their children. These will be amazing conversations that inspire volunteers and keep them coming back year after year.

5. Thank-you notes to those from their group who are giving (four hours)

The school will have the notecards for the volunteers to use. The message will be personal. These must go out within two weeks of the gift being received. Here are examples of thank-you notes that are clearly thoughtful and specific to the family / individual receiving them:

Dear Jason and Barbara:

I want to send you our heartfelt thanks. We asked for your support, trusted in your support, and have welcomed 45 children to our school family that your support is making possible.

A parent recently told me: "It means so much to have Gabby at the school. She is happier, more content, and doing so much better. I don't know what we would have done without this school."

This is your impact. Thank you.

Miranda

Dear Jim and Andrea:

What a blessing your gift is! Our students will experience spiritual growth as we invest this gift in their lives. Thank you for being a part of our community.

Miranda

Dear John:

Our school is a special community because of people like you. I wouldn't be who I am today if I also had not received a scholarship for my own education. Thank you for giving that gift to someone else. You're amazing!

Miranda

SIMON JEYNES

6. Attendance at a thank-you reception (60 minutes)

   Even though annual fund gifts will be accepted by the school through the end of the school year, the job of the volunteer Annual Fund Cabinet is over at the end of December. In January, the school's job is to thank / appreciate these volunteers at a face-to-face event.

The total time commitment for the Annual Fund Cabinet is about 10 hours total from August to December. Put that on a timeline:

August	I make my personal gift / pledge
Week of 9/27 to 10/8	Solicitation letter is signed and sent
October – December	Thank-you calls are made as gifts come in
October – December	Thank-you notes are sent as gifts come in
November	Reminder texts to those who have not yet given in my group
January	Appreciation reception and campaign report-to-date

The Annual Fund Case for Support

Your annual fund is the foundational driving force behind your philanthropy. But what's the case for your school's annual fund? What should people give to? Here are some real and current "cases" that Christian schools have created for their school fundraising in the actual words used on their websites:

1. *A donor selects a classroom and makes a contribution for the teacher to use and purchase much-needed resources for the classroom.*
2. *Funds from annual giving provide operating monies that support the ongoing work at the school and bridge the gap between tuition and the actual cost to educate a student.*
3. *The primary purpose of the Annual Fund is to support the school's operating budget for programs like tuition assistance, spiritual emphasis, athletics, music, yearbook, and other extracurricular activities.*
4. And then there are websites where the annual fund or annual giving has no page at all!

Money is an odd topic for Christians. Not sure why since Jesus certainly had no problems talking about it and, indeed, as we see in the Mary Principle, had his own Annual Fund Cabinet (Luke 8:3). For Christians, asking each other to be generous is both biblical and healthy. If what we have is "ours" entirely, then it is possible to believe that I can do what I want with it, including being selfish and spending it only on myself. That is how the secularist might think about it, although secularists can and do respond generously to the needs of others.

As Christians, we're excited about the potential of the resources that we have. If what we have is a gift of God for us to steward, then the question changes from what I want to do with it, to what does God want me to do with it. That is undoubtedly why research shows religious people give more than those who are not religious. The Giving USA Report on Giving to Religion in 2017 found that the difference was twofold – religious people give twice as much as those who are not religious.

Christians are stewards! God clearly intends us to take care of ourselves, our families, our communities, our neighbor, the widow, the orphan, the oppressed (cf. Psalm 9:9; Psalm 10:18; Psalm 146:7; Isaiah 58:10; Mark 12:31; Luke 10:36; 1 Corinthians 16:2; 2 Corinthians 8:1-15; 1 Timothy 5:4; James 1:27). Indeed, Jesus praises the generous giver in several stories and benefited himself from the fundraising that supported his own ministry.

If we have needs, we are to make them known to our God and to each other. James reproaches us: "You do not have because you do not ask God" (James 4:2-3). The early church was clearly highly focused on meeting each other's needs and asking those to whom God had given much to bless those to whom God had given less (cf. Acts 2:44-45). We should never be embarrassed about asking for money to help others.

The examples cited below are from different major denominational school systems and a nondenominational Christian school. It quickly becomes clear as we travel from website to website that schools are either embarrassed by the idea of asking supporters for money, and / or need the donations to make the operating budget work. Let's think about each in turn.

One of the website examples speaks to the way in which annual fundraising is needed to fill the "GAP." But needing donations to make the operating budget work defies logic, common sense, and good stewardship. The operating budget should work because those who benefit from it – the families who come to the school – pay for it. Asking them for less than it costs makes no arithmetical, logical, or fiscal sense.

We explicitly are telling our parents who pay the tuition (who are also the vast majority of our donors) that the school will close in March or April or May when we run out of tuition money unless we get more money in the form of donations. This is such a weak case for support! Why do schools so routinely do it?

The argument is that lowering tuition makes it more "affordable." What we don't want to admit, irrespective of the level of our tuition, is that our schools are **not** affordable. It's true! The moment that we ask for any money at all, a significant percentage of the population is unable to come. Even at a low $5,000 or $6,000 tuition level, a family has to have household income above the national average to afford one child's tuition, let alone two or three. We just are not affordable. That leads to the next point.

Ironically, the more you charge, the more you can help those who cannot afford it. We can see the contrast in this simple example:

Number of Students	150	150
Tuition	$5,000	$7,000
Income	$750,000	$1,050,000
Budget	$850,000	$1,050,000
Annual Fund	$100,000	$100,000
Financial Aid	0	$100,000

The seeming paradox is that the higher the tuition, the more the school can help those who can't afford the school either entirely or in part. Not only that, but the higher the tuition, the more likely it is that the classroom teacher has appropriate resources to support excellence (cases for support No. 1 and No. 3 above), that the teacher is paid at a level that doesn't mean applying for food stamps (as is lamentably true in too many Christian schools), and that the school is able to support families with several children and families with little disposable income (case No. 3 above), all through the operating budget.

The importance of this is significant. The reason for financial aid in Christian schools is not to support socioeconomic diversity. The reason is to ensure that any Christian family (in some schools, even non-Christian families) can bring up children with teachers who love Jesus, content that sees the world through a Creation / Resurrection lens, and a lifestyle / culture lived under and through grace. Financial aid is not to have more of "them." Financial aid is to support all of "us" – the whole Body of Christ (1 Timothy 5:8). The operating budget must be healthy to begin that support.

The case for support is not about the operating budget. The case for support demonstrates ways in which the donor's gift will directly benefit the children of the school. Des Moines Christian School, IA, wrote this on their website:

Many families are passionate about supporting DMC's annual fund, the Lion Fund, that provides resources for immediate enhancements of educational programs, athletics, fine arts and activities. Together your gifts impact all DMC students. Donations to the Lion Fund provide immediate resources that directly impact student life. The Lion Fund supports the continued enhancement of our academic and co-curricular programs and demonstrates community support of our school's mission.

Grace Christian School, VT, puts it a little differently but just as passionately and with the same sense of immediacy:

Each and every gift to The Inspire Grace Fund (TIGF) goes to helping our children! This year TIGF funds will help our school move forward in three specific ways. First, your gifts help more students come to GCS through financial aid. Second, your gifts help our teachers by offering continuing teacher training. This helps our teachers stay up on excellent education, and how to offer the very best school to our children. Third, TIGF also provides rich classroom resources. These tools help our students learn with excellence!

Neither example references the operations budget, suggests the school is in a weak financial position, or pleads. They are confident affirmations of what the school wants to achieve directly in the lives of children.

In creating your case statement:

1. Think and pray deeply as you determine the objectives for your case.
2. Engage the Leadership Team in identifying ways in which additional funding would genuinely move the children forward through enhancements to mission delivery.
3. Talk with the teachers about their ambitions for children in their classrooms. Tell them not to worry about their books or ongoing materials that they use each year. Ask them to tell you about the things they dream of having even though they "know it's impossible." The annual fund makes dreams come true.
4. Give the information to an excellent copywriter to put the case together. Bring it back to the team for comment (now so easy to do through digital access to a common document). Go through several iterations until everyone is happy to very happy with it.
5. Ensure the case is set up for the general population as well as for the leadership donors. Understand what each group wants to know.
6. Publish it on the website and in the email letters. Give it in print form to all your volunteers so they have it to reference – and to give away when appropriate.
7. Ensure the case has a variety of objectives to pique the interests of a diverse group.

Legacy Christian Academy, MN, (lcamn.org) laid it out simply on their website:

INVESTMENTS IN INDIVIDUALS
- *Award Scholarships*

INVESTMENTS IN INNOVATION
- *Foster PreK-12 innovative academic programs and resources*
- *Enrich faculty educational opportunities*
- *Provide educational technology*
- *Equip middle school science lab*
- *Expand academic intervention*

INVESTMENTS IN INFRASTRUCTURE
- *Design and install a new playground*

INVESTMENTS IN EXTRACURRICULAR
- *Enhance student experiences in athletics, fine arts, and after school clubs*

INVESTMENTS IN THE FUTURE
- *Develop a master site plan for Legacy*

Note: 10 percent of all fundraising goes to the Legacy endowment for generational change.

It takes a lot of work and time and skill to get your case to this point of simplicity. But the time you put into it will be well repaid by donor generosity.

Some donors will want to give their money to a specific category. Every donor has the right to say what they want done with their contribution. It is therefore wise to note in your case that money that is raised over and above the needs of any particular objective will be assigned to the next greatest need. Most donors though, in our experience, will give without restriction knowing that you will use the money on the objectives you have identified and being at ease and trusting your stewardship.

Make Giving Easy!

Followers of Jesus want to give. In fact, there are many generous people in the world who are not followers of Jesus who respond by virtue of being human and being convicted by the needs they see around them (Romans 2:14-15). Jesus followers are even more motivated since our giving begins with the ultimate gift of Jesus himself to us for the healing of Creation (Romans 8:20-21) through death's defeat (Romans 5:17). Giving is not painful but joyful – it is the ultimate stewardship of what has been given to us.

This is critical if we are to be successful in asking donors to give. If we are apologetic, embarrassed, unsure, tentative, our solicitations will be ineffective. When we are confident, respectful, thoughtful, and prayerful solicitors, donors will respond with inspirational generosity. And we know a lot about donors. We know that donors want to do six things:

1. Give to a *genuine need*, not to make up for poor stewardship by the school.
2. Give to *assist children* (as a part of that genuine need) to come to the school and experience God's love surrounding them as an integral part of their education.
3. Give because *they are inspired*, not because they are compelled, by the power of the school's mission in the lives of children.
4. Give *relative to their own prosperity* and as part of their own stewardship of the resources with which God has gifted them.
5. *Give in a way that is not judged*, but rather respected and honored.
6. *Give according to the heart*, not just according to the accountant.

So make it easy to give. Milpitas Christian School, CA, had a very useful visual on their website along with explanatory notes:

| Credit Card | Check | Stock | Pledge | Corporate Matching |

Credit or Debit Card	+
Check	+
Pledge	+
Stock and Other Securities	+
Corporate Matching	+

Most people will give by cash, check, or credit card. An increasing number of donors want to give by text, or one of the online applications. Give them whatever options they want! New Life Academy, MN, moved in that direction. Notice the simple format with easy-to-find additional information:

— Online Giving

Online giving is a safe and easy way to support New Life Academy. Click here to donate online now Also learn how your employer might double your gift through an employee gift matching.program

+ Send a check

+ Text 2 Give

+ Make a Pledge

+ Gifts of Securities

+ Gifts from your Estate

+ Matching Gifts

Ensure that, on the website and in person, you can capture the information you need without it being overwhelming. Here is a nice example from Catholic Central High School, MI. It is very clean; easy to click through, with prefills already there; and provides dropdowns for options.

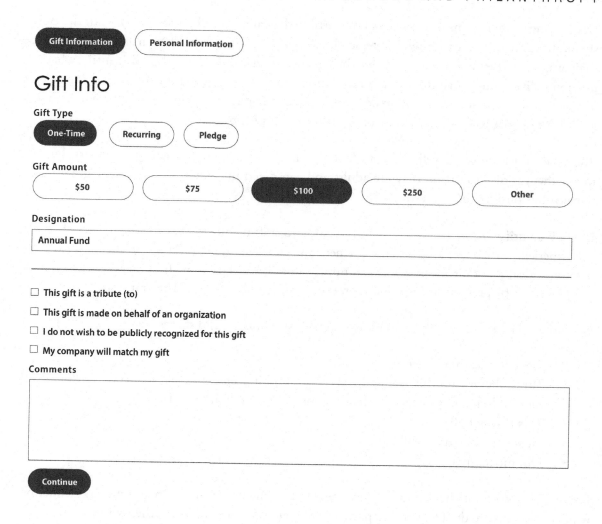

Giving by Teachers and Staff

Teachers and staff in many CSM schools do not give. There are a variety of reasons given for this:

- They are badly paid.
- They already buy classroom resources from their own pockets.
- The give generously of their time.
- They are not asked.

Just writing these reasons down shows how terrible they are. If teachers are badly paid, the Board should have an objective through Strategic Planning / Strategic Financial Management to increase their wages. If they buy resources from their own pockets, the school should identify what the mission-delivery budget actually is and raise tuition to ensure these items can be funded properly. Teachers work hard, it is true, and so do many people – that has nothing to do with giving. Giving is a faith response to God, not a tradeoff for some other purpose.

The final bullet stings as well. They are not asked. How they respond is in their court, but not to ask them is disrespectful. They are adults and can determine what action to take as they each prayerfully consider the request.

Instead, identify one or two teachers and one or two staff members who do give to the school. In our experience, there are always some teachers and staff who donate. At a staff meeting / teacher meeting (ideally a joint meeting), the administrators leave the room. It is inappropriate for the "employer" to be present during the ask or, even worse, make the ask. They must leave.

Now, the peer (remember it's all about relationships) stands up and shares:

- I give to the annual fund
- This is the case for this year and you can see how it deeply benefits us directly by supporting the children and providing enhancements to our program and facilities.
- This is why I give.
- This is the impact it will have.
- Join me in giving.

Provide easy ways for them to give. Some teachers / staff like to set it up as a payroll deduction, which is very easy to do. Deduct $5 a paycheck to go to the annual fund! Others will give in typical ways by credit card and the various pay service applications.

Teachers and staff are often second-income jobs, so the discussion will go back home to the couple as they consider their charitable giving.

It is both important and inspiring to be able to go to the community and state that giving to the annual fund means joining with both the Board and the school employees, all of whom support the children in this way.

The Annual Fund Cabinet includes peer teachers and staff who will make the thank-you calls and send the thank-you notes.

The Four Thank-Yous

There are four thank-yous given to every donor, irrespective of gift size:

1. The Annual Fund Cabinet has as one of their tasks a phone call to offer their thanks to a donor within 48 hours of receipt of the gift. The person making the phone call is the one who signed the solicitation letter.
2. The Cabinet writes a signed note for each gift that goes out within two weeks of the gift's receipt.
3. By the end of January, each donor receives their donation tax receipt with a warm note of appreciation from the business office.
4. The school produces an annual fund report after the end of the school year (some schools publish this in August). It includes at least three pieces of information:
   - A breakdown of what was asked and what was raised.
   - A clear identification of what the money was or will be spent on reinforcing that the promises made have been kept.
   - Direct examples of the impact of the annual fund in the lives of children, e.g., a testimony from a family that received financial aid and photos of children using materials purchased through the annual fund.

Note: do not include a list of all donors in the annual report. While this has been a standard practice for decades, it is now out-of-date. This is an incredible time-saver!

Since printing an annual report can be very expensive, a digital one, well-designed, is just fine. It can, of course, be communicated digitally to all families / donors; put on the school's website; used in social media, e.g., a link on the school's Facebook page.

This is not a full list of all the touches you might make, depending on the gift and donor circumstances. However, these four thank-yous must be received by every donor, without fail.

The Annual Fund Calendar

There are a variety of "calendars" that schools have used. This is probably the most typical. Consider it in the light of your own culture, history, current school calendar, and so on. The elements are common, however you actually time it.

June / July	Annual Fund Cabinet and the Principal finalize the case, the trifold brochure, and the ask letter. They make their own gift to the campaign.

August   The Board is personally solicited for an annual fund gift by the Board President / Principal or the person with the closest relationship to the Board member. Board members are taught that the school should be one of their top three philanthropic gifts. No other solicitations can be made until every Board member has given or pledged to give. The school administration is also asked and expected to give.

September   Teacher / staff leaders present to the employees together or separately. It may take a year or two to get to 100 percent if this has not been your practice to date. Note that this giving is primarily to demonstrate leadership to the school community at large. Teacher / staff solicitation must be done by a peer, not a member of the administration, because of the power issues involved.

Leadership gifts are solicited by the Philanthropy Committee / Board.

October   The letter to the school community goes out to ask for a gift. The trifold brochure is included in the envelope. This is a mailing, not an email. The letter is to the person by name (not a generic Dear Parent). The total amount already raised through Board, teachers / staff, Administration, and giving leaders is included, and so is the fact that 100 percent of these members of these groups have given – this is inspirational.

November   The Annual Fund Cabinet follows up with those who have not given, including personal and encouraging touches. This message is sent by text or email. Follow-up to those who have given or pledged is done promptly.

December   Recognizing the December 31 deadline, there is someone available to accept donations through the last day of December.

January to June (or the end of your financial year if not June 30)
    Gifts are accepted at any time, but your target ideally should be reached or well on the way to being reached by the end of December.

Note: many of our donors have a variety of designations, i.e., they might be parent, an alum, a staff member. Determine in which order to ask your donors by their level in the organization. Here is a simple order chart. No order is "absolute!"

- Board member / Principal
- Administration
- Staff
- Leadership donor
- Parent
- All others

Annual Fund Leadership Donors

As part of the organization of the annual fund, determine what a leadership gift is. A simple way to do this is to look at what the top 10 percent to 20 percent of donors gave. That becomes a leadership gift range, e.g., $700 or $1,000 or more. Another way might be to look at the size of gift that produced 80 percent or more of the annual fund and make that the leadership gift range.

It is typical for 20 percent or less of your donors to give 80 percent or more of the total giving. While we appreciate the smaller gifts as much as the larger gifts, and while we might like to personalize the relationship between the school and the donor for everyone, the reality of time and resources means that we are only able to take the in-person solicitation approach with the leadership group. Leadership donors are thus by definition in-person donors. Each donor should be solicited in person and each donor must be approached and thanked in a personal way.

This means that solicitation of the leadership donor is done by either inviting the donor to the school for the conversation or by meeting the donor individual / couple at a place of their choosing to make the request for a gift. The visit is in three parts: education (providing insight into the school's current situation and sharing the main points of the Strategic Plan as context); preparation (communicating this year's case for support); solicitation (asking for the gift). percent

Often, the visit is made by two people (Jesus sent his disciples out in twos) – one has the relationship with the donor; they will take on the roles between them of education, preparation, and solicitation. Key to the visit is giving the donor respect and finding the place where they would be most inspired to give. For some, helping families is deeply moving. For others, putting great opportunities into the lives of children is exhilarating. Of course, the donor may also just be happy to give (and unrestricted giving is always a bonus from the school's point of view).

Thank-yous to the leadership donors include the four described above, as well as a fifth:

- An invitation to a leadership donor reception hosted by the Principal, Board President, Chair of the Philanthropy Committee (and Philanthropy Director if you have one)

The Philanthropy Committee members who lead this level of giving do not do all the above —they will have their own portfolio of people to visit. Their role is to make sure everyone is provided with the materials for the visit, to ensure that everyone is trained in what they are to do (along with the Principal and Philanthropy Director if you have one), and to maintain the information about visits and outcomes so it can be put in the database.

While this section is simply about the "ask," it is crucial to reiterate that relational philanthropy requires that the ask is a natural outcome of many other actions represented by the Golden Rule Cycle. We place that here again as a reminder – it has been explained at length earlier in the book.

THE GOLDEN RULE CYCLE

©2024 Christian School Management

Coda

The annual fund in the Christian school must be done professionally, faithfully, and inspirationally.

Professionally means that the school is dealing with its operating budget well, covering its operating expenses with tuition and fees. Employees are paid professionally. Mission delivery is funded at a level of excellence. The school can account for its monies and is able to look after both tuition and gifts legally, spiritually, and morally in the right way.

Faithfully means that the school is planning forward with prayer and thanksgiving. Faithful does not mean leaning on God for financial "miracles" year after year (cf. Luke 16:11-12 and many other passages). It does mean being thankful for God's generosity, planning with God's blessing, and trusting in God's arithmetic.

Inspirationally means making a case that turns the eyes to the future with dreams, even small dreams, that suggest success and motion and hope. It is not asking parents and others to plug budget holes. It is asking your donors to know that you have thoughtfully and prayerfully foreseen what the school will need, and that the school's present success can be even greater in the future with their help.

May your annual funds be amazing opportunities for the grace of God to abound! (2 Corinthians 9:8). Ensure that at the end of every giving cycle, a central outcome is that the community has been strengthened, relationships have been deepened, and that children are still at the center of the conversation.

Summary

- The annual fund is the base of all the school's philanthropic efforts.
- Annual giving (all giving) improves when the school's own finances are in good order, following the Ox Principle. (See appendix.)
- There are two outcomes of annual giving:
  o A culture of philanthropy
  o Uncovering the next generation of leadership donors

- The Annual Fund Cabinet is a subset of the Philanthropy Committee. It is the volunteer organization that makes annual giving relational.
- Annual fund leadership donors are the responsibility of the Philanthropy Committee.
- Steward your volunteers through:
  o Prayer
  o Training
  o Thanks
  o Feedback
  o Holding accountable

DONOR RECOGNITION EVENT

Iₙ ᴛʜɪs sᴇᴄᴛɪᴏɴ, ᴡᴇ ᴛᴀʟᴋ about an annual event that is for all donors. In the last chapter, we spoke about the leadership donor reception. This is different. This is for every donor from smallest to largest. In one survey noted by Penelope Burk, "87% of survey respondents who had attended at least one donor recognition event within the previous year said that the event made them want to give again" (p. 213).

Key to this general event is the engagement of the school's children. First of all, from a practical point of view, since most donors are parents and almost all small donors are parents, they will come if their children are part of the event. Second, whether they are parents or not, the whole point of giving was to do something wonderful in the lives of these children. Consequently, having the children there is an opportunity to make giving visible, i.e., to see the "who" and identify again and connect again to that "why." Various schools have done it in different ways, for example:

- The choir performs during a meal or introduces the main speaker of the evening.
- Children help serve refreshments.
- Children act as greeters and show donors to their seats.
- Children are tour guides.
- All of the above.

The next most important thing is that the donors meet the staff and volunteers, particularly the members of the Philanthropy Committee and the Board. Both school staff and volunteers need to understand their role in "working" the room, ensuring they see as many people as possible, making each person feel "seen," and noting any valuable information they might gain in those conversations.

Obviously, those who have donor portfolios will ensure that they welcome and take care of their own donor(s). But this is an event for every donor, not just for those who gave the most. Today, everyone is on an equal footing. The $5 donor needs to meet the Board President, just as the $5 million donor does. It is easy to go to events where it is plain that the school leaders only have eyes for the most prestigious donors. Let that not be so for CSM schools.

At this event, we embody the life of Jesus, who says in Matthew 18: "See that you do not despise one of these little ones. For I tell you that their angels in heaven always see the face of my Father in heaven." As Paul says right at the beginning of his first letter to the Corinthians: "Brothers and sisters, think of what you were when you were called. Not many of you were wise by human standards; not many were influential; not many were of noble birth. But God chose the foolish things of the world to shame the wise; God chose the weak things of the world to shame the strong. God chose the lowly things of this world and the despised things –and the things that are not – to nullify the things that are, so that no one may boast before him. It is because of him that you are in Christ Jesus, who has become for us wisdom from God – that is, our righteousness, holiness and redemption. Therefore, as it is written: 'Let the one who boasts boast in the Lord.'"

As important is the opportunity for donors to meet each other. Since this is an invitation-only event, everyone who comes knows that everyone they meet has given financially to the school. Most donors are very curious to see who else has given and very encouraged when they see friends, or parents they may have worked with as volunteers, or people they met casually on the sidelines at games, and are able to identify them as co-donors.

Events should always be different year to year. One year, it may include a fabulous speaker about a topic of contemporary interest; another year, it may be an opportunity to tour the building under construction and hear from the architect; another year yet, it might be a picnic in the local park with games for the kids provided. There's no one-size-fits-all. Timing, of course, should recognize the needs of families. Typically, we do not advise a gathering that lasts longer than 90 minutes, with the opportunity to "hang around" if you want to. But we have seen successful Saturday events, breakfast events, and evening events.

Notice that this is an exclusive event. Only donors from last year / current year are invited. It may be that some of last year's donors have not yet given this year. Often, the event will encourage them to make a gift. Those who are not invited will be curious as to why not. The event should be widely publicized so that non-donors are aware of what they are missing out on. The point is not to make them feel bad; they have the right to give or not give. The point is to make a point about the commitment of the school's donors and the intentionality of the school in honoring them.

In no way is this an "ask" event. There should only be appreciation and thankfulness on display. Speakers, event organizers, Board members, Philanthropy Committee members, staff must all be warned not to make off-the-cuff remarks about giving, funny or not. This is all about appreciation. If someone voluntarily walks up to the Principal and says they would like to make an additional gift, of course that is an opportunity to grasp. But the reason should be only that they are a past-year donor and want to ensure that they make their gift for this year, or that they are so inspired by what the school is doing with the gift that they want to increase it.

To help ensure that there is no sense that it is an ask event, there is no speech from the Board President, no long welcome from the Chair of the Philanthropy Committee, no "state of the union" by the Principal (all parents should be invited to this type of address). The event very simply:

- Thanks those present for their support
- Identifies in concrete terms, typically through story, the ways in which the gifts have and / or are making an impact
- Gives each attendee a significant opportunity to meet and socialize with everyone else there (accompanied by appropriate refreshment for the type of event)

We do not recommend that this event be an opportunity to recognize individual donors. It is a community celebration and it celebrates every donor equally. If individual donors need to be recognized, that can be done through a different venue – maybe a private reception or a building-naming unveiling.

> ### TRUE STORY – the heart of the graduate
>
> One CSM school hosts a donor reception for the parents of the graduating class. Six years ago, we started hosting a breakfast for just the parents of the graduating seniors. The first time we had the event, parents thought it was a fundraiser. The second-year we did it, alumni parents started telling other parents it wasn't a fundraiser. By the third year, parents began to believe we were truly thanking them for choosing and bringing and entrusting the school with their child. Rather than watch parents drive away (maybe forever) after graduation - we are making heart connections, and using our words to thank them and then pray a blessing over their family.

The best events provide opportunities for testimonials. This could be from a student or several students about the impact on their lives. It could be from a couple who talk about what happened in their family. Hearing about real experience is a powerful emotional connector. If it is real and raw, it doesn't have to be polished in the professional sense. While it should be well prepared, testimonials are delivered from the heart, not the teleprompter. Testimonials are best not done by staff members. They can share stories in the social part of the event as they circulate through the room. That works well one-to-one, but it does not ring true when part of the main stage presentation to the group as a whole.

This is not a no-cost-spared kind of event. The donors don't want to think of their gifts being "wasted" in extravagance. At the same time, it does need to be professional and well done. You don't need an elegant four-course meal with wine. But you do need thoughtful attention to detail and an ambience that lends itself to celebration. Don't charge admission – ever! And don't spend a fortune. Make it tasteful! A caterer is a good idea when a meal is being served. While donors might not mind volunteering, you don't want to take them away from the experience of being thanked themselves. Just ensure that the budget is appropriate to the crowd and shows good stewardship.

The staff and the volunteers must prepare for the event carefully. By this we mean that they must understand the following:

- The event is for interacting with the donors, not each other.
- Everyone who walks through the door must immediately feel as if they were expected.
- Leadership donors must see their portfolio "owner."
- Staff and volunteers must constantly be on the lookout for attendees who seem to have drifted to the outside of the crowd and ensure they are included.
- While it is human nature to talk with those whom we know, and there is nothing wrong with that, every staff member and volunteer must commit to talking with at least four or five donors they have never met before.

Every donor should leave this appreciation event better informed and more enthusiastic than when they came in. Because every donor is invited, the $5 donor is rubbing shoulders with the $100,000 donor. That's a good thing in both directions.

Lastly, don't be downcast if some donors or even many donors do not come. They appreciate the invitation, the effort you are making to thank them. If this is your first general donor appreciation event, it may be that they think it is another solicitation. Afterwards, they will talk with those who did go and the enthusiasm of the attendees will bring a bigger crowd in consecutive years.

Note: this section speaks of an event. Sometimes schools want to run three or four smaller events at different times to accommodate the needs of the donors. Some can't make it in the evenings or on weekends. For some, a breakfast event is perfect; for others, work commitments make that impossible. Each school must decide what will work best for them. Test it out. Try what you think and see if it works. If not, no regrets, try something else until you have the formula that works for your community. The same rules apply!

Summary

- The donor recognition event is for all donors, whatever the size of the gift.
- Children should be a visible part of the event.
- Donors must meet the volunteers (Philanthropy Committee, etc.) and school staff.
- This is for celebration and thanks, not for asking.
- Keep is simple.
- Keep it nice but not wasteful.
- Meet everybody.

THE COMPREHENSIVE CAMPAIGN

WHEN YOUR SCHOOL'S PLANS FOR the future require fundraising efforts that go beyond the scope of annual giving – typically for capital and / or endowment needs – the annual fund becomes a component of what we now call a comprehensive campaign. This campaign becomes one of the three times, maximum, that we ask parents for money each year (second only to tuition / fees). And it's the annual outreach to other donors, both in the school and in the wider community.

In relational philanthropy, we are generous because we have been engaged in a story that we feel or are beginning to feel passionate about. We are generous because we have seen the school's mission impact the lives of our own children and are grateful. We are generous in response to our faith's call to follow our God who has made the ultimate generous gift of his own Son to us. We are generous fundamentally because someone asks us to be. More likely than not, this is someone whom we know pretty well personally and / or professionally.

Our schools sometimes forget that our donors, our philanthropists, don't segment their relationship to the school in the way we do. We have a Business Office and a Principal / Head of School and someone looking after this and someone looking after that, and so forth. Different communications come from different places. The school is, so to speak, many.

But the donor is one. The donor's budget is one.

Therefore, the school's approach to its donors must be singular – a comprehensive campaign encompassing all the asks for that year. For example, the school's constituency should not receive an annual appeal ask in October and a capital campaign ask in February. The request should recognize the donor is singular and respect and honor the donor's annual / singular budget. The ask in October is comprehensive, including the annual appeal and any other fundraising efforts (e.g., capital campaign, endowment campaign).

For schools like ours, the combination of annual fund and capital campaign (i.e. comprehensive) is the most likely scenario. We will continue to use the annual / capital approach throughout the rest of this section.

How do we handle that this type of campaign? We ask our Board and our leadership donors personally. Having stewarded our donors well, in the ask visit, we provide the donor with information related to both:

- The annual fund (this is how you have supported annual giving in the past and this is our current objective for these reasons)
- The capital campaign (you know we have a transformational opportunity to increase enrollment capacity and provide extraordinary facilities in which to deliver our mission)

The twofold ask is made at the same time: "Over the next three years, would you continue to support the annual fund at your current level? Last year, it was $1,500. Would you give $1,500 this year, $1,750 next year, and $2,000 in the third year? And would you make a capital pledge over the same three years of $15,0000 annually, totaling $45,000?"

One (edited) example of a case for support looked like this:

Case for Support – CSM Christian School

Objective Over Three Years:		$3,600,000 (Annual Fund)
		$13,400,00 (Reaching Out in Faith Campaign – ROIFC)
Breakdown:	Year 1 $6,300,000	($1,100,000 Annual Fund; $5 million ROIFC)
	Year 2 $6,300,000	($1,200,000 Annual Fund; $5 million ROIFC)
	Year 3 $4,700,000	($1,300,000 Annual Fund; $3.4 million ROIFC)

CSM Christian School's mission is to ensure children develop spiritual and intellectual maturity so they can be a positive influence in their families, classrooms, vocations, and travels.

Leadership donors have enabled the school to continue its quest for excellence and to meet the need for an expanding student body. Radical generosity to the Reaching Out in Faith Campaign will enable CSM Christian School to:

- Institute a Student Excellence Endowment so we can:
  o Enhance the richness of the student experience through experiential learning.

- o Provide ongoing and excellent professional growth opportunities to our Christian Professional Learning Community.
- o Enrich and support children through the expanding academic support program.
- o Deepen our growing performing and visual arts programs.

- Expand the Lower School facilities so we can grow God's Kingdom through welcoming the many children who want to attend CSM Christian School.
  - o Providing 100 more learning spaces for children.

The annual fund this year will:

1. Provide financial aid to over 220 families, opening our doors to all mission-appropriate Christian families without regard to income.
2. Further develop two outdoor classrooms.
3. Provide adaptive classroom furniture for all Middle School children – Year One of a three-year initiative.

We invite you to join us in continuing the story of God's redemptive power at CSM Christian School.

My Pledge

Year One	2025–26	Annual Fund _____	ROIFC _____
Year Two	2026–27	Annual Fund _____	ROIFC _____
Year Three	2027–28	Annual Fund _____	ROIFC _____

The outcomes for this unified approach to philanthropy are:

1. The donor is clear about all aspects of philanthropy at the school they support.
2. The number of "asks" per year continues to be controlled – one (plus tuition for parents).
3. There is clarity around the different kinds of objectives the annual fund and capital campaigns support, i.e., annual is present-tense giving, capital is strategic multigenerational giving with impact far into the future.
4. The annual fund continues to be strong and even grows during any capital campaign. The donor can see that when the comprehensive campaign ends, the annual fund continues.
5. Comprehensive campaigns allow the campaign to include all three kinds of giving – annual, capital, endowment.

It might be just a word. But changing from "capital" to "comprehensive" leads to a deeper practice of philanthropy in our schools, builds more sustainable philanthropy, and eliminates "surprise" in our relationships with our donors.

Running Your Comprehensive Campaign

Maybe oddly, there is not much more advice to give about running a comprehensive campaign than there is about running an annual fund. In relational philanthropy, the principles are exactly the same and the execution is parallel.

Responsibility

There is one key difference between the annual giving process and a comprehensive campaign.

- The annual fund is the primary responsibility of the Operations Team with the support of the Philanthropy Committee.
- A capital campaign (and/or endowment), is the primary responsibility of the Board of Trustees, carried out by the Philanthropy Committee and supported by Operations.
- In a comprehensive campaign, the two sides must be highly coordinated to ensure alignment in service to the relationship with the donor.

Note: there is no permission needed for the annual fund to run each year and there is no approval needed for its case for support, so long as the case either directly supports or does not take away support for the objectives of the Board's Strategic Plan / Strategic Financial Management.

The Board of Trustees must specifically approve any comprehensive campaign efforts other than the annual fund; each member of the Board must be completely committed to these efforts' success; the campaign must be part of the Board's Strategic Plan / Strategic Financial Management; the Board takes responsibility for their success / failure.

The following table compares the annual with the capital campaign:

	Annual Fund	Capital Campaign
Responsibility	Operations (Principal)	Board of Trustees
Duration	Year to year	3-5 years
Personnel (School and Board)	Principal / Annual Fund Manager / Annual Fund Committee	Board / Philanthropy Committee / Principal / Philanthropy Director
Case for Support	"Now" objectives	"Generational" objectives
Metrics for Success	KPI 10% of net tuition	Feasibility study
Leadership Donors	Give 80%+ of total	Give 80%+ of total
Source of Leadership Gifts	Income	Asset
Volunteers	Annual Fund Cabinet	Philanthropy Committee
Additional Resources	None	Campaign associate
Data	Essential	Essential

Quiet Phase of the Campaign

In the quiet phase of the campaign, the school is sharing its vision with a select group of the school's supporters. This process includes preparing the "case for support," carrying out the feasibility study, and actually finding out what the leadership donors will give / pledge to the campaign. It is quiet, not silent. The broader community is aware that plans are being made but is not given the details while the school does its due diligence.

The capital and annual fund cases are somewhat different. The annual fund case for support encompasses a wide range of very different outcomes – from financial aid to playgrounds to special projects to classroom resources to specialized professional growth activities, all at the same time. The capital campaign, on the other hand, is very narrowly focused on one or two major objectives, e.g., the middle school academic building and two new soccer fields. This narrow focus has two practical reasons:

1. It's all we think we can afford.
2. It's all we want right now.

This makes the campaign simple at its heart. We only need to think about these specific things.

However, the downside of this simplicity is that it narrows what the donor can give to. A percentage of donors will say they like the plan – and give. Essentially, they are saying that they trust the school (probably on the basis of excellent historical stewardship of funds) and that they will give so the school can spend as it needs to attain the objective. Another percentage of donors, however, wants to direct their funds to their own pet projects. The school accommodates this by splitting the large objective (the middle school academic wing) into smaller bites. This offers donors choice within the context of the single large objective, e.g.:

- Science / STEM labs
- Student commons
- Library
- Black box theater
- Entranceway

Then ask: What are you interested in?

The Leadership Case for Support

That conversation between the school and the lead donors is mediated by creating a leadership case for support. It is not the final case – the school will not develop that until the donor leadership has had an opportunity to comment. The leadership case is created to educate, inform, learn, and persuade.

1. Educate
    - Who the school is (mission, values)
    - What happened in the past leading to the current moment (e.g., previous campaigns)

2. Inform
    - What is the school's vision (why this, why now, how will it impact children)
    - What is needed (construction, renovation)
    - What is in the plan
    - What are the costs

3. Learn
    - What are your thoughts?
    - What advice would you give us?
    - What excites and motivates you?

4. Persuade
   - How the campaign will benefit children
   - Where they see themselves

This is not a fancy document. It doesn't need glossy photos or heavy design. It needs to be practical and easy to read. It needs to be thorough and data rich. It needs to look as if it has been thought through, but not as though money has been "wasted" on its creation. The school's leadership donors are not impressed by fancy. They are impressed by the evidence that solid homework has been done and all angles have been considered – including risks involved. They want to know the school is moving ahead in a professional way.

The Campus Master Development Plan – a Key Tool in Informing the Donor

Many leadership donors want to know the context of the current project and see how it fits into the overall vision of the Board / school. The Campus Master Development Plan (CMDP) is your background document. The Board has an ethical obligation to practice foresight. What is everything that the school will want over the next 50 years? Maybe that seems too heavy a lift but, for most schools, it's less complicated than it seems:

- How large do we want the school to become?
- What facilities do we have currently?
- Where are current bottlenecks (typically specialized spaces such as gym space, labs, art and music rooms)?
- What facilities will we need for the current and future size of school?
- What is the current program?
- What do we want in the future and what facilities does that imply?
- What is the school's current footprint?
- Where will everything go?
- What are the logical phases for this to happen?

While we can't really look into the future over a 50-year timeline, it's not hard to say that programmatically we need another practice gym space, that for two sections we will need another 10 classrooms, that choir and band need separate class spaces, and so on.

Maybe obviously, the CMDP should follow the Board's Strategic Plan / Strategic Financial Management documents, which include the Strategic Academic Plan.

When the donor sees, for example, the five phases of which the current campaign is phase two, they have the opportunity to understand how their investment will take the school to another level and how they can help the school move forward. Occasionally, that lead donor will give to the current campaign but fund an entire future phase because that phase is what motivates them.

The CMDP is a parallel document to the Board's Property Acquisition Plan. This includes:

- The current needs of the school
- Consideration of the strategic needs of the school as the Board's Strategic Plan might suggest, and in particular the impact of building plans on the school's natural context (what CSM terms Garden of Eden)
- A review of real-estate trends in the local area
- A look at regional trends
- Demographic trend information
- An understanding of the fiscal trends, interest rate environment, etc.
- A recommendation, as appropriate, for reserves accumulation beyond the three months recommended in the KPI to ensure the school is in good position to take advantage of opportunity

Feasibility Study

How can the Board move ahead if it doesn't know whether it will be successful? The leader case is tested in the feasibility study.

The Board and school are wise to **always** carry out a feasibility study to ensure that their leadership donors are brought into the campaign and are willing to support it at the level needed for success.

The typical way of doing a feasibility study has been to bring in a third-party consultant to personally interview the top 10 to 20 donors and report back to the Board. This has generally worked very well and is still an option to consider. CSM now thinks that this takes away a great opportunity for deepening the relationship between the donor and the school. We advocate for the school to carry out its own feasibility study.

It's valuable to have a consultant come in and train the Board and Philanthropy Committee in using a Structured Lead Donor Interview (SLDI) with faith and courage and prayer, then carry out the interviews themselves. The process is just as or more effective and far less expensive. There are thus two virtuous outcomes: deepening the relationship with your lead donors and reducing campaign administrative costs. The interview will ascertain the leadership donor's:

1. Relationship to the school to date and its impact in the donor's / donor's family's life
2. Involvement with the school over the previous five years
3. Philanthropic objects and interests
4. Interest in the leader case, including specific feedback
5. Willingness to invest
6. Estate plans

This is enormous stewardship of the donor. The school is respecting them, listening to their advice, as well as asking how they might act if this campaign went ahead.

Based on the SLDI outcomes, the school develops an online interview survey and sends it out to the next 100 to 200 donors to gain a sense of their excitement and commitment.

A useful schematic to provide the lead donor during the feasibility study interview is a gift chart. The example below is for a $5 million campaign. As gifts are given and / or pledged, an additional column can be added to the right to identify the number of gifts obtained in each category.

Number of Gifts	Size of Gift	Total	Cumulative
1	$2,000,0000	$2,000,000	$2,000,000
2	$500,000	$1,000,000	$3,000,000
4	$250,000	$1,000,000	$4,000,000
5	$100,000	$500,000	$4,500,000
5	$50,000	$250,000	$4,750,000
Many	Various	$250,000	$5,000,000

Leadership Donors by Longevity

In the above table, it is obvious who the "lead" donors are. And without them, any campaign will fail. Your school cannot be successful on the basis of $10 gifts. However, CSM truly believes in the power of the faithful widow's mite (cf. Mark 12). We encourage you to consider those who have given for seven years or more as a special category of leadership donor.

We know schools where donors give a "small" amount faithfully every month. Other donors make a faithful annual contribution without fail. Ten dollars a month for seven years is getting close to what most schools consider an annual fund leadership gift – $1,000. Pick your own longevity target (some schools use 10 years) and honor those donors in a very special way, giving thanks for their faithfulness. "Love and faithfulness keep a king safe; through love his throne is made secure" (Proverbs 20:28).

We note that, while these donors are not currently making major contributions, research suggests that a third are open to an ask that could impact the campaign, and the same percentage are open to putting the school in their estate planning. Your database needs to be good enough to be able to identify donors who have and are giving regularly, irrespective of the amount.

Making the Ask

Once the feasibility study is complete, the Board must decide on next steps. They can go ahead with the original plan, modify it, or scrap it. Assuming there is a green light for the campaign, it is time to go back to those donors and make the ask. They should not be surprised. And you should have at least an idea as to what they will give – if they ask you how much you would like. Relationships are predicated on knowledge of each other. The leadership donor expects you to know them well enough to not ask them for too much – or for too little!

Of course, sometimes we are disappointed at the gift when we think about the donor's capacity. Disappointment is maybe not the right emotional response. Rather, think about what was missed. Were they not engaged enough? Did they have the information they needed? Was the person who asked them someone they trusted? Was there a peer who could have inspired them? Is it just circumstantial – not at this time? How has the door been left open to ask again?

When the gift is received, as in annual giving, the response is crucial:

- Personal phone call within 48 hours
- Personal note of thanks within two weeks

Always remember the Golden Rule Cycle and check which elements have been covered and which still need to be done. Are you remembering to pray for your donor? Report back the great progress being made? Invite them to significant events for the campaign? Take them on a personal tour?

Hiring the Campaign Consultant

We would always advise that the school hire a professional consultant to assist in the campaign. Christian schools routinely underinvest in philanthropy. As we continue to stress, philanthropy requires an expert's understanding. Find a person that you believe understands the school and its mission, and is committed to working with you based on who you are and what you have.

Donors, of course, are rightfully concerned that their investment in the school goes directly into the campaign objective rather than administration costs. We advocate that in the Strategic Plan / Strategic Financial Management prior to the campaign, dollars are put aside into reserves to fund the administrative costs of the campaign to the extent possible, e.g., consulting costs, architect fees, design. At a few schools, we have even been able to use reserves to cover initial infrastructure improvements (water, sewer, utilities). But even if that is not possible, don't hesitate to hire professional counsel. The consultant will:

- Help you plan
- Hold you accountable
- Hold your hand in

Maybe the most important is the second bullet point. Boards and Philanthropy Committees are all composed of volunteers who have many other things in their lives. Even school employees can be drawn away from the "main thing" by the everyday matters that seem so urgent. The consultant will constantly hold you accountable to do what you committed to – and drive focus / energy in the direction where it will have the most impact.

The Public Campaign

The campaign has not been a secret up to this point, but there has been a lot of action to preparing for its success. You know when you are ready to go public because the leadership case for support is ready to become the community case for support that will be shared with all members of the community in order to complete the campaign. Yes, the campaign goes public when you are sure what the final amount raised is going to be and there is significant confidence that the campaign will be successful. Typically, this means that you have raised 75 percent to 90 percent of the total needed.

To put it negatively, the campaign does not go public until the school is sure of its success.

Utilize the same gift chart as you did during the leadership / quiet phase. In the public phase, expand it to show what has already been achieved, emphasizing that every contribution from here on is to complete the campaign. It's helpful to put a column in for both what has been raised at each gift level to date as well as a cumulative column. Anything that makes it easy for the person reading it is a good thing!

Number of Gifts Needed	Size of Gift Needed	Total Needed	Given To Date	Cumulative	Total Campaign Needed
1	$2million	$2million	$2million	$2million	$2million
2	$500,000	$1million	$1million	$3million	$3million
4	$250,000	$1million	$500,000	$3.5million	$4million
5	$100,000	$500,000	$200,000	$3.7million	$4.5million
5	$50,000	$250,000	$250,000	$3.95million	$4.75million
many	various	$250,000	$0	$3.95million	$5million

Social Media Mavens

In Penelope Burk's *Donor-Centered Fundraising*, she comments on what she calls "mass influencers" (p.183). Almost every school we know has a Facebook page with wonderful pictures and reports about what is happening every week in the lives of children. Often, they will include shout-outs to teachers and other adults who are contributing in some special way. Many schools have other social media outreach venues as well. Burk's research suggests that about 16 percent to 18 percent of those who follow you are "mass influencers." They are passionate and committed about the school and are active on social media, talking the school up and being willing to volunteer in a variety of ways. Burk writes: "If mass influencers know they are a coveted resource, they will do most of the work for you in growing your pool of followers, converting prospects into donors and even influencing followers who are already donors to give more often and more generously."

We suggest that either your social media professional or a member of the Philanthropy Committee, specially recruited because of their skills in this area, identify these people through their activity, and engage them proactively:

- Giving them previews of campaign information before it is released to the school community
- Asking for their advice about it
- Asking for their opinion about engaging the parent community as a whole

---

TRUE STORY – listening to an influencer!

As a new Head of School, I was sitting at my desk writing my first letter to the school's parents. We had met in a reception setting but I wanted to tell them how the first couple of days had gone and to give some idea as to what the direction of the school was. I finished the letter and passed it to my executive assistant to proof and get ready for sending.

Carrying on with my other work, I was interrupted by a soft knock at the door. In came Desi, a parent volunteer who was every school's dream of a helper: unassuming, powerful, totally connected into the school community, someone who had been linked to the school through her seven children for over 13 years. She said to me in a very kind manner: "You can't send this letter out to the parents like this. I know what you mean to say. Would you mind if I worded it in a way that our parents can hear it?" What a Godsend! Desi was my mass influencer and I ran every communication through her. She saved me from many mistakes!!

Running the Public Campaign

The public campaign is raising less than 25 percent of the total. This is a different group of people, however, than those who raised the first 75+ percent. They need:

- A well-produced campaign brochure
- A constant round of the Golden Rule Cycle – pray, thank, report, celebrate, ask
- Very visible signs of progress

Spending money on a campaign brochure for leadership donors is not a wise use of funds. It is still open to change, the objective hasn't been finally nailed down, the donor doesn't want funds spent in this manner. However, spending money on a really good-looking and well-produced campaign brochure for the $100 and $500 donor is worth it. While the leadership donor is giving from assets, most small donors are still giving from income. Their frame of reference is the annual fund and other fundraising events and campaigns run by other organizations.

The comprehensive campaign is the annual fund campaign on steroids. It requires 12 months of almost frenetic action.

- Establish a prayer group that meets regularly to pray for the campaign, for the donors, for the construction company, for the children who will be blessed, for safety, for success, for the campaign to be in God's will. This is, of course, a group that should be in place during the leadup to the quiet campaign and through the entire process.
- Establish minor and major celebration moments. Think about your objectives and create markers when there will be public acknowledgement of progress made. The ceremonial shovel at the beginning and the thanksgiving celebration at the end are the two obvious ones. Don't ignore what's happening in between – the footings are in, the roof is up, come for a family tour of the inside (wearing a hard hat). We recommend that these celebrations have a liturgical / worship aspect to them. For example, the final celebrations would include a Mass or worship chapel.
- Set up a camera and provide an internet link on your website that families can use to connect from their home computers. That way they can see what is going on and join in the celebration.
- Ensure that environmental concerns related to construction (think cutting down trees, for example!) are addressed openly and publicly. Maybe for adults it is or isn't an issue – for our children, it is. In a 2021, 10-country survey, the researchers found that 46 percent of USA teens were extremely or very worried about climate change. Fifty-seven percent felt sad about the issue and 46 percent felt helpless. In our schools, we should make that a part of our outreach to the children in our schools by identifying the environmental factors being considered and how they are being dealt with, e.g., wetlands, nesting birds, water runoff, power requirements.
- Thank and thank and thank again. For every gift, thanks is due with a phone call, a personal note, and a receipt including a warm letter. We have talked with schools that say they just don't have time to do that much thanking. If you don't thank, you don't deserve the donor. Remember that the public campaign is a mirror of the annual fund campaign and should include an equal or greater number of volunteers.

The Final Celebration when the Campaign Is Over

We find that our schools are very good at celebrations. There are prayers, readings of Scripture, food and drink, tours, exhibits, speeches, acknowledgements. All this is very good.

Almost always, there is one thing missing – children. We do not mean here the seemingly obligatory performance by the school's choir or band or both. There's nothing wrong with that, of course, even as it skirts with turning children into public relations cyphers. But it uses them more as props rather than as the main thing.

Consider:

- Children serving as representatives on the planning committee / meetings
- A high school student (or middle school in a K–8) making the opening speech
- The choir being introduced by a fifth-grader who really cares about the new project
- The food and drink being served by children of all ages who are learning the art of waiting on table
- The tours being led by children most closely impacted by the new construction or renovation

The point of the campaign was not the building or renovation or new facility. The point is mission delivery in the lives of the school's children. Assuming that they will lead in these celebrations, and that adults will take a back seat, transforms the celebration and faces it in a more generative direction.

THE MAJOR GIFT CAMPAIGN

T HERE ARE TIMES WHEN A "campaign" is too large a stone to break too small a nut. Let's imagine that you are a school with a $1.5 million budget and are raising $125,000 in annual giving. You had a capital campaign 18 months ago to build six classrooms and a new entryway with better security that cost $3.2 million. About 65 percent of your donors are still fulfilling their three-year pledges. As new families come into the school, you are engaging them to contribute to that campaign to pay off the final bridge loan and make the project debt free.

Now, the Strategic Plan / Strategic Financial Management is being renewed. The school is in a different place with a 15 percent increase in enrollment, a new facility inhabited, income over expenses approaching 102 percent, high morale and enthusiasm.

In the Strategic Academic Plan, the academic leaders have consulted with all the teachers and some student focus groups. The result of their research is that they would love to expand the outdoor program with an elementary adventure playground that would include elements for use in the science curriculum, a middle school reflection walk for personal use and to support the Bible curriculum, and a high school greenhouse to support the school's diploma in agriculture. Total cost for all three is $900,000.

Consider the following:

- The school is still wending its way through the last campaign.
- Many leadership donors have given willingly and to their limits.
- This is an important initiative but is too large for the annual fund to cover.

This is the kind of scenario where a major gifts campaign works really well.

1. Identify leadership donors who have fulfilled their pledges.
2. Run donor profiles on each of them to see which are highly motivated by these kinds of initiatives.
3. Develop a strong case with children and teachers at the forefront.
4. Ensure the Strategic Plan / Strategic Financial Management are rock solid and 100 percent supported by the Board.
5. Take the case privately to five or six donors asking them to fund these initiatives.

Major gift campaigns are private campaigns. They target objectives that are too small for a full-scale campaign or too large for the annual fund to support. They seek to motivate (and keep involved) leadership donors who have finished their commitment to one campaign and not started their commitment to another.

Summary

- Annual giving can be a stand-alone campaign, or it can be combined with other fundraising efforts in a comprehensive campaign.
- A unified campaign respects the donor, who should only be asked once for their gift.
- Comprehensive campaigns are run in a similar fashion to an annual fund. Differences include:
  o A feasibility study to test the case for support
  o A quiet campaign that runs before the public campaign

- The public campaign doesn't run till 75+ percent of the total has been raised / pledged from leadership donors.
- Celebrate successes.
- Consider a major gifts campaign when the objective is smaller, less appealing, or when donors are still giving from the last comprehensive campaign.

PHILANTHROPY AND SOCIAL CAPITAL

THIS IMPORTANT CHAPTER PULLS TOGETHER two concepts that hitherto have not been fully understood.

CSM continues to teach that Christian philanthropy is founded on relationships, not transactions. In simple terms, Christians do what St. Paul did when he was traveling the ancient world asking for money. He went directly to people and asked them for it. He didn't run raffles, organize bake sales, play 18 holes of golf. "So here is my opinion on this matter: It is to your advantage, since you made a good start last year both in your giving and your desire to give, to finish what you started, so that just as you wanted to do it eagerly, you can also complete it according to your means" (2 Corinthians 8). He had a relationship, he pointed to the relationship with Jesus that they had ("For you know the grace of our Lord Jesus Christ, that although he was rich, he became poor for your sakes, so that you by his poverty could become rich," v. 9), he asked them for money.

We continue to teach that philanthropy is a school activity, not a special-interest activity. Booster clubs, parent-teacher associations, support groups – all with the best intentions and motives – diminish philanthropy by connecting it so blatantly to self-interest. It is certain that self-interest is a powerful motivator and these groups point to significant successes as donations flow into the bank account. And donors have the right to direct their money wherever they wish. We do not dispute that; in fact, we endorse it. But there is a better way that both supports the needs these groups are interested in and moves the school as a whole community forward.

What does that mean for the association or club? Should they go away if their philanthropy role is subsumed into annual giving, where the whole community is engaged in the forward motion of the school in its delivery of mission into the lives of children? This is where the second concept comes in. In 1988, James Coleman wrote a seminal article called "Social Capital in the Creation of Human Capital." In this article, he wrote in the conclusion: "In explicating the concept of social capital, three forms were identified: obligations and expectations, which depend on trustworthiness of the social environment, information-flow capability of the social structure, and norms accompanied by sanctions. A property shared by most forms of social capital that differentiates it from other forms of capital is its public good aspect: the actor or actors who generate social capital ordinarily capture only a small part of its benefits" (p. S118). The actions of members of internal groups in your school, working together to create a community, in so doing create a stock of social capital (interconnections / networks) that create:

- Obligations (if you will work a shift making hamburgers, I will work a shift later in the year helping you)
- Increased trust (because we work together, we get to know each other and therefore are more likely to trust each other, for example, by leaving my child with you on the sidelines while I go to pick up my spouse)
- Knowledge (we share information that each of us has, information that overlaps in its extensiveness)
- Norms (this is the way we do things round here)

Interestingly, social capital is not an accountant's game. While we all benefit from this accumulation of capital, largely as a by-product of our actions, we do not necessarily benefit equally. Coleman writes: "the kinds of social structures that make possible social norms and the sanctions that enforce them do not benefit primarily the person or persons whose efforts would be necessary to bring them about, but benefit all those who are part of such a structure" (Coleman p. S116).

The following table (Coleman p. 115) illustrates the benefit of having a tight community from which children go to school. In this table, dropout rates are compared – religious schools where children come from unitary cultural and religious settings and public schools where backgrounds and connections are diffuse and arbitrary. It is clear that the social capital implicit in the religious families' interconnections has a significant impact on the chance of success for their children. This was true for Catholic schools, as well as Baptist and Jewish.

TABLE 2

DROPOUT RATES BETWEEN SPRING, GRADE 10, AND SPRING, GRADE 12, FOR STUDENTS FROM SCHOOLS WITH DIFFERING AMOUNTS OF SOCIAL CAPITAL IN THE SURROUNDING COMMUNITY

	Public	Catholic	Other Private Schools
1. Raw dropout rates	14.4	3.4	11.9
2. Dropout rates standardized to average public school sophomore[a]	14.4	5.2	11.6

	Non-Catholic Religious	Independent
3. Raw dropout rates for students[b] from independent and non-Catholic religious private schools	3.7	10.0

[a] The standardization is based on separate logistic regressions for these two sets of schools, using the same variables listed in n. 5. Coefficients and means for the standardization are in Hoffer (1986, tables 5 and 24).

[b] The tabulation is based on unweighted data, which is responsible for the fact that both rates are lower than the rate for other private schools in item 1 of the table, which is based on weighted data.

Christian philanthropy is relational philanthropy. School organizations that band together to support various objectives are best suited, not to fundraising, but to creating community and, in research terms, the social capital that community drives. And there is plenty of evidence to show that this work of community-building has direct impact in fundraising. We don't want the booster club raising funds. They're not very good at it, and it actually depresses the total the school could raise if philanthropy was a coordinated relational activity. We do want the booster club (and parent association and theater support group) organizing and enjoying activities that build community. By so doing, they create social capital (obligations, trust, knowledge, norms) that directly improve philanthropy outcomes. They improve relationships.

Robert Putnam writes in *Bowling Alone*: "More important than wealth, education, community size, age, family status, and employment, however, by far the most consistent predictor of giving time and money is involvement in community life. Social recluses are rarely major donors or active volunteers but *schmoozers* and *machers* are typically both" (p. 119). Here are some statistics to bear this out:

- Americans who regularly attend church and clubs volunteer 10 times as much as those who do neither.
- Volunteers in 1995 contributed 200 percent to 300 percent more than non-volunteers.
- Those who entertain friends at home are more likely to volunteer and work on community projects.
- In 1996, members of religious organizations gave 1.9 percent of income to charity, members of secular organizations gave 2.3 percent of income to charity. If you were not a member of either, you gave 0.4 percent of income to charity.
- Americans active in community affairs are twice as likely to give blood.

Putnam writes: "Social capital is a more powerful predictor of philanthropy than financial capital" (p. 120). There is a darker side to the data. It seems that the amount of money being given each year keeps going up. You may see that in your own school's data. Historically, the amount being given proportional to income is actually going down. Putnam again: "In 1960 we gave away about $1 for every $2 we spent on recreation; in 1997 we gave away less than $0.50 for every $2 we spent on recreation" (p. 123). Social capital in that period demonstrably decreased. In case we might think that this is "old" data, Putnam in 2015 reported on another study carried out by skeptical scholars: "both kin and nonkin networks have shrunk in the past two decades … America's social networks are collapsing inward, and now consist of fewer, denser, more homogeneous, more familial (and less nonkin) ties" (*Our Kids,* p. 211).

In other words, social capital is a predictor of giving of time and money; the various groupings in the school contribute strongly to the development of deep social capital, thus supporting philanthropy; if they act as isolated actors for their own benefit, their social capital will not benefit the school as a whole; if they are part of the school as an organism, they are powerful and important.

Let's go back to St. Paul. In 2 Corinthians 9, he speaks of the Macedonians using the term "they" over and over, i.e., collectively as a community: "Entirely on their own, they urgently pleaded with us for the privilege of sharing in this service to the Lord's people. And they exceeded our expectations: They gave themselves first of all to the Lord, and then by the will of God also to us." It appears that Paul was perfectly aware of the importance and power of social capital along with its connections of obligation, trust, knowledge, and norms. We should recognize the same.

This chapter should not be construed as saying that we should get together IN ORDER TO create social capital. Rather, we should support the building of community recognizing that we also benefit from the social capital it develops. It's not about the money. It's about the relationships that result in an overflowing of generosity out of gratitude to our God. We give Paul the last word: "This service that you perform is not only supplying the needs of the Lord's people but is also overflowing in many expressions of thanks to God. Because of the service by which you have proved yourselves, others will praise God for the obedience that accompanies your confession of the gospel of Christ, and for your generosity in sharing with them and with everyone else. And in their prayers for you their hearts will go out to you, because of the surpassing grace God has given you. Thanks be to God for his indescribable gift!" (2 Corinthians 9:12-15).

BOOSTER CLUBS AND CHRISTIAN SCHOOL PHILANTHROPY

THE SCENARIO IS A COMMON one. A bunch of parents are standing around one day talking about the soccer / volleyball / football / hockey / etc., team. The coach walks up and they say: "How's it going, coach? Is there anything you need?" The coach barely thinks for a moment before providing a list of items that would be great to have in practice but which they can't afford — more cones, practice balls so they don't have to use the match balls daily, new soccer net, five good whistles, and so on. The parents ask whether it would be okay if they found the money to get some or all of the items. The coach is excited and agrees.

This is how most booster clubs got started. Enthusiasm combines with a clear need, along with the desire to give kids the best experience possible, and it wouldn't do any harm to "my" kid who is on the team either.

Fast forward to today and families are now fully integrated into the process of support and encouragement through a booster club. In some schools, there is just one booster club for athletics. In others, there are multiple booster clubs — one for each sport, one for drama, one for art, one for music. There's a sponsorship secretary who approaches businesses to buy signs or business card ads. There's a travel secretary who organizes the food for teams when they go on the buses. There's a small fundraiser, just for parents, held during the preseason. It's actually not that small. It raises several thousand dollars each year.

How should we think about this outpouring of support and volunteerism? Maybe surprisingly, we should be appropriately skeptical. Here are the issues:

1. Budget: booster clubs come about because there is a need that the school budget is not meeting. After a while, the school comes to rely on the booster club's work to ensure that needs are met, which seems to allow tuition to be depressed.

2. Annual fund: the best fundraising is done through the school's annual fund. Booster clubs act as competition to the school's own fundraising and fragment the school's philanthropic efforts. Paradoxically, all these separate efforts actually result in less being raised than is possible.

3. Donors: it is the school's responsibility to look after each donor well. This is very difficult, even in the best collaborative circumstances that we have seen, when different organizations in the school are looking for and soliciting donors. While some are enthused, most are confused and irritated by the constant asks that come from all directions. Some of our schools have upward of 100 asks in a single year!

4. Power: booster clubs, unintentionally, build separate territories and power structures in a school. However, once built, they can be held onto tenaciously by those who "own" them. A donor becomes the "possession" of the club; the money raised "belongs" to the club; some clubs have their own bank accounts and decide how the money raised will be spent. The Athletic Director, in particular, can become a contentious figure in the school community. When clubs begin to operate autonomously, they no longer have all children in mind, only some; the club members become primarily interested in benefiting their own children.

5. Money: money becomes compartmentalized and control of money results in a distortion of the school's mission. The athletic team or other focus becomes the end, rather than the program and curriculum of the school leading to a mission end. When "I" own the money "I" raised, then the community takes a back seat and is fractured.

6. Prestige: with or without booster clubs, a hierarchy exists within the school where some things are overtly valued more than others. We can see this in resource allocation, time given, website positioning, and so on. Booster clubs accentuate that in ways that breed significant resentment. The football team has new uniforms every two years while the golf team has never had uniforms at all. The gym is beautiful while the music room is shabby. Piling more money into high-profile areas makes the disparities even more obvious and even worse.

Solutions:

1. Budget: the Board must make a commitment to fully fund all operating budgets; the Principal and Business Manager must ensure that all appropriate needs are identified and included in the budget for the Board to approve.

2. Annual fund: all philanthropy should flow through the annual fund and be organized as a single effort. Working together to engage the community builds community.

3. Donors: good philanthropy seeks to build a relationship with each donor. Such work honors and respects each donor's time, energy, and bank balance. Nickel-and-diming donors means that the gift being given is rarely optimal. Well done, philanthropy identifies and solicits the donor, but also ensures the donor is stewarded well so that the gift is repeated and increased year by year.

4. Power: the school belongs to God, and is there to serve the children. Money can pervert this attitude and make it about the adults. Within a servant-leadership community focused on what's best for all children, the power of the school is beneficial and loving. Assuring the program leaders that their budget will meet their needs takes away the need for the power conversation.

5. Money: all money belongs to the school. It is budgeted to meet the needs of all areas of the school's mission delivery. Additional needs are met on a prioritized basis where everybody will take a turn in special funding through philanthropy. In this way, all members of the community, whether high-profile or not, are cared for.

6. Prestige: it is true that more money will be spent on some areas than others. Some are just more expensive. The school has to make mission-based decisions on which areas it will or will not support. However, all children must feel they are valuable within the school community whether their area of interest is "popular" or not. The school's responsibility to each child is never negated by public relations or secular hierarchies.

While booster clubs began and continue with the best of intentions, their most effective work is in supporting and community building. They should not be involved in philanthropy except as part of the larger school community, and solely through the auspices of the school's annual giving efforts. All philanthropic efforts must flow through the school's annual giving program.

Summary

- Fundraising by parent groups through booster clubs is usually the result of an inadequate school budget.
- Solve the underlying issue by funding mission delivery programs properly.
- Focus parent support groups on building community.
- Align all philanthropy through the annual fund.
- All children must be served over time.
- Special-cause fundraising is toxic, inequitable, and inefficient.

GIVING TUESDAY

THIS IDEA BECAME A REALITY in 2012 as an antidote to the consumerism of Black Friday. It was an opportunity for the general public to consider how they might spend on others as well as themselves. There are two sites – givingtuesday.ca and givingtuesday.org – with the same excellent idea: "Everyone has something to give and every act of generosity counts." They were cofounded by the United Nations Foundation and thus this is a global phenomenon. It is very successful, bringing in $2.7 billion in the USA alone in 2021.

And we are not for it. Not for our schools. It is a great program and has benefited many. It has obviously struck a chord. But our Christian schools should not indulge in it. Seems counter-intuitive. After all, it's another opportunity for our constituency to participate in giving to our school – and many schools do utilize the idea of Giving Tuesday and do raise money in this way.

We want to use the idea of Giving Tuesday to emphasize the principles that we have been repeating over and over again. Christian philanthropy is about relationship building. It is not anonymous, disengaged, episodic, spur of the moment. It is about deeply respecting every one of the school's constituents from child to parent to grandparent to corporate sponsor to alumni. We want each investor in the school's mission on behalf of children to thoughtfully and prayerfully consider how they might use what God has given them to benefit the school's children. We want that thought and prayer to deepen and be part of a long-term and continuing relationship with the school that is as transformative for the donor as it is for the school.

Giving Tuesday has just become another way for organizations to ask their donors for money once again. This has led to over-solicitation in our schools. As we count the number of times our parents are asked for money, Giving Tuesday has just added to that number. Our donors do not need another ask. They need a better relationship.

One school we know raises over $68,000 on Giving Tuesday. Are we asking them to give that up? Well, it depends. First, no leadership donor should be asked to give on Giving Tuesday. Their relationship is personal to the point that any solicitation is going to be face-to-face. Second, no regular donor should be asked to give on Giving Tuesday. You are not winning friends by asking them to go to a competition for giving dollars. You should know the way in which they already give and support them in that. Third, for organizations that are trying to be intentional in their philanthropy processes, Giving Tuesday has become a lazy way of over-soliciting.

Leave Giving Tuesday as a means for the general public, people who have not yet seen themselves as donors, to have a way for them to get involved. For your school, pay attention to the relationship you have with your donors and ensure they are treated with honor and respect. They will thank you for not having to deal with yet "another" request for money.

CHILDREN AND PHILANTHROPY

CSM PROMOTES TWO BASIC PRINCIPLES around children and raising money:

1. The school's children should never raise money for themselves.
2. The school's children can raise money for others if they are personally involved.

1. The school's children should never raise money for themselves.

We often partner with schools that are underfunded. That is very clear because children are carrying out sometimes extensive transactional fundraisers for field trips (think the eighth-grade trip to Washington) or to fund student organizations (think the annual budget for the student government). These fundraisers almost always involve selling food at lunchtime or holding car washes or benefiting large companies by selling chocolate bars and the like. This is teaching children the wrong approach to philanthropy, We want them to learn that philanthropy is relational, not transactional.

If the program happens during the school year and during school hours, it must be funded by the school's operations budget. The Board's responsibility is to ensure that there are sufficient resources for excellence in mission delivery. However that happens, it must not be supported by asking or suggesting that children raise money for their own education.

There are many arguments we have been given as to why fundraising is good for children – character building, resourcefulness, planning, taking responsibility, etc. We respond simply by saying that children did not ask to go to school – they are forced to do so by adults who thus have the responsibility of caring for them while they are there. All those good outcomes should be taught in different ways. This is a bad way.

Having said that children should not raise money for themselves, there is a partial exception carried out by some of our schools that is an excellent practice. Bringing the high school students within the orbit of "adult" philanthropy is a critical education piece. We recommend that, having experienced the impact of making a difference for others, each member of the senior class be invited to make a gift for a financial aid endowment (the class of X endowment). The members of that class will then be asked annually to increase the corpus of that endowment so that other children can benefit from the same transformational education as they have. Of course, as class succeeds class, the administration of monies raised is in a singular endowment – the class has a piece of that. Alumni that become school parents can direct their annual gift to the annual fund and/or their class endowment.

2. The school's children can raise money for others if they are personally involved.

We prefer that this happen only at the high school level. Raising money is a skill and it is worth utilizing for the common good. Children should fundraise by focusing outside themselves. We have seen a steady rise in narcissism over the past 30 years, and they don't need their narcissism to increase even further – "it's all about me." Instead, we want to focus them on the needs of others.

Matthew 25 articulates this beautifully when Jesus says: "Then the King will say to those on his right, 'Come, you who are blessed by my Father; take your inheritance, the kingdom prepared for you since the creation of the world. For I was hungry and you gave me something to eat, I was thirsty and you gave me something to drink, I was a stranger and you invited me in, I needed clothes and you clothed me, I was sick and you looked after me, I was in prison and you came to visit me.' "Then the righteous will answer him, 'Lord, when did we see you hungry and feed you, or thirsty and give you something to drink? When did we see you as a stranger and invite you in, or needing clothes and clothe you? When did we see you sick or in prison and go to visit you?' "The King will reply, 'Truly I tell you, whatever you did for one of the least of these brothers and sisters of mine, you did for me.'"

When children raise money for others in an enterprise where they are personally involved, they are engaged in Kingdom work. We have articulated several times in this book the truth that donors who are involved typically give more than those who don't. We want our children to learn that giving themselves first matters, and that the gift then follows.

And they typically want to be involved. The CNN Heroes Young Wonder series tells inspiring stories that illustrate this wonderfully well. Here's one example.

When Campbell Remess was 9 years old, he asked his parents if he could buy Christmas presents for the children in his local hospital. His mother told him that it would cost too much. But Campbell, one of nine children whose family lives on the Australian island of Tasmania, was undeterred. He took matters into his own hands – literally.

He founded Project 365 by Campbell and, using his mother's sewing machine, started crafting one-of-a-kind teddy bears to give to sick children in the hospital and around the world. Now 13 years old, Campbell has made between 1,200 and 1,400 bears by hand. This year, he began auctioning some of his bears and using the proceeds to send children and their families on "Kindness Cruises," a much-needed escape from their battles with cancer.

"I think the magic in the bears is the hope," he said. "It's the hope that the bears give the people."

Affirm Films, a Christian film studio owned by Sony, released *5,000 Blankets* in 2022, telling the story of Phillip Bunch, whose father ended up on the streets with schizophrenia. As he and his mother searched for his father, Phillip, 7 years of age at the time, realized that many of the people he saw were not warm and he began to get blankets to give out to them. Phillipswish.com notes that "The first year 200 blankets were collected, by the fourth year, over 20,000 blankets were collected along with hundreds of hats, scarves, gloves, sleeping bags, toiletries and thousands of toys."

Summary

- Children should not fundraise for their school and their own education.
- Children must be directly involved in charitable action.
  - High school students should be incorporated into philanthropic efforts.

RETAINING DONORS

Donors are choosier and require greater accountability than they ever have. Keeping them is important for obvious reasons. But if you're not keeping them, it means you have probably:

- Treated them as a transaction, not a relationship
- Failed to thank them in a meaningful way
- Reported in a way that does not communicate responsible accountability
- Stopped praying for them

If you find that donors are not making a second and third gift, reread this book!

Ensure that you track retention of donors as assiduously as you track retention of children. Consider the following data points:

- Overall retention rate
- First-, second-, and third-year retention (remember that the first gift is the tryout gift)
- Number of new donors
- Retention by segment (parents, alumni parents, grandparents, Board, etc.)
- Number of donors in each gift category
- Number of donors that move up from one category to another
- Average gift size (split into leadership and non-leadership donors)
- Number of monthly donors and the number of years a donor has given
- Record of thank-yous made for each gift

These datasets should be part of the regular reporting regimen. It is part of the school's responsibility in getting to know the donor – establishing and strengthening the relationship. The relationship is in communication. Articulate / write down your communication plan each year for each segment of donors. Run surveys with donor segments each year to ask them a couple of questions with a simple 1–5 Likert scale to click on:

1. I love giving to CSM Christian School.
2. I appreciate the communication I receive from CSM Christian School.
3. I know my gift will be spent as promised.

An Net Promoter Style (NPS)-style question might be added:

4. I am committed to giving to CSM Christian School (0–10 scale).

Responses to these kinds of surveys and the regular interaction that you have with your donors will allow you to create a communications matrix for all donors. Identify the different kinds of donor groups that you have and what items will go to each group. There will be some that may go to all donors, such as the annual fund and invitation to the annual donor celebration BBQ. Some will go only to leadership donors. Only grandparents (or another significant adult in the child's life) will be invited to Grandparents Day (obviously). And so on. This matrix will ensure that no one is missed. Remember that your donors may be tagged with more than one designation, e.g., parent, Board member, alumnus.

WHY ARE CHRISTIAN SCHOOLS NOT LEVERAGING GENERATIONAL GIVING?

A<small>LL</small> C<small>HRISTIAN SCHOOLS MUST DEVELOP</small> an endowment. Why? Because at our typical tuition levels, we cannot afford to help all the families who need it. It's that simple. We want to be a community that embraces every aspect of the Body of Christ. We are constrained by the fact that we charge tuition. We are not embarrassed by that – and we are convicted by the limitations it places on us. While many schools seek donors who will support financial aid, that is a year-to-year strategy. It can and should be continued at the same time as more permanent funding is sought in order to drive revenues in addition to tuition that can help support an inclusive community from a socioeconomic point of view.

It can and should be continued at the same time as more permanent funding, in addition to tuition, is sought. The goal is to drive revenues that can help support an inclusive community from a socioeconomic point of view.

There are endowments for all kinds of reasons, for example:

- Endowment building to fund ongoing maintenance and improvement
- Teacher-endowed funds to support teacher leadership
- General endowment to support the work of the school
- Program endowment to provide additional support for mission trips, for example
- Endowed Chairs for important initiatives, e.g., the Chair of Biblical Justice
- Financial aid – trying to ensure that our Christian schools are need-blind

Irrespective of your school size, you must begin an endowment for that final reason. Financial aid should be the core of your endowment efforts. It's surprising that Christian schools are not doing this *en masse* because:

1. The boomer cohort was born between 1946 and 1964. They are therefore approaching their 80s at the leading edge; the youngest are pretty much at retirement age. This is a very large group of people.

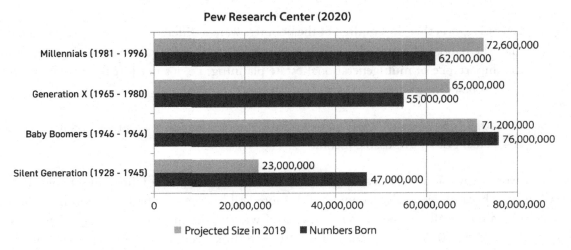

U.S. Living Adult Generations

Pew Research Center (2020)

2. During the Great Recession (2009–2010) and the COVID-19 pandemic, boomers became wealthier and millennials became poorer, i.e., overall, the boomers acted in ways that expanded their wealth.

3. The 2020 *U.S. Trust Insights on Wealth and Worth* uncovered that 31 percent of boomers said they would rather leave their money to a charity than to their family; only 55 percent thought it was important to leave an inheritance to their children.

4. Cerulli Associates research says that "U.S. households are expected to transfer close to $70 trillion to their heirs and charities by 2042. Baby Boomers are expected to pass on upward of 73% of this amount (a total of $51 trillion)."

5. From the same source, the importance of planning that transfer, including to charities (think your school) is paramount: "Advisors planning for clients who have significant capital gains exposure beyond the million-dollar threshold should consider stringently managing taxable income by realizing gains up to certain levels, if possible, and plan a strategic gifting and/or donation plan," says Chayce Horton, analyst.

SIMON JEYNES

6. Penelope Burk asks whether raising money is not holding back philanthropy, i.e., planned giving: "Among donors who had already assigned a bequest to a not-for-profit, only 20% said that a representative of the beneficiary had played some role in influencing their decision. And among respondents with a will but **with no assigned bequest to date** (emphasis added), 59 percent referenced issues that not-for-profits can influence, such as "being asked to include a gift in my will by a not-for-profit I admire" (2018).

7. CNBC reports that the children of the boomers want a different and more personal model than the hands-off approach many boomers take / took. Many advisers are talking about the importance of multigenerational estate planning, i.e, it's not just the parents schools need to be talking with.

8. The 2015 *U.S. News & World Report*'s Baby Boomer Report states that boomers control 70+ percent of all disposable income.

In other words, there is a great deal of wealth that is accessible to us in Christian schools. This is even more so because, generally, boomers with more children tend to be Christian. In addition, our families are typically in the top three deciles of wealth. The site dqydj.com says that average household worth in 2020 was $746,821. But in the top three deciles it was higher than that:

%ile	2020	2017	Difference	% Difference
70%	$314,920.61	$298,494.39	$16,426.22	5.5%
71%	$328,617.37	$314,859.74	$13,757.63	4.4%
72%	$349,362.49	$332,360.59	$17,001.90	5.1%
73%	$365,919.18	$346,527.00	$19,392.18	5.6%
74%	$382,911.64	$367,447.18	$15,464.46	4.2%
75%	$403,283.56	$394,492.37	$8,791.19	2.2%
76%	$428,623.03	$421,013.90	$7,609.13	1.8%
77%	$455,610.73	$441,910.73	$13,700.00	3.1%
78%	$485,176.88	$467,978.84	$17,198.04	3.7%
79%	$523,925.50	$500,978.37	$22,947.13	4.6%
80%	$558,189.68	$533,012.92	$25,176.76	4.7%
81%	$591,350.95	$578,522.31	$12,828.64	2.2%
82%	$637,050.12	$622,853.45	$14,196.67	2.3%
83%	$681,782.41	$666,924.42	$14,857.99	2.2%
84%	$737,122.98	$719,876.99	$17,245.99	2.4%

85%	$795,218.85	$788,261.25	$6,957.60	0.9%
86%	$854,908.75	$862,009.45	-$7,100.70	-0.8%
87%	$928,665.81	$941,483.86	-$12,818.05	-1.4%
88%	$991,188.75	$1,042,954.25	-$51,765.50	-5.0%
89%	$1,085,969.92	$1,141,861.62	-$55,891.70	-4.9%
90%	$1,219,126.46	$1,262,318.06	-$43,191.60	-3.4%
91%	$1,355,268.26	$1,407,054.31	-$51,786.05	-3.7%
92%	$1,541,905.98	$1,543,296.95	-$1,390.97	-0.1%
93%	$1,767,510.16	$1,791,063.57	-$23,553.41	-1.3%
94%	$2,080,569.86	$2,169,622.95	-$89,053.09	-4.1%
95%	$2,584,130.26	$2,538,733.22	$45,397.04	1.8%
96%	$3,294,388.49	$2,987,342.24	$307,046.25	10.3%
97%	$4,640,603.15	$3,954,145.12	$686,458.03	17.4%
98%	$6,557,022.79	$6,209,387.36	$347,635.43	5.6%
99%	$11,099,166.07	$11,075,297.97	$23,868.10	0.2%

Steps to take:

1. Most important, if you are still doing fundraising events (transactional philanthropy), move to an annual fund (relational philanthropy). CSM can help with onsite workshops that get you going the first year, raising thousands of dollars more than you do now.

2. Tithe your annual giving to endowment (a CSM KPI) to inspire donors and to already begin to support your financial-aid budget. Set a 10 percent spending policy.

3. Almost most importantly, if you are not collecting your data systematically, start right now. You can't have a relationship with someone you don't know, and your data should be able to tell you a lot, allowing you also to sustain relationships through personnel changes.

4. Improve your volunteer leadership significantly. A base number of volunteers in philanthropy is 24, irrespective of the size of school. Larger schools can integrate far larger numbers.

5. Profile and build personal relationships with the donors who give 80+ percent of your fundraising. Put all your donors into a table. Figure out where 80 percent of dollars is. Draw a line. Those are the donors you should be personally talking to, inviting into the school, understanding their passions, connecting their heart to the mission of the school.

6. Find someone, a volunteer as well as a professional if you can afford them, to focus entirely on endowment giving as part of the overall philanthropy of the school.

7. This is a caveat thing to do. If you are still fundraising to cover the operations expense gap, close the gap through Strategic Planning / Strategic Financial Management with tuition. Each year, include a .5 percent to 1 percent raise in tuition just to reduce that gap and free up philanthropic dollars to work miracles in the lives of children.

8. Top donors are giving to fewer charities than they have in the past, so you are totally privileged to have captured their interest. Don't disappoint them – thank them, tell them how their gifts mattered, show the impact in the lives of children. Don't hesitate to ask them whether you are part of their estate.

9. Ensure you continually mine your annual giving data to find the next leadership donors, recognizing that younger donors who might give less now are still eager to participate if they are inspired.

There is much to say and learn about planned giving. This chapter is not the place – but it can potentially serve as a wake-up call for you and your school. Think about this time as a God-given opportunity for radical change in your financial abilities because of this going-on-now transfer of generational wealth that will continue for the next decade or so.

TITHING TO ENDOWMENT IN THE CHRISTIAN SCHOOL

INDEPENDENT SCHOOLS ARE SOMETHING OF an exception in the nonprofit world. Most nonprofits operate almost exclusively on the basis of donations, grants, and government funding. We, on the other hand, operate largely on the basis of income from educational services provided – tuition. Donations of various kinds help us finish our annual budgeting, do something extra, or provide capital funds for buildings and land purchases.

Endowment is a special kind of donation. Donations to endowment build a corpus of money that provides the school with strategic (long-range) potential for investment back into the school. In Christian schools, the purpose of endowment should first be to support financial aid.

Your ability to provide financial aid is limited. Typically, a school with an $8,000 tuition level can only "afford" to spend 10 percent of gross tuition on financial aid.

While we work with schools that are spending 30+ percent of their gross tuition in financial aid, this is not because it is good economics. It is always at the expense of appropriate compensation and funding the school's programs, i.e., the money given away above 10 percent should have been spent on compensation and program. It is important for the Christian school to desire to include all families who are mission appropriate and who want their children educated within the love and care of a Christian community. It is not practical to include all within the context of the operating budget on its own.

This means that Christian schools typically are forced to restrict the amount of financial aid they offer, both absolutely (the percentage of gross tuition) as well as individually (the amount they are willing to give an individual family). This is where endowment comes in.

Let's take an actual school example where the school has a genuine, lived-out mission to inclusion:

Number of Students = 170
Full Tuition = $7,200

Actual Tuition Income: $568,600	Operating Expenses: $998,183	
Shortfall: $429,583	Donations: $429,600	Profit / Loss: $17
Gross Tuition: $1,224,000	Financial Aid: $655,400	Percentage: 53.5%
Number of Students times Tuition	*Gross Tuition minus Actual Tuition Income*	

It is clear from this example that, while donations are significant, they are not covering the actual financial aid. In other words, there is a mismatch of $225,800 (financial aid minus donations) that is not provided for in the budget and that is coming "out of" compensation and program. And the percentage of financial aid is very high (53.5 percent), also putting downward pressure on compensation and program.

One question might be to ask whether the level of donations is sustainable. But for this section we ask a different question: how might endowment help this school sustain its vision for inclusion? We believe that all Christian schools must be committed to radical inclusion – to admitting all mission-appropriate families who wish to come without regard to capacity to pay. That may be impractical in the here and now, but keeping it as the desired outcome aids us in thinking through the question of endowment. This leads to the first step to take if you have no endowment-building strategy currently.

We recommend to all Christian schools that the Board create policy to tithe (10 percent) of their annual fundraising to endowment. All requests to give to the annual fund and to any annual event designated for annual giving (such as the banquet, silent auction, etc.) should include the statement that the total of annual giving will be tithed to the school's endowment as designated by the Board.

We further recommend that the Board designate the annual spending policy for this endowment be also a tithe (10 percent). Let's take the example of an actual school. This school has created a plan (Strategic Financial Management) that will create a surplus, feeding a nascent endowment:

	Year 1	Year 2	Year 3	Year 4	Year 5
Income	2,067,866	2,120,300	2,261,909	2,402,969	2,537,743
Expenses	2,340,884	2,192,100	2,288,903	2,384,750	2,490,410
Operations +/-	(273,018)	(71,800)	(26,994)	18,219	47,333
Donations	86,498	95,147	104,662	114,082	124,349
Tithe to Endowment 10%	0	0	10,466	11,408	12,435
Profit / Loss	(186,520)	23,348	67,202	120,893	159,247
Endowment	0	0	10,466	21,874	33,263
Spending Policy 10%	0	0	0	1,047	2,187

Good financial management will take this school, based on its current enrollment, to a surplus position feeding both a cash reserve and an endowment. By the end of this plan, the school will be receiving a cash influx to support a greater-than-10-percent financial-aid program.

It is critical for the Board to understand that endowment is multigenerational in nature. While this looks tiny and insignificant right now, over two generations it can become strong and generative for families who wish to attend the school.

Building endowment is two-pronged. This first key step speaks to the school's seriousness about its generational mission. It gives evidence of the school's fiscal prudence. It provides confidence about the school's stewardship. The second step is for the school's Philanthropy Committee to develop endowment-building policies approved by the Board that lead to gifts from donors specific to the endowment.

Endowment is seeded by the school. Endowment gains speed and traction through planned giving. The Philanthropy Committee, once it has annual giving under its belt, can begin to develop a pipeline of donors who will give to endowment as part of their estate and / or in other ways.

As you reflect on whether your school is ready to begin its endowment, ask these questions:

1. Do you have a Strategic Plan in operation and underlying the Board's actions?
2. Do you have Strategic Financial Management, the financial plan providing discipline and stewardship to the vision?
3. Have you included the operations reserve as a key strategic item in both elements?

If the answer to these three questions is yes, then you are ready to think about your endowment.

Remember: the CSM Mary Principle articulates five standards for philanthropic giving:

1. Giving is in gratitude for what has been done.
2. Giving is done by people who are intimately involved with the action.
3. Giving includes involvement, not just the act of giving itself.
4. Giving galvanizes possibilities that otherwise could not be imagined.
5. Giving is recognized and honored.

THE ENDOWMENT LIFE CYCLE

Schools in their entrepreneurial stage give more thought to specific needs and create a title to fit that need. Examples include starting with an Admission Director, then adding a Database Manager, then a Philanthropy Director. Admission and philanthropy begin to fill parallel roles, with admission coming first and then handing over the parent downstream to philanthropy. Often the Business Office is the third spoke, from a parent perspective.

Stewarding the parent from the moment of admission inquiry through to their long-term relationship must be the priority of the school. Therefore, the school must revisit the staff positions and be encouraged to follow an advancement model, where admission, philanthropy, and marketing are under one department. The advantages:

- The database is shared.
- Expectations of the annual fund are communicated to parents during the enrollment process.
- Potential donors who surface during the admission phase are cultivated earlier.
- Marketing materials are designed with admission and philanthropy input. All branding is standardized.
- The team functions as one, supporting the calendar needs of each function.

We want to reiterate the importance of endowment for Christian schools. CSM does not believe that this is an optional extra but a key part of the school's strategy to fulfill its mission. Very simply, this is because the school can (and should) give away 10 percent of its gross tuition as financial aid. And that is not enough to meet the needs of every family that would come to our schools. So we need another source of income. Endowment is strategically the major source of that income. The reason for endowment in a Christian school is to support financial aid. That does not mean it cannot or should not support other causes. Those are "really nice to have." Financial aid is a necessity to fulfill our mandate from God.

We have written at length about the Christian value of "inclusion," the Christian idea that the Good News is for all nations, a phrase that occurs repeatedly in Scripture. Here are but a few examples:

- Abraham will surely become a great and powerful nation, and all nations on earth will be blessed through him (Genesis 18:18).
- Declare his glory among the nations, his marvelous deeds among all peoples (1 Chronicles 16:24).
- May his name endure forever; may it continue as long as the sun. Then all nations will be blessed through him, and they will call him blessed (Psalms 72:17).
- At that time they will call Jerusalem The Throne of the Lord, and all nations will gather in Jerusalem to honor the name of the Lord (Jeremiah 3:17).
- Therefore go and make disciples of all nations, baptizing them in the name of the Father and of the Son and of the Holy Spirit (Matthew 28:19).

This is emphasized in the ministry of Jesus, who spoke to and visited and welcomed and sought out as his Father expected him to "because he has anointed me to proclaim good news to the poor. He has sent me to proclaim freedom for the prisoners and recovery of sight for the blind, to set the oppressed free, to proclaim the year of the Lord's favor (Luke 4:18-19). Thus the Christian school is a welcoming place for all children, for all families who are attracted to the school's mission and want their children brought up in its embrace, in the love and fear of the Lord. This is not about socioeconomic diversity. It comes from a different place entirely – the basic premise that the Christian school wants every sheep to be brought back to the shepherd. Where there is a financial obstacle, the Christian school is honor bound to find a solution.

What if you currently don't have an endowment at all? Or what if you have a "large" one? We know Christian schools with tuitions less than $13,207 who have zero and who have almost $20 million.

Here is the CSM Endowment Life Cycle:

Entrepreneurial	Adolescent	Mature	Dying
Financial aid is >30% and funded from operations	Financial aid is >20% and funded from operations	Financial aid is 10%, funded from operations and additional aid funded from endowment	Financial aid is secular: it becomes about budget, not about extending God's Kingdom
No endowment	Some endowment (provides <10% additional financial aid)	Significant endowment (provides at least an additional 10% financial aid)	Having an endowment is more important than spending it
Tuition does not cover expenses and is tactical	Tuition almost covers expenses and is tactical	Tuition covers expenses and is strategic	Tuition becomes "greedy"
Event-based, transactional fundraising	Annual giving and missional relationship-building with donors	Major gifts and planned giving to expand opportunity	The donor has influence to affect and even direct the mission
Fundraising is to cover the budget	Fundraising is to enhance the student experience	Fundraising is to build for future generations	Fundraising is to impress society
Enthusiastic volunteers	Philanthropy Committee	Foundation Board	Independent and proud Board
Action to take	**Action to take**	**Action to take**	**Action to take**
Increase tuition income to cover operations expenses	Increase tuition income to cover operations expenses	Maintain value of tuition and raise it strategically	Review the school's mission and revert to needs rather than wants
Tithe fundraising to endowment	Tithe fundraising to endowment	Engage with donors around multigenerational impact	Refuse gifts that are not mission appropriate
Develop an endowment plan	Communicate the endowment plan	Develop a foundation to run the endowment	Refocus the foundation / school Board on servant leadership

Entrepreneurial Phase of Endowment

You may be a relatively new school in the first 10 years of existence, or you may be a school 30 or 40 years old now adapting to a fast-changing environment. In this phase, fundraising might include asking highly committed people for money, but mostly it revolves around transactional fundraising where money is exchanged for a benefit: selling goods like poinsettias, Easter lilies, chocolate bars; putting on gala dinners, golf tournaments.

This is often against a backdrop of financial insecurity. Tuition is designed to be so low that fundraising is required in order to make it through every year. Compensation is also low as a result, and there are rarely excellent supplies for the school's programs so they can deliver the mission. If there are extraordinary expenditures such as a leaking roof, this causes anxiety or even crisis. Planning, including budgeting, is done on a day-to-day, year-to-year basis. Financial aid is given away at a rate far exceeding 10 percent of gross tuition.

In these circumstances, typically everyone is working extremely hard and doing a great job. However, looking down the road, it is not sustainable either financially or from a workload standpoint. The Board and Principal must:

1. Lead using a Strategic Plan / Strategic Financial Management
2. Carry out the discipline of tithing to endowment
3. Carry out the discipline of beginning to create a reserve
4. Increase tuition and / or enrollment (including class size) with the objective of covering operations expenses with tuition and fees
5. Stop any growth in financial aid until the endowment can support it
6. Begin to create an endowment plan

Adolescent Phase of Endowment

You are leading from a Strategic Plan / Strategic Financial Management and you have instituted disciplines of tithing, creating operations reserves, and covering expenses. You are not there yet but the vector is clear. You are maximizing class size in order to serve the optimal number of students and that is making you more efficient financially.

You have significantly reduced or eliminated all but one of your fundraising events and turned them into community-building activities. In their place, you have instituted annual giving, a respectful way of approaching donors and asking them to support / invest in the school and its mission. Transactional giving is being replaced by missional giving.

As a result, fundraising receipts are going up and your ability to enhance the student experience by providing more and better resources for learning is growing. The standard of education you provide has increased and demand for your school in your community has increased with it. Teacher morale is up as they ask for resources and actually receive them without having to use their own funds.

In these circumstances, greater confidence means that the Board and Principal can move a little faster. Sustainability from a financial point of view now is possible, and improving finances means that the school can employ a team that more equitably and effectively shares the workload. The Board and Principal must:

1. Continue to lead using the discipline of a Strategic Plan / Strategic Financial Management and develop the Philanthropy Committee
2. Continue to carry out the discipline of tithing to endowment
3. Ensure that there is a clear objective of maintaining two or three months of operating reserves (a Key Performance Indicator)
4. Take the last steps to cover the gap between income and expenses so that fundraising can be applied directly to mission delivery (student experience and program)
5. Develop an emerging financial-aid policy and vector that supports an inclusive student body
6. Communicate the endowment plan as part of ongoing relationship-building with actual and potential donors – and as part (a small part) of the conversation during the admission process

Mature Phase of Endowment

You are leading from a Strategic Plan / Strategic Financial Management, and new members are being brought onto the Board to effectively carry the plan out. This highly intentional recruitment results in high performance in the execution of the Strategic Plan / Strategic Financial Management.

Leadership depth is evident in the Philanthropy Committee; it acts both in support of annual giving as well as proactively seeking leadership gifts for capital and endowment funding. Giving to the annual fund is optimal. The impact of annual giving on the school is visible since it is going to enhance the experience of the students while expenses are covered through tuition and fees. As a result, donors are highly motivated and participation rates are increasing.

The Board and Principal must:

1. Consider tuition within the patience and discipline of a Strategic Plan / Strategic Financial Management
2. Continue to carry out the discipline of tithing from fundraising to endowment
3. Meet the operations reserve objective of two to three months operating expense (a Key Performance Indicator)
4. Develop and sustain a focus on planned and estate giving to build endowment with large gifts
5. Consider setting up the endowment under a separate organizational structure with its own Board
6. Ensure that the funding of financial aid over the 10 percent in the operations budget continues to increase, ensuring the school is more and more inclusive

Dying Phase of Endowment

Success is a funny thing. As Christians, we rely heavily on the grace of God and pray continuously for his blessing. Once we believe that the blessing has been given, we ~~can~~ may forget that the real blessing was actually not the money but the children whose lives we had the privilege of serving. Once it appears the endowment is successful, the money that represents that success can become the same problem as it was for the rich man who "went away sad, because he had great wealth" (Mark 10:22).

The "dying phase" is not about making poor investment decisions or raiding the endowment to support the finances of the school during an economic downturn. It is about a change in the hearts and minds of those in the school and on the Board, including the foundation Board, if you have one. It is a spiritual death that represents the endowment, not as the gift of a generous and loving God, but as the means to prestige and power. This is not theoretical. This is based on observation of Christian school cultures and the effect that money can have on them if money is not subordinated to mission.

The Board and Principal must:

1. Refocus the school on the school's mission
2. Re-read and study the life of Jesus as one who came to serve (Matthew 20: 28)
3. Review the CSM Key Performance Indicators (KPI)

4. Eliminate the influence of those who do not understand that children are the point, not power or prestige
5. Maintain a strategic, next-generation, outlook
6. Ensure the endowment is part of a culture of generosity and inclusion / welcome

Last Words

Paying attention to endowment is an important aspect of leadership at a Christian school. It is neither tangential nor the last thing to be done but an essential component of what it means to be a welcoming community.

Notes:

1. A financial Key Performance Indicator (KPI) is that the Christian school tithes from its fundraising to its endowment – CSM teaches that 10 percent of all fundraising income from any source goes into the school's endowment. This is not the school's operations reserve, money that comes from surplus and a different Key Performance Indicator.
2. The concept of life cycle is based on organizational theory.

PAYING YOUR PHILANTHROPY STAFF

Schools are "odd" insofar as their income is not primarily derived from fundraising or grants. The vast majority of nonprofits have a dominant source of funding – individual donations, corporate donations, government grants. For schools, the dominant source of funding is tuition, i.e., selling a product – education – to a captive population (every child must go to school). Christian schools fund (or should fund) their operations from this dominant source, tuition. This means that our schools do not rely on philanthropy to stay open on a day-to-day basis.

Our philanthropy staff are therefore support positions, not the "main thing." Here's an example of pay in the average nonprofit.

Job Title	Average Salary (USD)	Average Salary (CAD)
Executive Director	$73,174	$68,493
Fundraising Manager	$58,326	$60,038
Program Coordinator	$48,368	$48,625
Administrative Assistant	$52,522	$44,603

Free Resources, Guides, Toolkits and More | Keela accessed August 28, 2024

This doesn't match what happens in our Christian schools where the Executive Director is the Principal and is paid in a marketplace not parallel to nonprofits. Education is the school's marketplace and our salaries reflect that reality. Be wary in trying to find examples. Looking online, unless you are looking at specifically private / Christian schools, is not that helpful.

The variables in administrative school salary include the number of children enrolled; the number of divisions; the geography of the school; the subset of schools the school belongs to, such as Montessori, or Christian Reformed or Catholic or Lutheran. Many of these groups have their own pay scales.

Sometimes we imagine that, because we are Christian, that salary is lower on the list of requirements. That may be true to the extent that the applicant is a second income. We can see the outcome of that in our teaching staff, who are majority female and second income. As soon as you move outside teaching and into administration, salary matters a lot. For most in these positions, salary is a major reason for applying for an administrative position. Of course, everyone is and wants to be mission aligned. Job satisfaction matters. Working in a Christian environment with fellow believers is usually crucial. And salary matters. A lot.

CSM advises that we think about salary on the basis of ratios and position. There is no clever justification for this except that of practicality and realism. This is what is expected in the industry. From top to bottom, we have these positions:

1. Principal / Head of School – highest-paid employee, salary at least 20 percent higher than the next highest salary
2. Philanthropy Director and Chief Financial Officer – "compete" for the next highest salary, based on who has greater experience and / or longevity within the organization
3. Academic leaders
4. Database Manager and Annual Fund Manager and Family Relations Manager
5. Alumni Relations Coordinator

The Planned Giving Officer can be a maverick in the compensation scheme. We have seen salaries all over the place. However, the skills implicit in this position usually put compensation into the second-tier level.

It is important in compensation for positions in philanthropy that there be no incentives or bonuses tied to the amount raised. We still see advertisements talking about receiving a percentage. CSM, along with all the other professional organizations in the field, consider this unethical and an invitation to very poor practices. It is unacceptable in Christian schools.

CSM ties the Database Manager to a five-to-seven-year teacher salary, and the Annual Fund Manager to a one-to-three-year teacher salary. This ratio is helpful in establishing the band of compensation the school is comfortable in offering.

Notice the importance of titles and salary / compensation. Our schools can be careless about the way titles are handed out. Establish your own hierarchy – CSM uses Director, Manager, Coordinator. Recognize that each level of title has its own salary expectations. Think this through carefully. Don't hand out grandiose titles where equally grandiose salaries may be expected, raising your administrative costs. Also, ensure that the responsibilities match the titles. It is very expensive to promote the Annual Fund Manager to Philanthropy Director with the salary jump, but see no correlating increase in skills and responsibilities. It's just a title.

Paying your Philanthropy Officers appropriately honors and respects them. Christian schools are expected to do that.

OTHER ROLES THAT IMPACT PHILANTHROPY IN CHRISTIAN SCHOOLS

Teachers

Teachers are the front line of philanthropy in the school. It's not surprising that neither the administrators, nor the teachers themselves, think about teachers when they are planning for philanthropy. Teachers are there to teach children, not to market or solicit. That's true. And, at the same time, in Christian schools teachers have to accept that their role is strategic as well as tactical. While they spend their time with the children, their communications and networking are crucial to both retention of children and to the success of philanthropy. If the parents, generally the primary donors to your school, do not have confidence in the school, they will not be strongly supportive. Confidence comes first through the relationship of family to teacher.

Teachers cannot support when they have not been engaged. Ensure:

- They are taught the basic tenets of philanthropy, i.e., that annual giving accomplishes two things: creates a culture of philanthropy and uncovers the next generation of leadership donors.
- They are the first to know what is going on – they should not hear news about the school from the parents.
- They understand the annual fund / comprehensive campaigns, seeing that these efforts are crucial to adding the next layer of excellence to what they do as teachers and support them directly in their work.

- They are giving. If they are not invited (by their peers) to participate, they will not see this as a personal commitment as well as a professional connection.
- They participate in developing the "teacher's list" of objectives that will influence how the annual fund is shaped each year.
- They are thanked in meaningful ways.

Teachers need and appreciate direction about their communications. If your teachers have come from the public system, they are not skilled in parent communication and are likely to see it as a distraction. If your teachers are new to teaching, parent communication is very low on their list of essentials – you must raise it to a high level. If well guided, teachers will immediately appreciate how communicating effectively will help them in their daily tasks as well as forward the strategic objectives of the school as a whole.

If your teachers are "experienced," i.e., they have been at the school for a while, they may have never been engaged in *marketing* and may be suspicious of the whole idea. They must know that their experience and influence is important and can be leveraged to benefit their children. Ensure that teachers know:

1. They are leaders in the interface between the school and its constituencies (current families, alumni families, alumni students, community connections, church relationships).
2. Their time is valued and should indeed be spent almost 100 percent with the children.
3. Their presence and participation in public events and in annual giving is inspirational to families and makes a difference.
4. We want them to focus their communication on mission benefit, not on "what" they do.
5. The time teachers spend on communication doesn't change; its focus shifts from features (day-to-day activities) into storytelling about the great (true) things happening in the lives of children (benefits). This leads naturally to children re-enrolling and parents making philanthropic investment in the school.

TRUE STORY

At a school CSM serves, the teachers were asked to share their elevator speeches. This was before any training had happened. The challenge was: you have 30 seconds or less to share about your school. What would you say? The result was boring, not easy to understand, and certainly not going to lead to further conversation. They tried to explain the philosophy of the school, talked about where the school was.

They were then asked to share a story about a child who had experienced something amazing at their school. The change was radical – they were far more animated, there were some tears, they talked about a real person, the time wasn't long enough.

Jesus told stories intended to engage, make the listener come back for more, teach something important, point the hearer back to himself as the storyteller. It was done so well, people would literally walk around the Sea of Galilee to get back to Jesus. That's what "benefit-based" communication is.

Athletic Director

Athletics has an outsize footprint and impact in U.S. Christian schools. It is important in Canadian Christian schools too but doesn't have the same dominance. In either place, the impact of athletics is significant in terms of the facilities it requires and the amount of money needed in relation to anything else in the budget. It is outside the school day and not every child participates. For the majority who do, it has enormous value and importance. It is a place of competition, of physical endeavor, of leadership opportunity, a potential entryway to university scholarships, a place where renown can be achieved. The entryway of many schools is often dominated by trophy cases with usually exclusively athletic trophies in them.

The connection between the Athletic Director / coaches and the athletes is often a deep one. They know the athletes in good and bad times. They push them to an extreme. They have fun together. They strive for excellence. At all levels, whether varsity, JV, or intramural, there is a connection between the coach and student that is palpable. What the athletes are asked to do places them at significant physical risk as the emergency departments at hospitals across North America attest. All this leads to an important bonding among the athletes themselves and between the individual athlete and coach.

This is paralleled on the sidelines or gym bleachers with the more hands-off relationship between the coach and the parents. Most schools now have agreements that parents must sign concerning appropriate conduct on their part at practices and games, attesting to the emotional importance of athletics in the lives of families. Bad behavior is more prevalent and collegiate-level recruiting now takes the parents and their involvement into account!

From a philanthropy point of view, this situation also places the Athletic Director and sometimes the coach in a position of great influence. We see this in the activities of booster clubs, dealt with earlier in this book. The willingness of parents to give to their own child's sport to benefit the possibility of success is significant.

It is crucial (CRUCIAL!) that the Athletic Director clearly understands his / her responsibility as a school representative. In a very few schools, but enough to make this point worthwhile, athletics becomes a kingdom unto itself and sees itself also as a competitor in the resources marketplace.

In those schools, the Athletic Director becomes an adversary to the school's annual fund or comprehensive campaign. Unwilling to wait for their turn in the line, athletics goes and seeks its own funding in direct conflict with its own school. Fortunately, this is rare but it is an ever-present threat. We have met many great Athletic Directors who are completely integrated into their school's philanthropic efforts, understand they are part of a team, are willing to make long-range plans for their own needs, and take their turn in having them fulfilled.

As always, the school's mission and a child-centered approach provide the athletics staff with the correct context and attitude.

- The child is there for the entire mission, not just the athletics part of it.
- The Athletic Director and coaches must see the student-athlete holistically, not just as an athlete. Just as the academicians have to realize that the child does not do math or social studies all day, athletics has to understand the child's larger context and honor and respect it.
- Relational philanthropy makes the pie bigger for everyone, when we operate as a team.
- We will raise more money together than through booster clubs or the like. Athletics will benefit much more in this community approach.
- The influence of the Athletic Director and the coaches must be used to support the school's overall goals. This influence motivates some leadership donors. Educating those donors that athletics will have its turn matters.
- The Athletic Director and coaches must evince the highest integrity when working with donors and potential donors.
- The relationships the Athletic Director and coaches have with donors must be honored by the philanthropy leaders and incorporated into the team approach.
- The Athletic Director must be part of the philanthropy team at the planning stage and in the implementation stage.

Visual and Performing Arts

Briefly, what has been written about athletics applies to a subset of children and parents in the visual and performing arts as well. There is incredible commitment and loyalty in these areas, and the comments above should be considered to be applicable here too.

Family Relations

The person in charge of the admission process has a privileged position. This is the person to whom the parents entrust the deepest of family secrets as they strive to ensure the school is the best fit for their child. They share behavior, medical, spiritual, and emotional characteristics. The conversations during the admission process can be the most raw / revealing in the child's entire time at the school.

The Family Relations Director (FRD), also known as the Admission Director, is often the person the parent will call one or two or even more years later if they are having an issue with the school. The parents believe that the personal knowledge the FRD has of the family's situation makes them a credible source of advice, and even an ally in advocating for the child. The vulnerability implicit in FRD conversations and the emotional connection that is created makes this a position that has a long-term relationship with many / most parents.

While that is not leveraged into raising money, it is insider knowledge that, appropriately shared, can have great meaning in the philanthropy relationship between the parent and the school.

School Receptionist

Your school receptionist, whatever their official title, is the first face every donor sees on entering the school. This person knows much more than it might at first appear because they:

- See every visitor and know who they typically need to see, what their style is, how they approach their business
- Talk to everyone who calls the school and understand the pattern of calls – the one-offs, the repeats, those who get irritated easily, those who can be cared for immediately.
- Connect with every child that visits the office for whatever reason.
- Know how everyone in the building deals with interruptions, with requests, with visits, with difficult questions and easy ones.
- Know the calendar and what is going on officially and unofficially.

The school receptionist is the master of patterns. People operate in patterned ways. The receptionist sees and can identify those patterns. This is important information. There are key moments when the school receptionist is brought into the conversation, including the identification of potential new leadership donors.

Appendix One

SELECT BIBLIOGRAPHY

Burk P., (2018) **Donor Centered Fundraising: Second Edition** Cygnus Applied Research, Inc.: Hamilton, ON

Carmody D. P., and Lewis M., **Brain Activation When Hearing One's Own and Others' Names** *Brain Res.* 2006 October 20; 1116(1): 153–158.

Cialdini R. (2021) **Influence: The Power of Persuasion** HarperBusiness expanded edition: New York, New York

Dillon M. R., (2012) **Giving and Getting in the Kingdom: A Field Guide** Moody Publishers: Chicago, IL

Giving USA: The Annual Report on Philanthropy for the Year 2022 (2023). Chicago: Giving USA Foundation.

Giving USA: The Annual Report on Philanthropy for the Year 2023 (2024). Chicago: Giving USA Foundation.

Grace K. S. (2005) **Beyond Fund-raising: New Strategies for Nonprofit Innovation and Investment** John Wiley & Sons: Hoboken, New Jersey

Greenfield, J. M. (2009) **Fundraising Responsibilities of Non Profit Boards** BoardSource: Washington, D.C.

Nouwen, Henri J. M. (2010) **A Spirituality of Fundraising** Upper Room Books: Nashville, TN

Putnam R. (2020) **Bowling Alone: the Collapse and Revival of American Community** Simon & Schuster: New York, New York

Scott S. (2002) **Fierce Conversations: Achieving Success at Work and in Life One Conversation at a Time** Penguin: New York, New York

CSM PROFESSIONAL CODE OF ETHICS

Professionals and volunteers who practice philanthropy in Christian schools make these commitments to their donors:

1. We promise to build a relationship with you as Jesus did with his own Philanthropy Committee (Luke 8:3).
2. We promise to cover our "ask" with a canopy of prayer.
3. We promise that we will use your gift to move the school forward on behalf of the children, within the context of a plan showing excellent stewardship and financial sustainability.
4. We promise to strategically ensure that philanthropy dollars go to extending the mission in the life of the child and will not be diverted to running the operations budget, except to support financial aid.
5. We promise not to show partiality to one over another because of the gifts they have or have not made.
6. We promise to accept only gifts that are mission-appropriate.
7. We promise to involve you, if you wish, as a partner with the school.
8. We promise that asking you to invest in God's work at the school will be accompanied by the school's accountability and good stewardship in spending your money in the way you intended.
9. We promise that we are paid a salary and not a commission.
10. We promise to be grateful to God and to you for your generosity to the "family of believers" in the school, ask you for gifts that fit your own prosperity, and honor you as a giver.

The Donor Bill of Rights (AFP)

Philanthropy is based on voluntary action for the common good. It is a tradition of giving and sharing that is primary to the quality of life. To assure that philanthropy merits the respect and trust of the general public, and that donors and prospective donors can have full confidence in the not-for-profit organizations and causes they are asked to support, we declare that all donors have these rights:

I. To be informed of the organization's mission, of the way the organization intends to use donated resources, and of its capacity to use donations effectively for their intended purposes.

II. To be informed of the identity of those serving on the organization's governing board, and to expect the board to exercise prudent judgment in its stewardship responsibilities.

III. To have access to the organization's most recent financial statements.

IV. To be assured their gifts will be used for the purposes for which they were given.

V. To receive appropriate acknowledgement and recognition.

VI. To be assured that information about their donation is handled with respect and with confidentiality to the extent provided by law.

VII. To expect that all relationships with individuals representing organizations of interest to the donor will be professional in nature.

VIII. To be informed whether those seeking donations are volunteers, employees of the organization or hired solicitors.

IX. To have the opportunity for their names to be deleted from mailing lists that an organization may intend to share.

X. To feel free to ask questions when making a donation and to receive prompt, truthful and forthright answers.

The donor Bill of Rights was created by the Association of Fundraising Professionals (AFP), the Association for Healthcare Philanthropy (AHP), the Council for Advancement and Support of Education (CASE), and the Giving Institute: Leading Consultants to Non-Profits. It has been endorsed by numerous organizations.

Commitment Form

School Name: _____

Principal Name: _____

Board President Name: _____

On behalf of our school, we commit to the philanthropic ethical standards as identified in the CSM Philanthropy Code of Ethics and the AFP Donor Bill of Rights. We agree to put them on our website and display the CSM Certified Code of Ethics logo acknowledging the high standards to which we are called as we engage with our community.

Date: _____

CSM Mission: For Jesus; Through Mission; With Students

THE OX PRINCIPLE (2024)

Scripture notes the Ox Principle specifically and directly. It comes from both the New Testament and Hebrew Scriptures. How we treat people in relationship to stewarding money is an important part of excellent Christian school leadership resulting in sustainably excellent education.

> 1 Timothy 6:17
> "Do not muzzle an ox while it is treading out the grain."

> Numbers 18:21 (NIV)
> "I give to the Levites all the tithes in Israel as their inheritance in return for the work they do while serving at the tent of meeting."

> 1 Timothy 5:8
> "Anyone who does not provide for their relatives, and especially for their own household, has denied the faith and is worse than an unbeliever."

> Proverbs 22:7
> "The rich rule over the poor, and the borrower is slave to the lender."

> Exodus 41:33-36
> "And now let Pharaoh look for a discerning and wise man and put him in charge of the land of Egypt. Let Pharaoh appoint commissioners over the land to take a fifth of the harvest of Egypt during the seven years of abundance. They should collect all the food of these good years that are coming and store up the grain under the authority of Pharaoh, to be kept in the cities for food. This food should be held in reserve for the country, to be used during the seven years of famine that will come upon Egypt, so that the country may not be ruined by the famine."

The Christian school thinks about money a lot. It enjoys the thought that God provides richly for his people. It wants to have the best resources it can to serve its children. It is neither embarrassed nor ashamed to talk about God's gift of money. The school has an obligation to:

- Meet the Kingdom / moral / arithmetic needs of the strategic budget.
- Compensate its employees honorably and respectfully.
- Provide a safe and optimal learning environment.
- Minimize / eliminate debt.
- Maintain an operations reserve.

Let's start with the last item first: maintain an operations reserve. The Minnesota Council of Nonprofits discovered that "nonprofits with minimal or no reserves were more likely to have cut budgets, eliminated staff positions, reduced wages and benefits. They were also less likely to increase services to respond to growing demand." That is, if your school has no cash reserves, it is in a constantly unstable situation, whether it needs to deal with economic hard times in a healthy way or to respond to economic good times by being able to take advantage of opportunities. Each Christian school needs a cash operations reserve equivalent to three months of operating expenses.

And there is no justification in the Christian school for taking the attitude that the Lord will provide. Certainly, there are times when the widow's jar of oil stays miraculously full. And we rejoice in the goodness of our God. At the same time, it is clear that trust can often (often!) be a misnomer for poor management, with the result that our schools go out of business because they lacked the cardinal virtue of prudence. Aristotle defined prudence as *recta ratio agibilium*, "right reason applied to practice." And St. Thomas Aquinas considered it the first of the virtues. Our schools have never gone out of business because they charged too much. Reserves are one of the ways in which the Christian school exercises prudence and foresight in order to ensure that the school will still be here for the next generation. Whether used or not in "my" time of service, they will provide Joseph's sustenance in the time of famine.

With that in mind, we can turn to the issue of the school's budget. The Ox Principle and the Kingdom Principle overlap here. The budget's first task is a Kingdom task: to support excellence in mission delivery. The school's end is the budget's mission: extending God's Kingdom here on earth as in heaven. The Board and Principal / Head of School have first a Kingdom obligation – budget is not merely about being balanced. It is first about ensuring that the art teacher can deliver her program with excellence. And the science teacher, hers. And the Athletic Director, hers. Etcetera.

The Board's second task is to ensure that the budget is a moral document. Let there be no error here. Budget for many Christian schools means eking out a painful existence on the backs of poorly paid workers. We don't have to go to the prosperity preachers to know that this is bad economics of body, mind, and spirit. There is no Christian character in being paid below the poverty level or having no retirement benefits to assist a dignified old age. The budget is a moral document before it is a balanced document.

The Board's third task is arithmetic. The budget must balance. But note that a balanced budget does not presuppose Kingdom / mission excellence. A balanced budget can "support" mission mediocrity and be highly immoral in how it treats its people. Balance is third. After Kingdom. After Moral. And then balance.

We are called to excellence, and we witness that to our own people / community as well as to those who are watching us from the outside. "But you are a chosen race, a royal priesthood, a holy nation, a people for his own possession, that you may proclaim the excellencies of him who called you out of darkness into his marvelous light" (1 Peter 2:9). Witnessing to excellence means exemplifying excellence in our own financial practices.

There are then very clear steps to take in thinking about the budget:

1. Understand your own mission statement – what does it mean when we apply the standard of "excellence" to each of its words and think about the investment that is necessary to make that happen? (cf. the CSM Kingdom Principle)
2. Don't assume that the budget you have had for so many years is, de facto, the best budget. In fact, assume that there are deficits that you want to improve over time.
3. Unless the school is new, debt is typically the wrong way to raise money.

    -   This includes lines of credit required because there is not enough money to get through the year.
    -   Necessary building improvements and new construction must be supported by money raised through philanthropy.
    -   Debt payments are a tax on tuition and degrade the school's budget.
    -   Tuition must be set such that operations expenses are paid for 102 percent.

4. The issue of compensation is important. It is just wrong not to compensate Christian workers professionally. The notion that they should be "underpaid" because it is a ministry fails to honor them. Certainly, it is a ministry. We will not try to define a fair wage. But we do know this: when our workers are paid at a level that does not allow them to raise a family, or that forces them to rely on income from a spouse who works in a "secular" occupation, or has to take on more than one job, or that results in them not having benefits or any kind

of retirement opportunities, or requires them to be supported by the government through food stamps and the like, then our budget lacks a moral foundation. We can go further and say that in order to attract and retain the best teachers and staff, we commit to paying them competitively, recognizing their value and honoring it.

A note about philanthropy: CSM believes that the school's operational expenses must be paid for through tuition and fees. Philanthropy is the gift of the heart that invests in the future of the school and to the direct benefit of the children. God has made us generous people. It is part of the way in which we are created. The school should joyfully ask its supporters for their gifts, given because of God's generosity to us (cf. the CSM Mary Principle).

We are committed to being great stewards of the riches that God gives to us. We need to think of God as generous and thus that he will meet our needs. We have a responsibility to express those needs in such a way that we exemplify excellence in our mission delivery, professionally pay and provide benefits to our people, maintain prudence in our reserves and debt management, and meet the Kingdom / moral/ arithmetic needs of the budget. That is the Ox Principle.

THE MARY PRINCIPLE (2024)

The Mary Principle is so named because Luke identifies those who were part of Jesus' Philanthropy Committee in his Gospel. Mary is the first person named and the Mary Principle honors that. It is equally named the Mary Principle because philanthropy is not about gifts, it is about relationships. Luke articulates emphatically that the relationship these women had with Jesus came first. The gift followed.

> Luke 8:3
> "Mary (called Magdalene) from whom seven demons had come out; Joanna the wife of Chuza, the manager of Herod's household; Susanna; and many others. These women were helping to support them out of their own means."

Philanthropy has deep roots in Scripture. Moses himself is identified as a Philanthropy Director. And his obedience to God leads to the only known time when there was such abundance that the donors were asked to stop giving.

> Exodus 36:6-7
> "Moses instructed them to take his message throughout the camp, saying, "Let no man or woman do any more work for the offering for the sanctuary." So the people were restrained from bringing any more. Now the materials were more than enough for them to do all the work."

Christian schools need supporters who will give of their abundance (at whatever level that indicates) to further the work of the school. Tuition and fees should pay for all operational expenses of the school. Operational expenses typically do not include the purchasing of property, the building of new facilities or renovating old, providing items that are over and above normal everyday expenses. Strategically, every Christian school needs a culture of philanthropy in order to raise money over and above operating income. The Mary Principle calls the Christian school to enjoy raising money, to treat donors honorably and respectfully, and to follow the highest ethical standards.

From our perspective at CSM, it is no casual statement to call this the Mary Principle. The women mentioned in Luke's Gospel had been "cured of evil spirits and diseases" (v. 2). They had experienced an astonishing change in their circumstances and were giving out of gratitude for deliverance. These women were the same ones who, in Luke 23 and 24, gave Jesus' body its final ministrations and were the first at the tomb the next day. Certainly, having someone as wealthy as Joanna in the ranks would have been enormously important in order to cover the expenses of this work. It is one of the great ironies of history to note that Jesus' ministry was funded in part by Herod!

Why pick the name Mary? Mary Magdalene, a member of this influential group, is so important that she is mentioned at least 12 times in the Gospels, more than many of the apostles, and mentioned in connection with the key events of Jesus' life. She and the other women were not just appurtenances, but key and vital members of Jesus' work, with characteristics that one might find in other Bible passages such as Proverbs 31. Connecting philanthropy to these women is to honor their importance in the Biblical narrative.

Luke's brief narrative is very rich and establishes four operating principles for the work of raising money for Christian schools.

1. Giving is in gratitude for what has been done. (Mary gave because of what Jesus did for her.)
2. Giving is done by people who are intimately involved with the action. (The women were with Jesus on the road, not sitting back at home.)
3. Giving galvanizes possibilities that otherwise could not be imagined. (Their gifts meant Jesus' ministry could move forward eventually toward Jerusalem.)
4. Giving is recognized and honored. (Luke honors them through naming them and it is hard to imagine Jesus didn't say thank-you.)

We don't know if these women were asked to give or if they initiated the conversation. We can imagine, however, that once someone like Joanna had been healed, she asked in what way she could be part of what was going on with Jesus. There was obviously some kind of organizational structure to Jesus' ministry such that when he arrived at a place, preparations had been made: a place to stay the night, food bought for the road, fresh clothing to replace what was wearing out, new sandals on occasion, even transportation such as the special time that Jesus told his disciples to seek out the ass for his entrance into Jerusalem.

It can't have been a simple thing for 13 men and many other followers to travel around the countryside living a peripatetic lifestyle. Joanna would have been gratefully welcomed into the company of donors who kept things on an even keel. Maybe she asked; maybe she was asked. What we do know is that she and others (many others) were directly involved in supporting Jesus through their giving.

Historically, stewarding the money of others well has not been a strong practice on the part of Christian schools. Christian donors often (very often) become disillusioned because their money, given thoughtfully and hopefully, vanishes into a black hole that has these characteristics:

- It is not accountable – how it was spent is not identified.
- It does not solve problems; in fact, it merely papers over the problems the school continually fails to address.
- It does not move the school forward. It does not create space for creative solutions or visionary possibilities. Far from opening up opportunity, it reaffirms the school in thinking that its "faithful prayer" has been answered. The future is not a new day but only the present day repeated.
- It does not support building capacity in the administration, teachers, and staff of the school. The gift is used to cover deficits in the current budget. It does not fund "moving forward" items such as providing significant professional development, impacting the child's experience, building endowment, supporting the impactful use of consulting services, professionalizing operations, implementing technology systems to collect and manage data.
- Even when it is applied to new buildings and renovations, it often papers over the reality that it is really funding deferred maintenance, i.e., poor stewardship.

No, Christian schools must manage and think about donors and their gifts in a different way. Even the manna in the desert enabled the Jewish people to move toward the Promised Land! Christian schools must know how to look after the gift legally and ethically. Christian schools must know how to use the gift in a way that moves the school from the present into the future. Gifts that only serve the present, by definition, mask underlying management and leadership problems that the Board of Trustees and Principal / School Head are not addressing effectively. Gifts are about the future, vision and direction.

Interestingly, Christian schools have trouble asking people for money. It would seem that Jesus and his disciples were not shy about money. Mary, Joanna, and many others supported their work. The Mary Principle implicitly states that many want to support the work of Jesus in the Christian school and need to be asked. Penelope Burk in her research into giving says that, for example, "9 to 10 percent of people say they have put bequests in their wills, but more than 30 percent say they would definitely do it or take it under serious consideration if asked."

It is clear that our schools do not have the confidence, or they do not think it is right, to ask their potential supporters for money. There is sometimes the thought that these people SHOULD give and we shouldn't have to ask them. We do not take a position on that. What we do know is that if the school does not ask them, many who would give will not. After all, they ARE being asked by many other organizations and individuals, sometimes on a weekly basis, to contribute to many worthy causes.

The Christian school needs philanthropic dollars. It is not a "love of money" that leads to asking for investment into the lives of children in the school. It is an appreciation of the needs that truly exist in the delivery of the school's mission. It is because the school can clearly and authentically identify a future-oriented need. It is done with complete integrity and open accountability. It is done transparently and without embarrassment.

The donor wants to give. The donor has no problem with giving but wants to be asked. Donors want their philanthropy to be an excellent investment in the future. They want to be asked within the context of a plan, to be included appropriately in the conversation, to be thanked, to be told that their gift was used as asked, and to be given evidence that children benefited as a result of the gift. When donors are treated in this way, they will want to be equally or more generous the following year. A "tired" donor is typically someone for whom these things have not happened. Burnout among donors is a result of bad practice, not a general decline in generosity.

The Mary Principle is built on the Ox Principle. A school that balances its budget, limits its debt, compensates its employees professionally, and has a reserve is a school that is positioned to succeed in raising money optimally. The school that manages its budget poorly, fails to charge tuition that pays the bills, goes into debt, and asks its employees to work "sacrificially," i.e., without sufficient income to raise their families, is positioned to fail in any meaningful fundraising. These two principles work hand in hand.

Every Christian family that is involved with a Christian school wants to support it. The Mary Principle, and the Ox Principle that underlies it, give them every opportunity to do so. They will be eager and excited to see the miracles of what God has given them translate into the miracles that God will perform through their school.

THE CHILD PRINCIPLE (2024)

Let's consider some verses about children in the Gospels.

> Matthew 19:14
> "Jesus said, 'Let the little children come to me, and do not hinder them, for the kingdom of heaven belongs to such as these.'"

> Mark 10:14
> "When Jesus saw this, he was indignant. He said to them, 'Let the little children come to me, and do not hinder them, for the kingdom of God belongs to such as these.'"

> Luke 18:16
> "But Jesus called the children to him and said, 'Let the little children come to me, and do not hinder them, for the kingdom of God belongs to such as these.'"

> Matthew 18:3-5
> "And he said: 'Truly I tell you, unless you change and become like little children, you will never enter the kingdom of heaven. Therefore, whoever takes the lowly position of this child is the greatest in the kingdom of heaven. And whoever welcomes one such child in my name welcomes me.'"

As the Christian school strives to implement the Child Principle, it recognizes that all three of the Synoptic gospels tell adults to stop getting in the child's way. The Child Principle requires the Christian school to:

- Put the child first (be student-centered, the object of the school's mission purpose).

- Instruct adults to meet and support the child where the child is first, and only then to challenge the child to meet the adult where the adult is.
- Recognize that authority is there to serve the child, not to lord it over the child.

We are clear that child-centeredness means operating with the child at the center under the authority of God. Being child-centered should never be considered outside of the context of God's love and grace. First comes the recognition that we believe / trust in God and that knowledge of God is primary: "Only be careful, and watch yourselves closely so that you do not forget the things your eyes have seen or let them fade from your heart as long as you live. Teach them to your children and to their children after them" (Deuteronomy 4:9). The cry to not forget is key to our status as a faith, embedded in a teleological history centered in incarnation, crucifixion, and resurrection.

But when we think of the child within the context of the Christian school, we quickly recognize that adults create school often to their own benefit, not to the primary benefit of the child. Let's think of a couple of actual examples:

- We create schedules that fit the convenience of teachers and administrators rather than the clear needs of the child.
- We teach in a way that is comfortable for "me" and reflects "my" particular style rather than necessarily fitting and meeting each child's unique needs.
- We allocate time to meet bureaucratic requirements and arbitrary rules (such as the 120-hour Carnegie Unit) rather than considering how much time – more or less – makes sense from the child's point of view.

We must remember that school is a mandatory place for children but an optional place for adults; it is a place where children have little or no power and adults have much. Children continually move through and have no necessary sense of permanence, while adults might stay for an entire career / vocation. It is often, to our shame, a place where well-meaning disciples "hinder" the children from coming to the Father.

Being child-centered helps make us sensitive to our adult self-centeredness. Indeed, it is only within the context of God's love and grace that leaving the self-centeredness of adults behind makes any sense and, indeed, is possible. When we stop being self-centered as adults, we are freed to become immersed in the lives of our children. Then, we can "teach (the laws) to your children, talking about them when you sit at home and when you walk along the road, when you lie down and when you get up" (Deuteronomy 11:19). This all-encompassing embrace of the teaching life is what turns it from mere career into vocation.

Being child-centered is deeply biblical. God takes the same approach, considering us his children, embracing us and being with us (Emmanuel) through the indwelling of the Holy Spirit, through the law written on our hearts, through the reality of knowing we are created beings, and teaching us (Psalms 25:4-5; 27:11; 32:8; 86:11; 94:10; 119). He was with us at the beginning of time teaching the man (Genesis 2:16) while in Eden and apprenticing the man and woman in the making of clothing (Genesis 3:21). He came to us in Jesus, a child teaching in the Temple (Luke 2:46) and a man teaching the multitudes. We note that God the Father came to Adam and Eve within his creation, Jesus came to us in the context of embodied human history, and the Spirit comes to each of us within the context of our own lives. This is our biblical model of how we should approach children – within the context of their own lives, teaching them in the place they are, and being with them in a way they can understand.

Child-centeredness thus asks us to leave behind our own adult selfishness (which scripturally is always attached to ambition, cf. 2 Corinthians 12:20; Galatians 5:20; Philippians 2:3; James 3:14). It asks us to come toward the child within the child's own context and in a way that makes sense to the child. And it asks us to exercise authority in order to serve the child, not to dominate the child.

We are reminded in our speaking of authority that Jesus remarked that we should receive the kingdom of God "like a child" (Mark 10:15) or not enter in. His last evening with his disciples was spent teaching them about foot washing. "Do you understand what I have done for you?" he asked them. "You call me 'Teacher' and 'Lord,' and rightly so, for that is what I am. Now that I, your Lord and Teacher, have washed your feet, you also should wash one another's feet" (John 13:12-14). Our authority is then to serve, a paradox in any age but no less in our own – where authority means lording it over others and exercising our privilege.

None of this is to take away the difference between an adult and a child, the person who has been trained and the one who has not, the administrator who has been promoted and the one who has not. All these reflect our talents and gifts (given to us) and their developmental growth. It is not to take away the authority that has the sense of judgment – there are plenty of places to go in Scripture to demonstrate the validity of that. But in our schools, the dominant impulse is always to look at education from the child's point of view, through the child's eyes, and with the child's best interests at heart. The dominant impulse is, thus, to love and to serve.

In our schools, that means actually paying deep attention to what we say we are doing and what we are actually doing; to recognizing our missions as being almost exclusively and correctly about helping the child; to asking children their thoughts, fears, dreams, aspirations and finding them of value and acting on them; to beginning each conversation with the admonition to keep the child at the center; to coming to decisions and asking the question as to whom the decision primarily benefits; to running meetings that focus on mission delivery to the child, whatever the topic of conversation.

Schools with children at the center are fun, happy, high-achieving, extraordinary places. Adults in them are vocation-driven, selfless, wise, pure. James warns against being a teacher, noting how many pitfalls there are. But for those who know that is their calling, he also encourages in James 3:13, "Who is wise and understanding among you? Let them show it by their good life, by deeds done in the humility that comes from wisdom. But if you harbor bitter envy and selfish ambition in your hearts, do not boast about it or deny the truth. But the wisdom that comes from heaven is first of all pure; then peace-loving, considerate, submissive, full of mercy and good fruit, impartial and sincere." That is the Child Principle.

Appendix Six

KEY LISTS

Three Promises

Promise One: We promise to be grateful to God and to you for your generosity to the "family of believers" in the school, ask you for gifts that fit your own prosperity, and honor you as a giver.

Promise Two: We promise that asking you to invest in God's work at the school will be accompanied by the school's accountability in spending your money in the way you intended.

Promise Three: We promise that we will use your gift to move the school forward on behalf of the children within the context of a plan showing excellent stewardship and financial sustainability.

Five Operating Principles

1. Giving is in gratitude for what God has done for each one of us.
2. Giving is done by people who are intimately involved with the action.
3. Giving includes involvement, not just the act of giving itself.
4. Giving galvanizes possibilities that otherwise could not be imagined.
5. Giving is recognized and honored.

The Rule of Three Asks

Ask One: tuition / fees
Ask Two: the school's annual fund as part of annual giving
Ask Three: an opportunity to give to annual giving through an event / experience

The Philanthropy Committee's Mission Statement

The Philanthropy Committee is a partner with the school community in providing solicited resources to enhance and strategically benefit the students of the school for this and succeeding generations, acknowledging and being thankful to a generous God.

What Donors Expect

- A telephone thanks within 48 hours of the school's receiving the gift
- A thank-you note that arrives within two weeks of the gift being received
- Tax receipts (mailed by the end of January) with a warm note
- Report of use of money, demonstrating that the school's promises were kept and showing the impact on the children
- Annual report – this can be digital and should be published no more than two months after the end of the school's fiscal year; we note that it is not best practice any more to include a list of all donors, saving you immense amounts of time!

The Annual Fund

1. Raising money by any method is improved when that money is not needed to support the school's operating budget
2. We approach philanthropy by considering each individual donor rather than donors in aggregate
3. Raising money is best done through Christian philanthropy – building relationships
4. The annual fund is the mechanism by which relationship building leads to fundraising

Two Outcomes

1. To widen the donor base, developing a culture of philanthropy
2. To uncover potential leadership donors

Two Keys to Success

1. Peer-to-peer relationship building
2. Immediacy

Three Things Donors Want (Penelope Burk: *Donor-Centered Fundraising*)

1. Prompt, meaningful acknowledgement whenever they make a gift.
2. Confirmation that each gift, regardless of its value, will be assigned to a project, program, or initiative narrower in scope than the mission as a whole.
3. A report on the measurable results achieved to date in the program or project they are funding before they are asked for another gift.

Appendix Seven

THE DATABASE MANAGER

The Database Manager is responsible for coordinating database activities that serve the needs of current and prospective families, current and prospective donors, and various other constituencies in all areas of philanthropy. Responsibilities include: (1) the oversight of strategic plans for database utilization and optimization (serving family relations and philanthropy); (2) the provision of donor and constituent research (for both current and prospective donors); (3) the integration and optimization of the school's multiple databases, including the school's Student Information System(s); and (4) the stewardship of all constituents.

Responsibilities

- Knows how best to find, develop, track, maintain, recognize, record, and grow current and future constituency opportunities.
- Coordinates database activities, overseeing strategic plans for database utilization and optimization.
- Develops and monitors business rules for use and ownership of data within information systems, as well as manages training for internal database use and management of data.
- Supervises school staff in the use of the database.
- Gift Management—Enters and acknowledges gifts, assisting in account reconciliation, and producing regular reports as to the status of relational philanthropy efforts.
- Research—Provides prospect research services for Philanthropy.
- Prepares briefing reports for the Philanthropy Director / Chair of the Philanthropy Committee, and the Principal, as needed.
- Possesses expertise in the use of the database, particularly focusing on gift entry, so as to be able to identify donors for gift acknowledgement and detailed analytics

- Helps the staff and / or volunteers develop appropriate and efficient ways to track prospective donors, their gift capacity, affiliations, and interests.
- Admission and Enrollment Management / Family Relations—Records admission funnel data–from inquiry to enrollment; maintains enrollment records; and maintains re-enrollment records.
- Produces regular reports on enrollment activity.
- Marketing Communications—runs reports, queries, and lists for targeted mailings—for all sectors of family relations.
- Maintains re-enrollment records.
- Produces regular reports tracking the performance of social media and web-based communications.
- Is the "keeper of the plan," adjusting the plan as necessary (under the leadership of the Principal), tracks plan metrics.

Accounting Duties

- Processes credit card payments and online gifts.
- Provides demographic and prospect research to guide recruitment efforts.
- Stewardship—Proactively establishes, manages, and implements stewardship activities, including the creation of letters and reports for restricted, departmental, and endowed funds.
- Writes reports for donors on the use of their gifts.
- Develops and manages a reporting system for ongoing stewardship activities and customizes reports based on donor's needs.
- Ensures appropriate documents are filed and tracked with the Principal and / or Philanthropy Director and the Chief Financial Officer.
- Identifies, plans, and tracks stewardship and cultivation activities.
- Reports—Compiles giving reports for annual and capital giving and the annual report.
- Provides month-end reports for Business Office reconciliation.
- Prepares and mails pledge reminders.
- Provides support for phone initiatives, including preparing calling cards, and the setting up and tracking of results.

Qualifications

- Has five years' database experience.
- Is fluent in the latest technology pertinent to job duties and is knowledgeable of database systems, structure, and best practices.
- Is highly analytical and has an inherent attention to detail.
- Has the ability to understand and meet reporting needs and to manipulate data.
- Possesses general accounting and bookkeeping knowledge.

Performance Characteristics

- Is imbued with a deep sense of the school's mission and culture.
- Has an unflagging commitment to accuracy.
- Demonstrates extreme commitment to data privacy and donor confidentiality.
- Loves "order."
- Is a "data hound" – i.e., enjoys collection, analysis, and manipulation of data to generate meaningful information for decision-making purposes.
- Is committed to recording both qualitative and quantitative data.
- Is proactive and is obsessed with the timely capture, recording, and retrieval of data.
- Is committed to the CSM Code of Ethics and the Donor Bill of Rights.
- Is committed to their own professional growth and renewal.

Appendix Eight

PHILANTHROPY AND THE
PARETO DISTRIBUTION

Vilfredo Pareto lived between 1848 and 1923. He worked across a wide variety of fields – mathematics, economics, sociology, politics. Investopedia.com identifies key components of Pareto's Principle:

- The 80-20 rule maintains that 80 percent of outcomes come from 20 percent of causes.
- The 80-20 rule prioritizes the 20 percent of factors that will produce the best results.
- A principle of the 80-20 rule is to identify an entity's best assets and use them efficiently to create maximum value.
- This rule is a precept, not a hard-and-fast mathematical law.

This idea began in Pareto's garden. He was picking his peas and discovered that 20 percent of the pea pods contained 80 percent of the healthy peas. This was before genetics and the Agricultural Revolution! This is called the Pareto Distribution. As an economist and political scientist, Pareto applied this garden finding to the distribution of land in his native Italy and discovered that 20 percent of the people owned 80 percent of the land. It becomes apparent as we look around us that the Pareto Distribution seems to be everywhere. In schools, we might identify that:

- 20 percent of the children cause 80 percent of the behavior issues.
- 20 percent of the teachers take up 80 percent of the administrator's time.
- 20 percent of the school's potential volunteer force does 80 percent of the heavy lifting.
- 20 percent of the "curriculum" has 80 percent of all mission impact.

And related to philanthropy,

- 20 percent of donors give 80 percent of the money.

In the 21st century, that has skewed even further so that it is not unusual to do an analysis of giving and note that 10 percent of donors have given 90 percent of the dollars raised. In the general population, as Putnam identified in *Bowling Alone*, fewer people are giving a smaller proportion of their wealth than the generations before: "In 1960 we gave away about $1 for every $2 we spent on recreation; in 1997 we gave less than 50 cents for every $2 we spent on recreation" (p. 123). The Fraser Institute in its 2021 Canada Generosity Index noted: "The percentage of aggregate income donated to charity by Canadian tax filers has also decreased from 0.58% in 2009 to 0.53% in 2019."

Pareto's Distribution helps us in philanthropy to understand the sociological effects of a population that has become more individualistic and less "social." In our schools, we talk about the greater difficulty in finding volunteers – this has little to do with dual-income families. The proportion of dual-income families is about the same now as it was in the late 1990s. It has much more to do with the unwillingness of the individual to become involved and committed to an organization.

We have the same issue with donors. There are fewer people giving to our organizations, and we are relying more heavily on leadership donors to make up the difference. We used to aim for 100 percent participation in the annual fund. Now, we are delighted with 75 percent. Many schools we go to have far less than 50 percent participation, including the school's own employees, who should be the most motivated.

Joseph Juran took the Pareto Distribution in the 1940s and coined Pareto's Law. By this he meant that we should focus on the "vital few" and not on the "trivial many." Simply, in philanthropic terms, we should spend 80 percent of our time on the 20 percent of donors who can make a difference. This concept is used almost universally in all areas of human endeavor. Twenty percent of software bugs, when eliminated, will fix 80 percent of the issues. Let's fix those. Eighty percent of the problems we have in relationships are caused by 20 percent of our interactions. Let's focus therapy on those. Twenty percent of the clothing in our closets is worn 80 percent of the time. Let's change our buying patterns. Twenty percent of your goals will actually make a difference in your life. Let's prioritize what to pay attention to. And on it goes.

CSM would, however, take it in a different direction.

Pareto's Distribution recognizes the fact that some can and do give more than others. We are grateful for all our donors, large and small. This is an observable phenomenon.

Pareto's Law suggests that we should therefore focus on our larger donors and not worry too much about the others. We should ignore what Robert Putnam called in his 2020 book *The Upswing*, the "metastasizing self-centeredness among middle-class Americans since the peak of our generosity in the 1960s" (p. 143).

CSM says that we should pay attention to that self-centeredness and make the Christian school a place of change. Scripture says that we can change, that the person coming in our school entrances in September can be transformed during that year and the years that follow. Our lodestone is Paul's pleading in Romans 12:

"Therefore, I urge you, brothers and sisters, in view of God's mercy, to offer your bodies as a living sacrifice, holy and pleasing to God – this is your true and proper worship. Do not conform to the pattern of this world, but be transformed by the renewing of your mind. Then you will be able to test and approve what God's will is – his good, pleasing, and perfect will."

We urge you to take this encouragement from Romans and call our families to make this offering. Take the following direction:

1. During the admission process, message that the family is joining a community with mutual obligations that help all grow, the child first, but also the parent.
2. Follow that up with opportunities for the family to participate in community celebration on a regular basis. Participating, joining, communing, all fight the sociological trend of self-centeredness.
3. Invite parents to invest themselves in the life of the school through playing a role. While in Kindergarten, that might include hours at the school being a room parent, at high school, that might include hours after school coaching. It can be as simple as being on the concession stand once a season, or showing up at an Open House with a name badge that says Parent – Talk to Me! All the research shows that investing time is associated with investing resources. If you do not ever see the parent/s, they will hardly ever give.
4. Invite the community to invest in the school through annual giving. Ensure giving is simple to do, the school is quick to thank and celebrate, and the parent knows the impact of the gift over time.
5. Lead the parent/s to more leadership roles in their second and subsequent years, whether formally as a Parent Ambassador or part of the PTA, or informally in being faithfully present (cf. James Davison Hunter: *To Change the World*) – cleaning up at events, setting up chairs, coming in to be interviewed. Maturing in a sense of community is the objective here. We are not spectators; we are involved.
6. Appreciate all donors all the time – make it a distinction to be a donor that is honored and recognized, through the school desiring always to be in relationship with the donor.

7. As we recognize that we only have time to spend one-on-one with our leadership donors, we also draw those leaders into our community as we show them all those who follow them up the hill. We invite our leadership donors to be part of the action as well. We have seen such people acting on the Board, providing construction services, showing up to student-led activities, and participating in packing Christmas boxes, speaking to other potential and actual donors about their "why."

8. Lead the small donor to becoming a leadership donor through one or more of the following:

    •   Increasing their gifts
    •   Becoming a 10-year donor
    •   Sharing their testimony

Giving will reflect the Pareto Distribution. However, Christian schools should not follow Pareto's Law. Instead, we should strive for a Christian "renewing of the mind" and a transformation of the donor. We do not have to despair because of sociological trends but hope that we can reverse them in our communities. We do not despise the "poor" but follow God's leading:

"He has brought down rulers from their thrones but has lifted up the humble" (Matthew 1:52). In so doing, we will bring about the Kingdom on earth as it is in heaven: "After this I looked, and there before me was a great multitude that no one could count, from every nation, tribe, people and language, standing before the throne and before the Lamb. They were wearing white robes and were holding palm branches in their hands" (Revelation 7:9-10).

THE PHILANTHROPY CYCLES

The CSM Relational Philanthropy Cycle

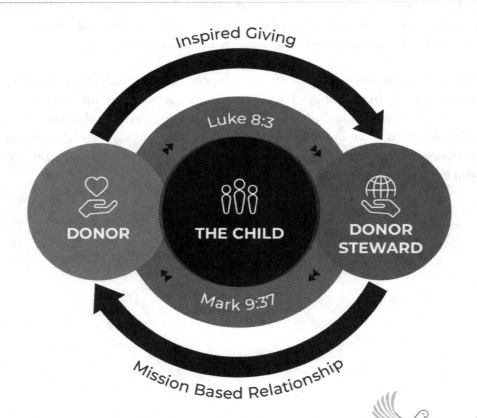

Inspired Giving

Luke 8:3

DONOR

THE CHILD

DONOR STEWARD

Mark 9:37

Mission Based Relationship

© Christian School Management 2022

CSM
partnership · leadership · transformation

The CSM Golden Rule Cycle

©2024 Christian School Management

Printed in the United States
by Baker & Taylor Publisher Services